Consumerism in the Ancient World

T0331332

Greek pottery was exported around the ancient world in vast quantities over a period of several centuries. This book focuses on the Greek pottery consumed by people in the western Mediterranean and trans-Alpine Europe from 800 to 300 BCE, attempting to understand the distribution of vases, and particularly the reasons why people who were not Greek decided to acquire them. This new approach includes discussion of the ways in which objects take on different meanings in new contexts, the linkages between the consumption of goods and identity construction, and the utility of objects for signaling positive information about their owners to their community. The study includes a database of almost 24,000 artifacts from more than 230 sites in Portugal, Spain, France, Switzerland, and Germany. This data was mapped and analyzed using geostatistical techniques to reveal different patterns of consumption in different places and at different times. The new approaches explored in this book mark a movement away from reliance on fragments of ancient authors' descriptions of western Europe, remains of monumental buildings, and major artworks in order to investigate ancient Greek social life and more "ordinary" forms of material culture.

Justin St. P. Walsh is Assistant Professor in the School of Art at Chapman University. He has worked for more than a decade at archaeological sites across the Mediterranean, especially Morgantina in Sicily, and has been the recipient of a Rome Prize, a Fulbright Grant to Greece, and numerous other awards. He is the author of several articles on Greek pottery, cross-cultural interactions, and the protection of cultural heritage.

Routledge Monographs in Classical Studies

Consumerism in the Ancient World
Imports and Identity Construction

Justin St. P. Walsh

Routledge
Taylor & Francis Group

LONDON AND NEW YORK

First published 2014 by Routledge

2 Park Square, Milton Park, Abingdon, Oxfordshire OX14 4RN
52 Vanderbilt Avenue, New York, NY 10017

Routledge is an imprint of the Taylor & Francis Group, an informa business

First issued in paperback 2019

Copyright © 2014 Taylor & Francis

Cover Image: Athenian red-figure stemless cup attributed to the
Amphitrite Painter, ca. 450–440 BCE (KAS 113, Landesmuseum
Württemberg). This cup was broken and repaired in antiquity, at which
time it was also given gold appliqué decoration in the La Téne style. It
was found in a secondary burial in the mound at Kleinaspergle, Asperg
(Kr. Ludwigsburg), Germany. Photo: P. Frankenstein, H. Zwietasch;
Landesmuseum Württemberg, Stuttgart, by permission.

Library of Congress Cataloging-in-Publication Data
St. P. Walsh, Justin.
   Consumerism in the ancient world : imports and identity construction / by
Justin St. P. Walsh.
      pages cm. — (Routledge monographs in classical studies ; 17)
   Includes bibliographical references and index.
   1. Mediterranean Region—Commerce—History—to 1500.
2. Commerce—History—To 500.   3. Consumption (Economics)—
Social aspects—Mediterranean Region.   4. Pottery, Greek—Mediterranean
Region.   5. Pottery, Ancient—Mediterranean Region.   6. Mediterranean
Region—Antiquities.   I. Title.
   HF381.S7 2014
   382.09182′200901—dc23
   2013031937

ISBN: 978-0-415-89379-4 (hbk)
ISBN: 978-0-367-86645-7 (pbk)

Typeset in Sabon
by Apex CoVantage, LLC

To Carlie, for her love and infinite patience

Contents

Figures

Tables

Image Credits

Digital and printed maps were created using open-source data supplied by the Global Administrative Areas database (http://www.gadm.org/), Natural Earth (http://www.naturalearthdata.com), and the European Environment Agency (http://www.eea.europa.eu).

All photographs were taken by the author. Fig. 3.8 is used by kind permission of Dr. Simone Stork. Figs. 3.14 and 5.1 are used by kind permission of Dr. Sebastián Celestino Pérez. All printed maps and charts were designed by Summer Woodward from data created by the author; all digital maps were created by the author.

Abbreviations

DK = Diels, H.A. 1962. *Die Fragmente der Vorsokratiker*, 6th ed., rev. by
   W. Kranz. Berlin: Weidmannische Buchhandlung.
FGrHist = Jacoby, F. 1923–1998. *Die Fragmente der Griechischen
   Historiker*. 4 parts. Berlin/Leiden: Weidmannische Buchhandlung/Brill.

Preface

This book owes a heavy debt to the scholarship of Professor Michael Dietler—not only his recent magnum opus, *Archaeologies of Colonialism: Consumption, Entanglement, and Violence in Ancient Mediterranean France,* which was published just after the proposal for this book was accepted by Routledge in 2010, but also his extensive series of articles over more than 20 years on consumption, exchange, and the social importance of alcohol and feasting. He has undoubtedly been one of the most successful scholars at bridging the traditional divide between classical archaeology and the discipline as it is practiced in other parts of the world and in other periods, a quality that I find particularly admirable.

I have relied on many of Dietler's ideas and findings for more than a decade, first as I wrote my dissertation on the site of Morgantina in Sicily, and since then in several articles on Greek pottery in colonial contexts. I see this book not as a repetition of *Archaeologies of Colonialism,* or even a counterpoint to it, but rather as a continuation of it and a supplement to it. In some respects, my work is much more constrained than Dietler's, since it leaves aside most discussion of subjects that have often formed part of comparative colonial studies, such as urban planning, construction techniques, funerary rites, or linguistics, and concentrates instead only on one type of evidence: Greek pottery. On the other hand, this book is also more expansive than his, dealing, as it does, with a much wider area than the south of France and thus more cultural groups. The broader geographic range is particularly useful for identifying whether patterns that were found could be considered typical or unusual. I have introduced a few new ideas from other scholars to build upon the framework for consumption proposed by Dietler, and I have used a new tool, kriging, from the world of geostatistics to provide evidence for analysis.

All of my data and the results of my analysis are publicly available online for download from the Routledge website (http://www.routledge .com/books/details/9780415893794/). Anyone who is interested in using that material for their own research, or who wants to check my methodology, may do so freely under an international Creative Commons license as long as they agree to share their modifications to the data to the public in the same way (CC BY-SA 3.0). Any use of my data or results must credit their initial creation to me. Those who have questions or comments are invited to contact me at jstpwalsh@chapman.edu.

Culver City, CA
July 2013

Acknowledgments

This book could not have come to fruition without the help of a wide array of people and institutions. I am grateful for financial support to Chapman University for a course release from teaching and two Scholarly and Creative Activity Grants that enabled me to travel to archaeological sites and museums in Spain and Germany and to spend a month in Athens during 2012, to purchase GIS software in order to analyze my data, and to produce maps and charts for publication. Between 2007 and 2011, Louisiana State University funded my travel to several conferences where I was able to develop the theoretical approach used here. I also owe thanks to the University of Cincinnati's Department of Classics for a Margo Tytus Summer Residency Fellowship in 2010, which I used partly to define the scope of this study. In addition to the Burnam Library at Cincinnati, I was fortunate to be able to use a number of other phenomenal library collections during my research, including the ones belonging to the American School of Classical Studies at Athens, the American Academy in Rome, the University of California at Los Angeles, and the Getty Research Institute. I thank their librarians, as well as those in Chapman's Leatherby Libraries Interlibrary Loan office for all their assistance (and patience).

I am also extremely grateful to the staff of Routledge and their associates for their professionalism, patience with a first-time book writer, and faith in the project: Laura Stearns, Lauren Verity, Stacy Noto, Emily Johnston at Apex, and many others behind the scenes as well. Summer Woodward, a graphic design assistant in the Chapman Ideation Lab, was responsible for turning my GIS layers and spreadsheets into publishable maps, charts, and tables.

I owe a debt of thanks to many scholars for their wise advice and constructive criticisms on some of the topics covered here over the years: Carla Antonaccio, Malcolm Bell, Jenifer Neils, Barbara Tsakirgis, Mira Green, Lin Foxhall, Tamar Hodos, Andrea Berlin, Sarah Morris, John Papadopoulos, Adria LaViolette, Jeff Hantman, Fraser Neiman, Tyler Jo Smith, Elizabeth Meyer, Clive Orton, Rob Fornango, Vladimir Stissi, Lisa Nevett, Bradley Ault, Franco De Angelis, Katharina Rebay-Salisbury, Melissa Vetters, and Scott Kiesling. Special thanks go to Michael Dietler and Marcelo Castro López for welcoming me so kindly to their excavations at Lattes and Cástulo, respectively, to Sebastián Celestino Pérez and Simone Stork for permission to publish images from Cancho Roano and Hochdorf, and to Armin Krüger for his tour of Asperg; also to my colleagues at LSU and Chapman: Mark Zucker, Nick Camerlenghi, Jeremiah Ariaz, Rod Parker, Catherine Wells, Chenta Franklin, Jeanie Randazzo, Wendy Salmond, Kent Lehnhof, Ann Gordon, and Patrick Fuery. Eric Chimenti deserves special praise for being an incredible problem-solver, finding money for software, and expertise for graphics when they were needed.

Finally, I must express my thanks to my family and friends for their support and understanding over the last few years. Above all, Carlie Galloway has kept me on an even keel and given me extraordinary love and patience at stressful moments, and for those gifts I am eternally grateful.

1 Introduction
Greek Pottery in New Contexts

WHY GREEK POTTERY?

Greek pottery has been found in archaeological contexts throughout the western Mediterranean and trans-Alpine Europe. What reasons persuaded people in these regions to buy vases from Athens, Corinth, Massalia, or other Greek cities (Figs. 1.1–1.2)? For even the mere fact that this long-distance trade occurred seems noteworthy. Vases from Athens, for example, were purchased in significant quantities for several centuries, not only by Greeks who were not Athenian, but also by people who were not Greek at all. Everywhere that Greek pottery was imported, people had their own local ceramic traditions with distinct shapes and fabrics extending back centuries or even millennia, yet they decided to acquire vessels made in Greek cities that were often thousands of kilometers away. What qualities did these imports have that convinced buyers to choose them? What, if anything, did these consumers know about the culture where the imported vessels had been made, or about the use of those vessels in their home societies? What, ultimately, did these imports mean to their buyers? And what did they mean to other people in the community who saw the consumption of imported Greek vases?

In order to answer these questions, we can examine the distribution of vases, casting attention towards different variables, such as the fabrics and shapes of the imported pottery that appeared in the West. These were of almost every shape produced by Greeks. They were used for drinking, eating, storage, and household tasks, and for transporting liquids like wine and olive oil. They came in fine wares, decorated with shiny surfaces and sometimes even images, and in coarse wares for utilitarian purposes. They traveled from as far away as Asia Minor, and from as close as the Greek colonies of Massalia and Emporion. Studying the distribution of the vases can show whether patterns emerge that show different kinds of consumption and use of Greek vases. For example, the distribution might have varied with proximity to Greece or to Greeks, so this factor should be taken into account. As for preferences, we might wonder whether people wanted large vases rather than small ones, or painted ones but not unpainted ones, or vases designed for some functions but not others—or perhaps some other variable (or combination of variables) was more important.

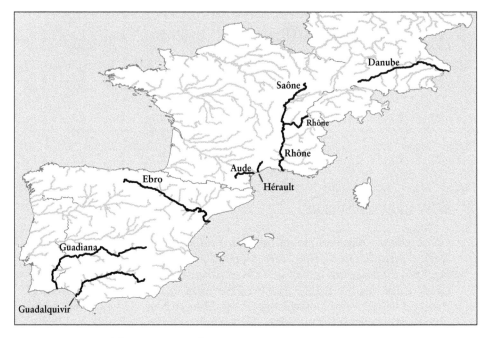

Figure 1.1   Map of the survey area showing river courses

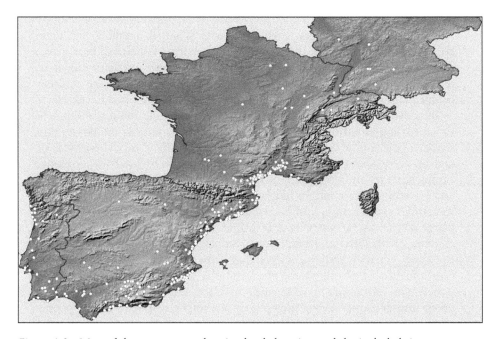

Figure 1.2   Map of the survey area showing land elevation and the included sites

The context in which vases appeared can be significant, too, for helping us learn how the vases were used by their new owners, whether in homes, burials, sanctuaries, or somewhere else.

The consumption of Greek vases with which this book is concerned occurred in the areas of modern Portugal, Spain, France, Germany, and Switzerland, primarily between about 700 and 350 BCE, with some examples also appearing both before and after these dates. During this period, visitors from the eastern and central Mediterranean—Phoenicians, Etruscans, and Greeks—traveled widely as merchants, but also as colonists, settling towns of all sizes along the coasts of Spain and France. Non-Greek traders sailed from town to town, but they also sometimes lived for short or long periods in or near indigenous villages while conducting business. It was a time of transition for the region's indigenous societies, too, as they added iron technology to their existing knowledge of bronze casting, developed wheel-made pottery, and underwent social, political, and economic upheavals during this period. Exchange therefore encompassed a wide range of experiences, depending on the period and location; it also included tangible goods and raw materials as well as more intangible things such as ideas. Trade also had both micro- and macro-scale components, since it was the result of interactions between individuals, but it was also carried out according to the plans and needs of complex polities such as villages, towns, and even city-states or kingdoms. Consumption of imports therefore occurred against a backdrop of constantly shifting power relations between people and between communities, often from a diversity of cultural backgrounds. Study of the ancient trade in Greek pottery therefore demands the investigation of a very wide array of data beyond the vases themselves, including geography, settlement patterns, ancient literary sources describing these regions and the people who lived there, material evidence of local populations, and the raw materials and finished goods that were exchanged for Greek pottery.

For more than a century, scholars of the classical world have devoted a great deal of attention to cross-cultural interactions such as the ones that happened in this area. The field has slowly evolved, sometimes under the influence of work carried out by peers in related subjects in science and the humanities (especially in the last thirty years). Their interests have shifted away from being solely concerned with the Greeks as bringers of civilization (meaning literature, philosophy, art, architecture, and military prowess) to the West and to the populations that would eventually become the great European powers—making this part of the world "classical," in fact. Now, great interest is directed at the reactions of indigenes to Greek presence, and to looking at indigenous cultures as interesting in their own right. The development of these new approaches has resulted in a shift away from reliance on the preserved fragments of ancient Greek authors' descriptions of western Europe, remains of monumental buildings, and major artworks, and toward investigation of social life and more prosaic forms of material culture. It has also led to the introduction of new archaeological methodologies that no longer privilege Greek material over other kinds of evidence.[1]

CONSUMERISM IN AN ANCIENT COLONIAL SITUATION

The genesis of this project lies in research conducted on a smaller scale, but in a related context, at the site of Morgantina, in east-central Sicily (Walsh 2006, 2011–2012, 2013). An indigenous Sikel settlement, Morgantina was founded on a hill called Cittadella around 1000–900 BCE (Leighton 1993, 2012). Contact with colonizing Greeks first appeared in the archaeological record in contexts dating to around 550 BCE, where Greek pottery was present. Greek building types (particularly *naiskoi*) appeared, with painted terra-cotta antefixes (Kenfield 1990, 1993a, 1993b, Greco 2005). The amount of Greek material present at the site steadily increased until the middle of the fifth century, when habitation seems to have ceased (Lyons 1996a, 1996b, Antonaccio 1997). According to the historian Diodorus Siculus (XI.78.5), the site was seized in 459 by an indigenous league bent on removing Greek influence from the island's interior, a sign that not all native groups welcomed the arrival of Greeks. A new town was founded on a neighboring ridge known as Serra Orlando, probably around 440–430, this time with a Greek-style orthogonal grid plan (Bell 1984–1985, 2000, 2006, 2008). Strong signs point to a joint indigenous and Greek colonial expedition initiating the second Morgantina, in contrast to the destruction of the first town, since Greek pottery (some of which may have been made nearby in coastal colonies, or even at Morgantina itself) as well as indigenous fine and coarse wares were discovered within the same contexts there (Bell 2006, 255–257; Walsh 2011–2012, 128–131).

Perhaps the most striking aspect of the two collections of Greek pottery—one from Cittadella, the other from Serra Orlando—was the difference in the distribution of shapes, despite the geographic and temporal contiguities between the sites. In a comparison of the Athenian black gloss ware from Morgantina, it became clear that although vessels for drinking were far more prominent than other categories at both towns, people in the later settlement bought and used a wider variety of shapes—many more different kinds of cups, bowls, and other types of vases—than in the later settlement. The single most popular shape at Cittadella, the stemmed cup (approximately a quarter of the total), was practically absent at Serra Orlando (less than 2 percent). There were roughly three times as many stemless cups and ten times as many cup-skyphoi at Cittadella as at Serra Orlando. Bowls formed only 1 percent of the assemblage at Cittadella, but 6 percent at Serra Orlando. These differences require an explanation (Walsh 2013).

It is clear that geography cannot be taken as the determining factor in the availability of various shapes, since the sites are directly adjacent to one another. The costs are not likely to have been significantly different for one shape relative to another, either, given that all the pottery would have had to travel the same or similar routes. The differences are also not likely to be related to the fact that two periods of importation of Athenian pottery to Morgantina are represented by the sample, either, as the same shapes were made at Athens throughout both periods (for the continued production of stemmed cups, particularly Acrocups and Vicups, through the end of the fifth century, for example, see Sparkes and Talcott 1970, 88). Looking at the evidence from Serra Orlando by itself, one might suspect that the absence of stemmed cups might be due to their fragility compared to cups that lacked a delicate stem—but comparison with Cittadella negates this possibility, too.

If cost, availability, location, and chronology cannot be identified (either singly or in combination) as decisive factors determining the distribution of Athenian pottery at Morgantina in the archaic and classical periods, then what other possibilities remain? The agency of consumers at Morgantina, and specifically their ability to make choices from among available options, seems to me to offer the only compelling explanation. This is not the place to enter into a detailed discussion of the reasons why consumers might have chosen one or more shapes preferentially over others—a survey of important factors in any consumer's decision-making process can be found in the theoretical approach outlined in chapter 4—but one group of vases can be mentioned here as an example. The prominence of shapes with certain features seems particularly connected to local expressions of preference (Walsh and Antonaccio 2014). These features, specifically offsets, carinations, and fragile strap handles, were formal links to the design of vases in metals such as gold, silver, and bronze. The presence of these features did not merely make reference to more costly and higher-status materials. They also made reference to local ancestral traditions in vase design, as similar features appeared in Sicilian repertoires going back into the Early Bronze Age. In other words, local concerns and interests endowed foreign products with new meanings that made some of those products preferable to others.

EXPANDING THE QUESTION

If such a seemingly modern behavior as consumer choice can be identified at Morgantina, in a milieu where Greeks and indigenes lived in close contact—and, indeed, where they became indistinguishable from one another in the archaeological record by the fourth century BCE (Antonaccio 2001)—it seems appropriate to expand the scope of study, and to try to discover what patterns might emerge from an investigation of the consumption of Greek pottery in a broader geographic area, where, in some cases, Greeks and indigenous people lived side by side (even in the same communities), and in other cases indigenous people might only ever have seen a single Greek product, let alone many Greek vases or even Greeks themselves. This book seeks to address that problem by gathering data on the locations of Greek pottery found in archaeological contexts across the western Mediterranean and trans-Alpine Europe. That data can be compared on a site-by-site and region-by-region basis in order to see whether traces of consumer choice exist, and whether the role of Greek vases in different communities can be discerned.

Economists have long been interested in the problem of how people make their decisions to buy things, but have rarely tried to understand the reasons behind why people want some things and not others, especially when those things are not necessities. Douglas and Isherwood (1996), however, applied anthropological research to this question. In neoclassical economics, consumers are often considered to be rational actors (the so-called *homo economicus* derived from John Stuart Mill's pursuer of wealth). The choice, which can be identified in most, if not all societies, to spend resources in seemingly unnecessary ways, would indeed seem to need some justification. Douglas and Isherwood made important advances by arguing for the importance of goods not as ends in and of themselves but as "less objects of desire than threads of a veil that disguises social relations under it" (152). They focused attention on the symbolic values and meanings that might be attached to goods, perhaps especially to luxuries. Objects can function as markers of relationships, in their exchange as well as in their use and display. A primary relationship associated with luxurious goods is likely to be the status of their owner relative to the rest of the community, given the need for greater expenditure of resources to acquire them.

The pottery studied in this book comes from 233 sites in five countries (Figs. 1.3–1.9). Information was recorded about almost 24,000 vases or

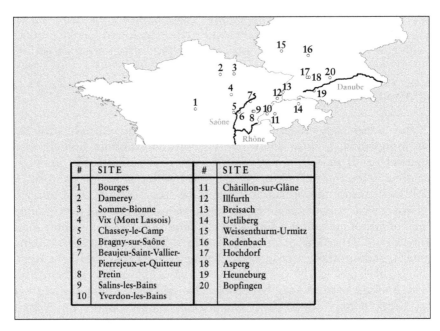

#	SITE	#	SITE
1	Bourges	11	Châtillon-sur-Glâne
2	Damerey	12	Illfurth
3	Somme-Bionne	13	Breisach
4	Vix (Mont Lassois)	14	Uetliberg
5	Chassey-le-Camp	15	Weissenthurm-Urmitz
6	Bragny-sur-Saône	16	Rodenbach
7	Beaujeu-Saint-Vallier-	17	Hochdorf
	Pierrejeux-et-Quitteur	18	Asperg
8	Pretin	19	Heuneburg
9	Salins-les-Bains	20	Bopfingen
10	Yverdon-les-Bains		

Figure 1.3   Sites in northern France, Germany, and Switzerland

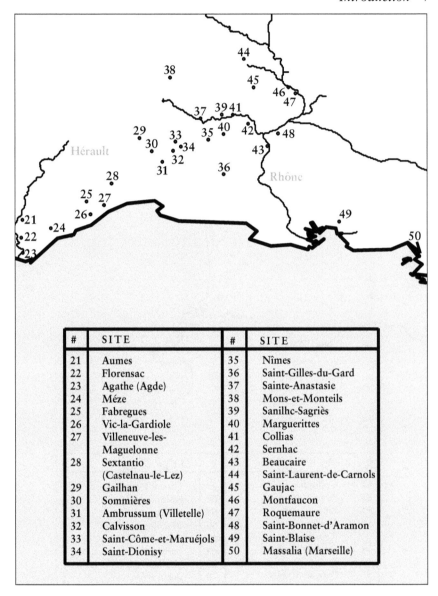

#	SITE	#	SITE
21	Aumes	35	Nîmes
22	Florensac	36	Saint-Gilles-du-Gard
23	Agathe (Agde)	37	Sainte-Anastasie
24	Méze	38	Mons-et-Monteils
25	Fabregues	39	Sanilhc-Sagriès
26	Vic-la-Gardiole	40	Marguerittes
27	Villeneuve-les-	41	Collias
	Maguelonne	42	Sernhac
28	Sextantio	43	Beaucaire
	(Castelnau-le-Lez)	44	Saint-Laurent-de-Carnols
29	Gailhan	45	Gaujac
30	Sommières	46	Montfaucon
31	Ambrussum (Villetelle)	47	Roquemaure
32	Calvisson	48	Saint-Bonnet-d'Aramon
33	Saint-Côme-et-Maruéjols	49	Saint-Blaise
34	Saint-Dionisy	50	Massalia (Marseille)

Figure 1.4 Sites in the south of France between Massalia (Marseille) and the Hérault River

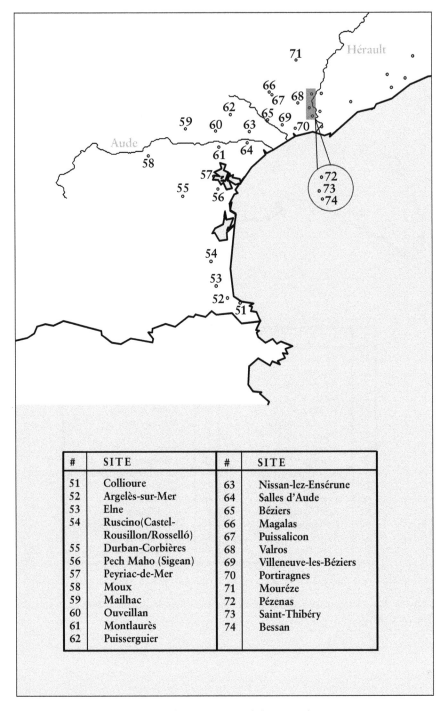

#	SITE	#	SITE
51	Collioure	63	Nissan-lez-Ensérune
52	Argelès-sur-Mer	64	Salles d'Aude
53	Elne	65	Béziers
54	Ruscino(Castel-	66	Magalas
	Rousillon/Rosselló)	67	Puissalicon
55	Durban-Corbières	68	Valros
56	Pech Maho (Sigean)	69	Villeneuve-les-Béziers
57	Peyriac-de-Mer	70	Portiragnes
58	Moux	71	Mouréze
59	Mailhac	72	Pézenas
60	Ouveillan	73	Saint-Thibéry
61	Montlaurès	74	Bessan
62	Puisserguier		

Figure 1.5   Sites in the south of France west of the Hérault River

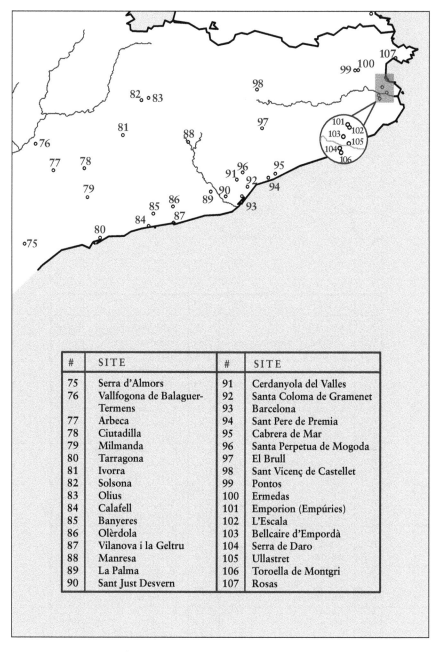

#	SITE	#	SITE
75	Serra d'Almors	91	Cerdanyola del Valles
76	Vallfogona de Balaguer-Termens	92	Santa Coloma de Gramenet
		93	Barcelona
77	Arbeca	94	Sant Pere de Premia
78	Ciutadilla	95	Cabrera de Mar
79	Milmanda	96	Santa Perpetua de Mogoda
80	Tarragona	97	El Brull
81	Ivorra	98	Sant Vicenç de Castellet
82	Solsona	99	Pontos
83	Olius	100	Ermedas
84	Calafell	101	Emporion (Empúries)
85	Banyeres	102	L'Escala
86	Olèrdola	103	Bellcaire d'Empordà
87	Vilanova i la Geltru	104	Serra de Daro
88	Manresa	105	Ullastret
89	La Palma	106	Toroella de Montgri
90	Sant Just Desvern	107	Rosas

Figure 1.6 Sites in Catalonia

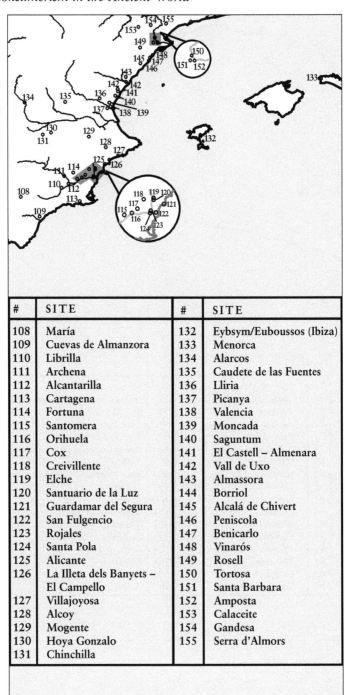

#	SITE	#	SITE
108	María	132	Eybsym/Euboussos (Ibiza)
109	Cuevas de Almanzora	133	Menorca
110	Librilla	134	Alarcos
111	Archena	135	Caudete de las Fuentes
112	Alcantarilla	136	Lliria
113	Cartagena	137	Picanya
114	Fortuna	138	Valencia
115	Santomera	139	Moncada
116	Orihuela	140	Saguntum
117	Cox	141	El Castell – Almenara
118	Creivillente	142	Vall de Uxo
119	Elche	143	Almassora
120	Santuario de la Luz	144	Borriol
121	Guardamar del Segura	145	Alcalá de Chivert
122	San Fulgencio	146	Peniscola
123	Rojales	147	Benicarlo
124	Santa Pola	148	Vinarós
125	Alicante	149	Rosell
126	La Illeta dels Banyets – El Campello	150	Tortosa
127	Villajoyosa	151	Santa Barbara
128	Alcoy	152	Amposta
129	Mogente	153	Calaceite
130	Hoya Gonzalo	154	Gandesa
131	Chinchilla	155	Serra d'Almors

Figure 1.7   Sites along the east coast of Spain

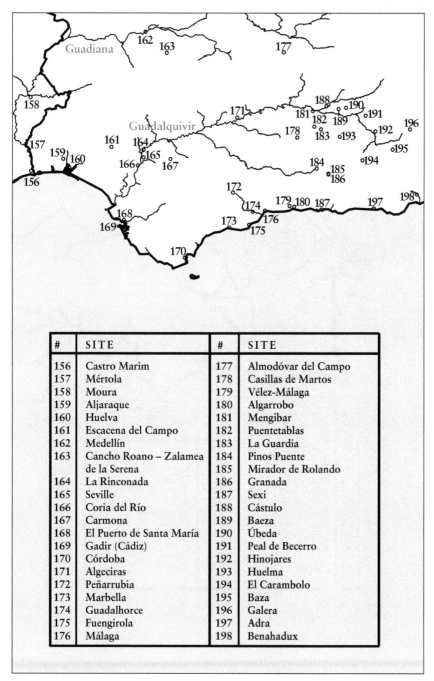

#	SITE	#	SITE
156	Castro Marim	177	Almodóvar del Campo
157	Mértola	178	Casillas de Martos
158	Moura	179	Vélez-Málaga
159	Aljaraque	180	Algarrobo
160	Huelva	181	Mengibar
161	Escacena del Campo	182	Puentetablas
162	Medellín	183	La Guardia
163	Cancho Roano – Zalamea	184	Pinos Puente
	de la Serena	185	Mirador de Rolando
164	La Rinconada	186	Granada
165	Seville	187	Sexi
166	Coria del Río	188	Cástulo
167	Carmona	189	Baeza
168	El Puerto de Santa María	190	Úbeda
169	Gadir (Cádiz)	191	Peal de Becerro
170	Córdoba	192	Hinojares
171	Algeciras	193	Huelma
172	Peñarrubia	194	El Carambolo
173	Marbella	195	Baza
174	Guadalhorce	196	Galera
175	Fuengirola	197	Adra
176	Málaga	198	Benahadux

Figure 1.8   Sites in Andalusia and southeastern Portugal

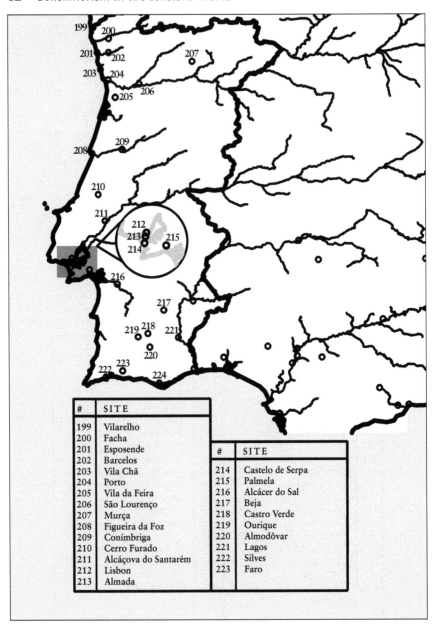

#	SITE
199	Vilarelho
200	Facha
201	Esposende
202	Barcelos
203	Vila Chã
204	Porto
205	Vila da Feira
206	São Lourenço
207	Murça
208	Figueira da Foz
209	Conímbriga
210	Cerro Furado
211	Alcáçova do Santarém
212	Lisbon
213	Almada

#	SITE
214	Castelo de Serpa
215	Palmela
216	Alcácer do Sal
217	Beja
218	Castro Verde
219	Ourique
220	Almodôvar
221	Lagos
222	Silves
223	Faro

Figure 1.9   Sites in Portugal

fragments of vases. This study will examine the values, meanings, and relationships associated with Greek pottery as a luxury good (a role that will be identified for it in chapter 5). It will also investigate the ways in which imported vases might have been used by individual consumers in very different societies to construct their identities. Particular attention will be paid to status as a kind of identity. As a widely published and easily identifiable "marker" that has been published at a large number of sites over a broad geographical area and chronological period, Greek pottery is an almost ideal subject for such research. At the same time, ancient western Europe is an appropriate place for the study to be situated because it has been the locus of some of the most interesting recent developments of theoretical approaches in archaeology, from the world-systems theory advocated by Patrice Brun and Barry Cunliffe; to the postcolonialism of Maria Eugenia Aubet Semmler, Paloma Cabrera Bonet, and Adolfo Domínguez, among others; to Peter van Dommelen and Carla Antonaccio's views of the hybridity of cultures in colonial contexts; to Michael Dietler's interest in the entanglement of goods and people, the transformation of meanings associated with things as they cross cultural boundaries, and the social importance of feasting and alcohol. All of these perspectives, and many of the ones that preceded them, will be discussed for their potential utility in answering the question of why people bought Greek pottery. Before that, however, it will be necessary to spend some time describing the historical and cultural milieu in which Greek pottery arrived in the West, both through an account of Greek colonization and through a description of the material cultures in which Greek pottery appeared archaeologically.

NOTE

1. This study admittedly relies for its dataset on that long-standing bias of excavators toward Greek pottery in their publications, but it does so in the hopes of continuing to turn attention toward non-Greek groups.

2 Greek Colonization in the West
A Historical and Cultural Survey

INTRODUCTION

A number of issues must be tackled before any degree of access can be gained to the significance of imported goods in ancient societies. First among these issues are the geographical, historical, and cultural contexts in which consumers made their choices to select certain goods over others (including the problems for understanding that are presented by the particular circumstances associated with colonization and the other kinds of cross-cultural interactions that happened in this region more than two millennia ago). Intercultural contact happened in different ways at different places and times, ranging from the forced imposition of colonial settlements in lands where they were not welcome to cooperative intermingling between two or more groups carried out to mutual benefit. Such interactions could also be either temporary or long-standing. At the same time that we consider ancient historical patterns, it is important throughout to be aware of the modern history of prior scholarship on these regions and the goods chosen for this study. Each of these subjects will be discussed and evaluated below.

GREEK CONTACTS WITH THE WEST

Trade and the First Wave of Colonization

Trade between Greece and the central and western Mediterranean was a feature of economic life as early as the Bronze Age. The first examples were Mycenaean products, particularly ceramics, such as those found in several Middle Bronze Age levels (ca. 1500–1250 BCE) at Thapsos in Sicily (Voza 1973a, 1973b), and on the island of Lipari (Leighton 1999), among other locations. A Mycenaean krater and cup also appeared as far west as Spain, at Llanete de los Moros, near the town of Montoro in the province of Córdoba (García Martín 2003, 94). The identity of the traders carrying these goods is not clear, though long-distance trade seems to have been practiced by sailors from the Levant, Cyprus, Crete, and mainland Greece in this period (Gale 1991, Pulak 2008). The trade in goods from Greece dwindled with the collapse of the Mycenaean palaces, but it reappeared as the Greek population began to grow again in the eighth century. Some of the earliest evidence of these contacts comes from a burial in the Osteria dell'Osa cemetery at Gabii, east of Rome. One pot in Tomb 482 had an inscription that seems to use the Greek alphabet—the earliest writing of any kind known from Italy—and was dated to around 770 (Watkins 1995, 37–39). Around the same time, Greek cups began to appear in Sicily, also in tombs. The earliest of these was a Euboian chevron skyphos of around 775, found at Villasmundo, near Augusta, but there were also Corinthian cups dating to the middle of the eighth century (Voza 1973a, 1973b). The earliest Greek vase in the far western Mediterranean was an Athenian Middle Geometric II pyxis found at Huelva dating to around 780, with a few other pieces following at El Puerto de Santa María (Pellicer et al. 1977, Shefton 1982, Domínguez 2001).

These imports increased throughout the eighth century and were soon followed by the first Greek colonists in the west. The earliest settlement was Pithekoussai, which was founded around 750 on the island of Ischia, north of the Bay of Naples. This settlement was seemingly an *emporion,* or a trading post that lacked the surrounding farmland needed to make it a politically independent and self-supporting community (Ridgway 1992).[1] The choice of this location may have been made as a way of balancing competing demands for access to new markets and security from attack. Pithekoussai, together with Kyme, the town that succeeded it on the mainland by 730, was the farthest north of any Greek settlement in Italy. Kyme, like most other Greek colonies, was an *apoikia,* a town that consisted of both an urbanized center and a *chora* (a hinterland suitable for intensive agriculture) to sustain it, rather than simply an emporion. *Apoikiai* were not just independent with regard to their economies; they also were autonomous city-states (*poleis*) whose ties to their founding cities were largely restricted to cultural affinities.[2] Etruscan domination of southern Lazio and northern Campania is likely to have prevented or dissuaded the Greek colonial expeditions from pushing any farther north.

Numerous colonies were founded on Sicily in this period as well, beginning with Naxos, Syracuse, Leontinoi, Katane, and Megara Hyblaia, all on the east side of the island around 735–725, and continuing into the seventh century with Gela, Messana, Akragas, Selinous, and Himera (Thuc. VI.3–4). The overall effect of these foundations was that by 625, the Greeks controlled all of the island's best harbors and riverine routes to the interior (except at the western end of the island, where Phoenicians were more active), as well as the largest agricultural zones, especially the Plain of Catania. A similar process occurred in south Italy, from Naples (ancient Parthenope/Neapolis) all the way along the coast to Taranto (ancient Taras) and Gallipoli (ancient Kallipolis).

In no instance, either during this first wave of western colonization, or later, did settlers found their new towns in a *terra nullius*. There were non-Greek groups living throughout these regions. It is difficult for modern scholars to study these other groups in the same way that they investigate Greeks because non-Greeks so rarely left written testimony of their lives and societies. Sometimes non-Greeks adopted the Greek alphabet to write their own languages, as happened in Sicily and Italy. But these inscriptions are usually brief, consisting of only a few words at a time. In only a few cases—notably the Etruscans in northern and central Italy, and the Iberians in eastern and central Spain—are there significant written records that survive. In the first example, while many Etruscan texts can be deciphered, they tend to be brief legal or religious inscriptions (land deeds and sales, dedications, etc.; Steinbauer 1999, Facchetti 2005). There are no narratives giving detailed mythologies, descriptions of social life, or historical accounts. As for Iberian texts, the writing can be sounded out phonetically, but the meaning is not yet understood (Sanmartí and Santacana 2005, 26–29).

We are left with the descriptions recorded by Greeks and Romans, often written many centuries after the colonization process began. Our under-standing of non-Greek native groups is therefore compromised on several levels: first, by the lack of native accounts of their own world; second, by the variable survival of Greek and Roman descriptions of the western Mediterranean since antiquity; and third, by the biases of the writers whose work did survive, since they portrayed events from their own culturally and socially determined perspectives, which cannot always be identified with certainty by modern scholars. The multiplicative nature of the problem is evident from the fact that ancient writers themselves sometimes disagreed even on the relatively simple question of how to identify large ethnic groups. In the case of Sicily before Greek settlement, Strabo (writing in the first century BCE) wrote that one group living there were the Morgeti (6.2.4). Diodorus Siculus (writing at the same time as Strabo, and being himself from Adrano, in the Sicilian interior) mentioned another group, called the Ausoni, who settled Sicily from the Aeolian Islands (V.8.1). Thucydides (writing in the late fifth century BCE, probably using the work of another fifth-century historian, Antiokhos of Syracuse) described three other groups, the Sikans, the Sikels, and the Elymians (VI.2.2–5).[3] None of these writers explain which characteristics (language, customs, social or political struc-tures, or something else) they used to identify one group from another. It is therefore unclear whether non-Greeks would have agreed with the divi-sions that were perceived by Greeks (Antonaccio 2001, 2003, 61). Did their system of self-identification follow a similar hierarchy as that of Greeks, who typically would identify individuals first by patronymic, then locality (deme, village) or tribe, *polis* or region, linguistic group (Doric, Ionic, Aeolic, etc.), and finally as Hellenes—or did it follow some other pattern of affiliations? Lacking independent evidence, we cannot pose an answer to this question—and without an answer, we must question the reports of Greek and Roman authors regarding the motivations and actions they attributed to non-Greeks, as well as the relationships that existed between them, and with Greeks.[4]

Classical writers reported that early interactions between colonizing Greeks and native populations covered a broad range, from violent conflict and upheaval, as documented at Naxos, Katane, Leontinoi, and Syracuse (Diod. Sic. XIV.88.1, Thuc. VI.3.2–3), and shown archaeologically at the last of these (Orsi 1919); to cooperation in the case of Megara Hyblaia, where a hapless group of Greek colonists who had tried and failed twice previously to found a settlement were ultimately granted land by an indigenous leader for their new town (Thuc. VI.4.1–2).[5] In later periods, Greeks and non-Greeks could, albeit infrequently, act together for mutual benefit, as in the case of the Syracusan colony of Kamarina and its neighboring indigenous population, which formed alliances in wars, even against Kamarina's metropolis (Philistos, *FGrHist* 556 F 5).[6] In the second half of the fifth century, there was at least one historically documented example of a colony founded by a mixed group of Greeks and natives, Kale Akte, on Sicily's north coast (Diod. Sic. 12.8.2). As described in the introduction, the refoundation of Morgantina in east-central Sicily at about the same time also seems likely from archaeological evidence to have been a mixed venture (Walsh 2011–12). Intermarriage seems to have formed a significant part of relations between natives and Greeks at many sites in this first wave of colonization (Shepherd 1999).

The Second Wave of Colonization in the West

Although colonial foundations continued to be made in south Italy and Sicily throughout the seventh century, Greeks do not seem to have attempted new foundations farther north or west until 600 or even slightly later. They may have been blocked from proceeding further with colonial foundations by Etruscans along the mainland coast of the Tyrrhenian Sea and by Phoenicians at the western end of Sicily and on Sardinia, as will be seen shortly. Some Greeks are likely to have traveled around the western part of the Mediterranean as traders, however, even if in limited numbers. Scholars have been divided as to the specific identity of these Greeks, with some suggesting from a linguistic analysis of place-names in the West and in the southeast Aegean that Rhodians were the first in the area, while others have noted the prominence of Euboian and, to a lesser extent, Attic Geometric pottery in early contexts in the Iberian Peninsula (Domínguez 2013, 14–16). Analysis of the dataset in chapter 6 will show how the import of Greek vases was a mere trickle in the eighth century (only singletons, practically speaking), just slightly more substantial in the seventh century, and the trade then exploded in the sixth century.[7] Domínguez (2013, 24–25) has recently argued that the increase in Greek imports in the seventh century reflects the presence of Greek merchants as far west as Huelva at least by the period between 630 and 530, but the origin of products may have little or nothing to say about the identity of the merchants transporting and selling them.

The first Greek colonial settlement to move beyond the early limits of south Italy and Sicily was Massalia, founded around 600 on the coast of southern France by colonists from Phokaia.[8] As in the first wave of foundations, good harborage seems to have been the most important priority, as the earliest evidence for settlement was found on the north side of the harbor now known as Marseille's Vieux Port—but there seems to have been less interest in agriculture. Strabo remarked on lack of high-quality farmland in the vicinity, relative to other Greek colonial foundations:

> Massalia is situated on a rocky place. . . . [The Massaliotes] possess a country which, although planted with olive-trees and vines, is, on account of its ruggedness, too poor for grain; so that, trusting the sea rather than the land, they preferred their natural fitness for a seafaring life (4.1.4–5, trans. Jones).

This description raises questions regarding the settlers' intent. What kind of town was Massalia supposed to be: an emporion or an apoikia? And how reliant was Massalia on native neighbors for grain to survive? In addition to the excellent harbor, the settlement was within easy sailing distance to the mouth of the Rhone River, which provides access to the interior, and where the trading center of Saint-Blaise was located.

The story of Massalia's foundation was recounted in the pseudo-Aristotelian *Constitution of the Massalians* preserved in Athenaios (13.576) and by Pompeius Trogus, summarized by Justin (43.3–8). As it is told, the Phokaian founder, who was named Euxenos ("Good guest") or Protis ("First"), depending on the version, was visiting a local indigenous leader, with whom he wanted to negotiate for land on which to settle. At the same time, the leader's daughter was to choose a husband from the assembled men, identifying her choice by giving him a cup of water. The young woman, named Petta or Gyptis, again depending on the source, ignored the men from her community and chose the Greek visitor. It should be noted first that these accounts come to us at least third-hand and are at a remove of several centuries from the time of the foundation. The story seems to reflect an interest in intermarriage between the groups, and possibly also a period of peaceful interactions between colonizers and indigenes, though it also carefully analogizes the relationship between Greeks and indigenes to the relationship between dominant husband and submissive wife (Dougherty 1993, 9, Dietler 2010, 25).

Almost immediately following Pompeius Trogus's description of the engagement of Protis and Gyptis, he told how relations between Greeks and natives broke down.[9] The cause of this breakdown was the rise to power of a new Celtic king who was concerned about the growth of

Massalia. He and other indigenous leaders attempted to attack the city on multiple occasions, but each time, a female figure interceded to save the Massaliotes: first, a young woman who was in love with a Greek revealed the deceitful Celtic plot before it commenced; second, a feminine deity appeared to the king in his sleep and induced him to cease his attack (afterwards, she was revealed to be Minerva). Such descriptions cast natives as untrustworthy and dishonorable. The Greeks, by contrast, were described as friendly and possibly even naïve (having left their city gates wide open to potential attack during a festival). They taught the Celts to grow grapes and olives, and brought harmony to the land.[10] Pompeius Trogus went so far as to state that because of the colonial foundation, "such a radiance was shed over both men and things, so that it was not Greece which seemed to have immigrated into Gaul, but Gaul that seemed to have been transplanted into Greece." Descriptions like these were undoubtedly self-serving and self-justifying, as Dietler has already commented (2010, 24–26).

Massaliotes did not only have to contend with natives and their interests. Greek historians' descriptions of conflict between Greeks, Etruscans, and Phoenicians in the face of Phokaian expansion in the western Mediterranean during the sixth century show that there was strong competition for the location where Massalia was founded, or more likely a desire to keep Greeks from expanding into the region more generally. Thucydides described a naval battle between Phokaians and Carthaginians at the time of Massalia's foundation (1.13.6). When the Phokaians in Ionia abandoned their hometown during the Persian invasion around 540, some of the population moved west to join the relatively new colony at Alalia on Corsica (it had been founded twenty years earlier). Herodotos says that the Phokaians provoked their neighbors through five years of "harassment and plundering" (Hdt. 1.165–166). A joint Phoenician and Etruscan navy attempted to block this growth of Greek presence by waging battle at Alalia but they were defeated; the Phokaians, too, lost many of their ships in what was described as a "Cadmean" victory. The Phokaians abandoned Alalia, moving to south Italy and eventually founding the colony of Elea.

Unlike in Italy and Sicily, where the earliest colonies were quickly followed by many expeditions from several other metropoleis, few other Greek settlements were immediately founded along the coast of France and Spain; those that did emerge came from Phokaia and Massalia.[11] Agathe (modern Agde) was the only one west of Massalia in France that is well attested in ancient literature (Strabo 4.1.5, Pliny, *Nat. Hist.* 3.5.1). At least two colonies were also founded to the southeast, on the coast of what is today Catalonia: Emporion (Empúries) and Rhodes (Rosas). Ancient authors record the names of several others that have not yet been conclusively identified with any archaeological remains, particularly Hemeroskopeion and Mainake (which apparently was no longer inhabited by Strabo's time, but whose ruins reportedly preserved evidence of a Greek plan; 3.4.2). The zone north of Valencia and south of Emporion, by contrast, was an almost uninterrupted region of indigenous settlement, with some Phoenician and apparently little, if any, Greek interaction (Carme Belarte 2009, 91). There were no Greek colonies at all in Portugal, or in the interior of France, Switzerland, or Germany.

The competitive nature of trade relations in the region is the likely reason for the sparseness of Greek foundations along the French and Spanish coastline, relative to the distribution of colonies along the Italian coast in the earlier wave of settlement. Etruscan and especially Phoenician traders seem to have focused much greater attention on France and Spain in the eighth and seventh centuries than on areas where Greeks had founded new towns, such as south Italy. Though Etruscans seem not to have founded any colonies (Lattara and Saint-Blaise may be exceptions to this, although the evidence is mixed; see Dietler 2010, 97–100, with references, and Bouloumié 1982), Phoenicians and Carthaginians did settle permanently, especially on Spain's southern coast. These settlements included Ibiza (ancient Eybsm; in Greek, Eubousos), Cartagena (Qart Hadasht; in Latin, Karthago Nova) and Cádiz (Gadir), the last of which may have existed already by the end of the ninth century.[12]

There seem to have been significant patterns that can be identified with regard to the size, location, and form of foreign settlements in Iberia— whether Greek, Phoenician, or Etruscan. First, they tended to appear at certain coastal locations, often at river mouths. These settlements, though small, included members from one or several foreign groups, though the settlements often seem not to have been unified, but rather separated into quarters. Iberians usually occupied a defensible higher ground or an interior position, and foreigners were placed close by the water on lower ground or on nearby islands (Domínguez 2003b, 21–23). There are numerous examples of this pattern. Emporion was initially founded on a small island very close to an Iberian settlement (in fact, it seems to have dislodged Iberians who were already there; see chapter 3); La Illeta dels Banyets (at El Campello, near Alicante) is a small peninsula jutting out to sea that shows strong evidence of both Phoenician and Iberian presence.[13] Gadir was founded on a small strip of land that extends sharply from the mainland. Some examples from farther afield also seem potentially relevant: Pithekoussai, located on a small island close to the Italian coast, has already been mentioned. It was primarily Greek, but seems to have included Phoenicians as well (Ridgway 1992). The colony of Syracuse was founded on the island of Ortygia before it spread onto Sicily proper, and Motyon, a Phoenician colony, was on a small island at the western tip of Sicily. Another Phoenician settlement in Iberia seems to have been identified by recent archaeological work at Cerro del Villar, formerly an island in the mouth of the Guadalhorce River. This may have been the location of the original Phoenician settlement of Malaka (Aubet 2005). In a story that mirrors the narrative describing the foundation of Kyme from Pithekoussai, it was abandoned for an unknown reason in the first quarter of the sixth century, with a new and larger-scale town founded at modern Málaga, four kilometers north. The overarching pattern, then, was for traders—either Greek or Phoenician, but perhaps not Etruscans, for whom there is little specific evidence—to settle in or near protected locations that were also geographically privileged for trade by virtue of their proximity to routes into the interior.

A highly interesting feature of Cerro del Villar was its orthogonal grid plan, highly unusual in the context of a Phoenician town. Aubet has drawn parallels with Greek cities in North Africa, implying that Phoenician contact with those examples might have inspired an experiment in Iberia. I wonder whether the plan is not rather a sign that Cerro del Villar was a cooperative effort, or at least whether a few Greeks might have been involved in its foundation. This explanation might also help account better for ancient confusion over the relationship between Mainake and Malaka. Strabo (3.4.2) placed Mainake to the east of Málaga, and also notes contemporary confusion over its name, saying that some believe it to be the same as Málaga, which he states is incorrect. Domínguez (2013b, 25) sees the name "Mainake" as referring to a Greek emporion located at Málaga, with the name ultimately coming to mean both the emporion and the Phoenician city to the Greeks.

The abandonment of the town at Cerro del Villar may relate to a break identified by Domínguez (2009)—or perhaps better, given the long time span over which the process occurred, the unraveling of relations—in which increasing competition and, ultimately, violence between groups with interests in trade (including the battles at Alalia and, in the fifth century, Kyme) led to the collapse of the emporion system. Struggles between Greeks, Phoenicians, and Etruscans for commercial opportunities via the implantation of emporia became manifest in accusations of piracy and then war. The introduction of new, specifically Greek settlements such as Massalia, Agathe, and Emporion may either have sparked this rupture, or simply been a symptom of it. Possible destabilization within the Phoenician diaspora caused by Babylon's siege of Tyre around 575, and the rise of Carthage within that context, may also have had some effect; likewise with the foundation of Kyrene in north Africa during the second half of the seventh century, followed by the threat presented to that city by Carthaginian expansion into Libya in the sixth century. Previous instances of side-by-side trade in the western Mediterranean, as at Huelva, and perhaps, as I suggest, at Cerro del Villar, too, would thus have become untenable. At the same time, however, Etruscan, Greek, and Phoenician/Carthaginian goods continued to be found throughout the region into the classical period.

Phoenicians and Carthaginians seem to have interacted and perhaps even mixed with native Iberians to a greater extent than Greeks did, apart from the colonies just noted. Indigenous architecture shows changes following contact, from rounded plans or plans that show no particular geometric design to rectangular plans (Ruiz and Molinos 1998, 46–50).

In some cases, Phoenicians may have moved into Iberian villages alongside their native customers to smooth the flow of trade; Huelva and La Illeta dels Banyets seem to be a strong candidates for this model (Domínguez 2003b, 201, García Martín 2003). In other examples, smaller new Phoenician settlements apparently attracted Iberians to move in close by, as at modern Guardamar del Segura, where the Segura River empties into the Mediterranean (Azuar et al. 2001, Domínguez 2002, 72, Rouillard et al. 2009, Vives-Ferrándiz 2010). Among the Greek settlements, only Emporion was clearly located adjacent to an indigenous settlement, although Agathe was later founded at the location of a previous indigenous settlement, close to Bessan and Béziers in a densely occupied Hallstatt landscape (Nickels 1982, 1995).[14]

The presence of early Phoenician emporia seems to have ensured their dominance of trade with Iberians, and this fact must have been noticed by Greeks. Before 550, the amphorai discovered in Catalonia (which themselves constituted 98% of all imports), were almost entirely from Phoenician producers in Andalusia, with much smaller proportions from Etruria and Phoenicians in north Africa, and essentially none from Greek producers (Sanmartí and Santacana 2005, 128–130; Sanmartí 2009, 59–61). Within about 100 years of the foundation of Emporion, the importation of vessels other than amphorai climbed substantially, from almost none to 65% of the total, and Greek vessels from Italy, Massalia, and other areas now made up 75% of the imported amphorai.

THE INDIGENOUS POPULATIONS

Greek vases have, of course, also been found in archaeological contexts far from the Greek colonies and emporia described above. They appeared throughout the hinterlands of western and central Europe. This study includes Greek vases found in Portugal, central and southern Spain, eastern and central France, western Switzerland, and the west and southwest of Germany.[15] In these places, there were no Greek settlements, but there were numerous towns and villages belonging to people of other cultural traditions. Wherever vases have been found in these areas, speculation has emerged regarding the extent of direct contact with Greek traders, and thus with Greek practices. The number of vases found in hinterland contexts is significantly lower than on the coast (a point that will be more fully developed in chapter 6).

Hallstatt Culture

Interpreting the ethnic groupings of non-Greeks in France, Germany, and Switzerland is as problematic as the situation encountered in Italy. Once again, the names that survive for groups are those given by Greeks and

Romans. Greek traders seem to have applied the term *Keltoi,* which they first used to describe a tribal group in southeastern France, to all the non-Greeks they met along the coast of France. Hekataios of Miletos, a late sixth-century writer preserved in Stephanos of Byzantium's *Ethnika* (*FGrHist* 1 F 54–55), is the earliest source to record this name. Greeks recognized cultural affinities between the populations of southern France and others extending inland to what is now central France, Germany, Switzerland, and beyond. By the time Greeks settled in the western Mediterranean, the Keltoi inhabited all of central Europe. In later migrations they moved south into Italy (culminating in the famous sack of Rome in 387 BCE) and southeast into Greece and Asia Minor.

Herodotos (2.34 and 4.48), another early user of the word Keltoi, referred to people in the far western Mediterranean as well as the area around the source of the Danube River, in southwestern Germany. Likewise, the Romans called the people of France and northwestern Italy Gauls, even though they also recognized more specific tribal divisions within that group (Pliny, *Nat. Hist.* 3.4–5). Archaeologists have identified a broad cultural group that inhabited this area during the Iron Age, one that underwent a transformation in the middle of the fifth century BCE. In the early phase, this group is known as the Hallstatt culture, after a type-site in western Austria that gained prominence for the salt mining that took place there (Spindler 1991, Müller-Scheessel 2000). Hallstatt sites were scattered across the landscape from central Europe as far as Galicia and even northern Portugal (Cunliffe 1979, Almagro-Gorbea 1997). They were often arranged within sight of a central hilltop that controlled its surroundings. In the Hallstatt C (Early Iron Age) period, beginning roughly 700, the most elaborate sites were in Bohemia, Austria, and southern Germany. In the succeeding Hallstatt D period (ca. 600–450), when Greek imports appeared, similar articulations spread west into Switzerland and central France.

The presence of rich individual graves, typically with a tumulus mound erected over them as a marker, as at Hochdorf, Asperg, Heuneburg, and Vix (Mont Lassois), among many others, has led to the interpretation of these sites as being ruled by regional elites who have been described as princes, or *Fürsten.* The graves often included the wagon on which the deceased was brought to the tomb, metal adornments such as fibulae or torcs, furniture, and drinking vessels, all placed in a built timber structure that was subsequently covered with earth. In addition to the tumulus graves for aristocrats, a strong emphasis was placed on warriors in tombs, with weaponry such as swords and daggers frequently placed alongside burials. High-status women received large quantities of gold and bronze jewelry in their burials (e.g., Éluère 1997, Joachim 1997). Metal objects were also used as votive offerings, occasionally deposited in rivers. Low-status burials included few, if any, objects; these were ceramic rather than metal. They were also distinguished by the use of cremation rather than the inhumations favored by elites. According to one theory, the great displays of wealth seen in elite late Hallstatt burials were a manifestation of the enormous burden borne by the lower classes to supply economic support to the elites (Cunliffe 1979, 40). As more wealth was buried and removed from circulation, and as the population grew to the point where it could not be supported by locally available resources, new territories had to be sought out for exploitation.

Prior to 600, there is hardly any evidence for the presence of Greek vessels in Hallstatt zones, especially in the interior. About 30 vessels from the seventh century were represented at Saint-Blaise, though these are late enough (all with median production dates of 615 or later) that they may actually belong to the period around Massalia's foundation. A few vessels appeared just west of the Hérault River at Pézenas, Bessan, and Mailhac, and in the Gard valley at Calvisson, but none moved farther up the Rhône or beyond before 600. The foundation of Massalia must therefore be seen as a catalyzing event that led to Greek products appearing in non-Greek contexts. Yet it is far from clear that when Greek pottery did eventually move inland, it did so accompanied by Greek merchants. Diodorus Siculus recorded that wine was brought to central and northern Gaul by Italian traders (5.26, perhaps referring only to his own time, the first century BCE, though see also Arafat and Morgan 1994). The materials sought by Mediterranean traders were mostly minerals; Wells lists iron, copper, tin, graphite, coral, stone, lignite, jet, sapropelite, amber, gold, and silver (1995, 230). Salt was also a significant exchange product, coming from mines such as those at Hallstatt itself (Zeller 1997).

Following a transition around 450 whose precise cause is still unknown, but which was linked to destruction of many of the most important *Fürstensitzen,* including Heuneburg and Vix, the Celtic culture of western Europe changed. The new culture is identified with a new type-site, La Téne, in Switzerland. The La Téne period continued down to the time of Roman conquests of what is today modern France and southern Germany in the first centuries BCE and CE, and was characterized by fortified hilltop settlements called *oppida*. A strong decline in the number of imports, particularly Greek ones, is associated with the transition from the Hallstatt to the La Téne period (Wells 1979), as is a gradual shrinkage in the disparity between wealthy and poor burials (Cunliffe 1979, 23).

Several scholars have noted distinctive differences between the Hallstatt cultures of central France, Germany and Austria, and those of Mediterranean France (Duval et al. 1990, Dietler 1997, 275). At the same time, no satisfactory nomenclature has been agreed upon to separate the two groups; scholars have often resorted to referring to groups by chronological periods rather than names. For the purposes of this investigation, groups in the upper Rhône and points farther north and west will be referred to as North Hallstatt, and those near the coast as South Hallstatt. Lusitanians, too, seem to have been related to Hallstatt culture, at least by language (Lenerz–de Wilde 1995, 533). These names undoubtedly smooth over subtle (or even major) differences between populations in each region, but they are useful for allowing the hypothesis that there might have been significant differences in the consumption of Greek pottery between otherwise related groups to be tested more easily.

The Iberian Peninsula

In Spain and Portugal, the situation can be even more complex. Here there seem to have been several different indigenous cultural groups that mixed to varying degrees with one another. It is difficult to find signs of sharp divisions between these groups in the material record, despite the existence of some detailed literary descriptions dating from later ancient periods, primarily by Strabo and Pliny the Elder. Part of the problem stems from the approaches taken by some scholars, especially in Spain in the first half of the 20th century, which ranged from "pan-Celtic" perspectives to nationalistic tendencies focusing on the Iberian culture (Ruíz and Molinos 1998, 10–12).

The name "Iberia" was given to the peninsula by Greeks, from their name for the Ebro River (Strabo 3.4.19). The name by which the region was known to indigenes is no longer extant; the Phoenician name may have been *i-shephanním*, which may have been the source for the later Latin name "Hispania." The dominance of such foreign names has been identified as colonialist "geographic violence," as defined by Said (Domínguez 2002, 68–69). The name "Iberian," like "Celtic," collapsed many other identifications into one more convenient for the Greeks—and as with "Celtic," "Iberian" has had a long afterlife in modern scholarship.

The people known to scholars as Iberians seem to have been located primarily along the east coast of Spain, from Catalonia all the way to the Phoenician towns of Sexi or Malaka in Andalusia. Hundreds of Iberian inscriptions have been found throughout this entire region, showing the presence of a common language. The inscriptions use various scripts whose phonetic values are generally known, but their meanings remain a mystery (Sanmartí and Santacana 2005, 26–29). In some cases in the southern area of Iberian habitation, a Greek alphabet was used for the Iberian language, but otherwise the two primary scripts were locally developed. Many inscriptions feature non-Iberian proper names, suggesting that in fact the linguistic situation was not unified, but rather more complex (de Hoz 1993). In many cases, Hallstatt people (usually described as Celts in scholarly literature describing this region, just as they are in scholarship on southern France) inhabited the interior and northern sectors of the Iberian Peninsula. In addition to these groups, scholars also frequently mention "Celtiberians" (in the northeastern interior, crossing over the Pyrenees) and "Ibero-Tartessians" (in the southern interior) (Cuadrado Díaz 1969; Sanmartí and Santacana 2005, 7), which signify the mixing of groups in this period.[16] Such mixtures emphasize the importance for archaeologists of recognizing local patterns and variations. The Ibero-Tartessians are associated with inscriptions in a semisyllabic text derived from the Phoenician alphabet (Domínguez 2002, 83).[17] Iberian habitation also extended north from modern Spain into Pyrénées-Orientales, Rousillon, and western Languedoc (see Ibero-Languedoc, below).[18] As will be seen in chapter 6, the various regions show markedly different consumption patterns for Greek pottery.

Iberian culture, like Hallstatt culture, developed out of the Urnfield culture of the Late Bronze Age. It is first identified around 900 BCE by reference to three major developments: growth and urbanization of settlements, the introduction of wheel-made pottery, and the appearance of iron technology (Cabrera Bonet 1996, 49). The catalyst for these developments has often been seen as external, spurred on by contact either with Phoenicians (Sanmartí and Padro 1976–78, Aubet 1993), or by contact with both Greeks and Phoenicians (Ruiz Zapatero 1983–84), but— importantly—the transition should not be seen as a mechanistic one formed or caused by Phoenicians or Greeks, or by Iberians rotely copying them. The appearance of Phoenician trade alongside or soon after the emergence of Iberian culture, particularly associated with metals—not only iron, but bronze, too; finished objects as well as raw materials—implies a diversified economy of agriculture and metallurgy to supply it. Iberian society seems to have been stratified, with elite control over the production of metal and prestige goods (Cabrera Bonet 1996, 51). As both Cabrera Bonet (1996, 52) and Aubet (1993, 24) have noted, the roots of these social and economic structures were local, existing already in the Urnfield period. The stratification of society may only have increased over time, as it appears from a drop in the number of tombs discovered per site between the Early Iron Age (700–500) and the Late Iberian Period (400–200) that burial rituals became reserved for an ever-shrinking portion of society, with the greatest change happening between the sixth and fifth centuries (Sanmartí and Santacana 2005, 45). At the same time, a hierarchy has also been detected in the range of settlement types that emerged in this period, from isolated rural houses, to small fortified villages, to large regional centers like Ullastret, which had dozens of houses within massive city walls (Sanmartí and Santacana, 60–66). The regional centers controlled large territories of up to 2000–3000 square kilometers, comparable to—if not actually larger than—many Greek poleis and Etruscan city-states (Plana i Mallart and Martín Ortega 2001, Sanmartí and Santacana 2005, 70–71).

Ibero-Languedoc

It has become increasingly clear over the last two decades that Iberian populations lived north of the Pyrenees mountains as well as on the Iberian Peninsula proper (Dietler 2010, 80). Strabo indicated some awareness of this, saying that "historians of former times, it is said, gave the name of Iberia to all the land beyond the Rhodanos (Rhône) and that isthmus between the Galatic gulfs (i.e., the modern Iberian peninsula)" (3.4.19, trans. Jones). The precise extent of their territory has not been determined precisely, although it appears that the Hérault River, rather than the Rhône, may have demarcated a boundary between Iberians and Hallstatt groups. One sign of the distinction between the Hallstatt and Iberian regions was the use of different alphabets (Untermann 1992), but material differences seem to have existed as well. Local ceramic assemblages were different at the transition from the Bronze Age to the Early Iron Age in the seventh and sixth centuries (to the east of the Hérault, the Suspendian *facies*, and to the west, the Mailhac II/Grand Bassin II; Py 1992, 29–30, Garcia 1993, 316, Dietler 1997, 277). Such differences, as will be shown in chapter 6, are forcefully apparent in the distribution and use of Greek pottery as well—not only between Ibero-Languedoc and the South Hallstatt region, but also between Ibero-Languedoc and other Iberians.

Tartessos

In the southwestern Iberian Peninsula, probably approximately equivalent to the area now within the Spanish provinces of Cádiz, Sevilla, and Huelva, was the area Greeks called Tartessos.[19] It seems to have been composed of a subgroup of Iberians. Modern scholars have directed attention to it because it is the first polity in the western Mediterranean that was described by Greek authors in any detail (Schulten 1959, 74–99; Maluquer de Motes 1985). It was reportedly endowed with extraordinary metal wealth. At the same time, very little is known for certain about the indigenous population of this region, their organization, and their culture. Herodotos and Strabo form the most important ancient literary sources for this region prior to and during the period of intercultural contact, but their descriptions leave much to be desired. Herodotos's first account (1.163) comes in the course of describing the earliest Phokaian voyages:

> Now the Phokaians were the first of the Hellenes to make long sea voyages; they are the ones who opened up the Adriatic, Tyrrhenia, Iberia, and Tartessos to the Hellenes. They did not sail in round-sided ships, but in pentekonters. When they went to Tartessos, they made friends with the king of the Tartessians, whose name was Arganthonios. He ruled as tyrant of Tartessos for 80 years, and lived for all of 120 years. The Phokaians became such good friends with this man that he urged them to leave Ionia behind and settle wherever they wished in his country; then, when he could not persuade them to do that, and learning that the growing power of the Mede was beginning to threaten them, he gave them a very generous amount of money to build a wall around their city (trans. Strassler).

From this account, it is hard to tell much of anything about Tartessos, except that it was wealthy and purportedly not just open to trade but friendly to it (at least, from Greeks), even if the traders arrived in warships (a probable sign of worry about competitors). It was apparently located on the far side of Iberia. The text also presents a justification for Phokaian colonization in the west, even though no colonies were made as far west as Tartessos is thought to have been. Herodotos does not reveal whether Tartessos was the name of a city or a region (Maluquer de Motes 1985, 16–26), nor does he describe Tartessos's size, its population, or the type or quality of its land. There is no mention of Phoenician traders.

The name of the Tartessian ruler, Arganthonios, probably a word meaning something like "Silver Man", however, is a hint of the area's wealth. It falls in line with many other names given by Greeks for important foreign people. The names given for the Sikel *hegemons* Archonides and Douketios, for example, probably are more like titles than given names (the latter probably from a Sikel word related to the Latin *dux;* Walsh 2011–12, 120 n. 36 and 122 n. 50). In the case of Arganthonios, his name may reflect the linkage between political power and control of resources already noted in northeastern Iberia by Aubet and Cabrera Bonet above. It may even be a Greek version of a local title, which could explain the long reign attributed by Greeks to the "master of silver"—in this way, Arganthonios would refer to multiple holders of the office, each in turn, whose role was of greater interest to Greek authors than their individual identities.

Somewhat later in his narrative, Herodotos told a second story that also purports to describe the first interactions between Greeks and Tartessians. It occurs in the midst of a larger account of the colonization of Kyrene (4.151–152). In this description, a ship from Samos (not Phokaia), blown off course, encounters a stranded Cretan murex fisherman named Korobios on an island named Plateia, which he had been left to hold by the colonization party. After listening to Korobios tell his story, and giving him a year's worth of provisions, the Samians departed for Egypt, but were

> again driven off course by an easterly wind which did not abate until they had passed through the Pillars of Herakles and by some divine guidance came to Tartessos. This trading post had not been exploited (*to de emporion touto ēn akēraton*) at this time, and so these men returned with a profit from their cargo greater than any other Hellenes of who we have an accurate account, except for Sostratos son of Laodamas of Aegina, since it is impossible for anyone to challenge his record! The Samians took a tenth of their profits, six talents' worth, and had a bronze bowl made in the Argive style, with griffin heads projecting around it. They dedicated it in the sanctuary of Hera and set it upon three gigantic bronze kneeling statues, over ten feet tall (trans. Strassler).

Tartessos is described explicitly as an emporion, and thus perhaps it was the name of a single settlement that was also applied to its surrounding territory, though it is also possible that this Tartessos refers specifically to Huelva (see chapter 3). In either case, it is notable that Herodotos makes the claim that the emporion had not yet been exploited, since Phoenicians are known to have been trading in this area since the ninth century (Arruda 2000, 170). The earliest Greek goods date to the middle of the eighth century, but these are sporadic.

The story of the Samian arrival in Tartessos seems to have parallels with the colonization story into which it intrudes. In the preceding sections of Herodotos's history, the Therans who hope to colonize Libya find out from Korobios that he had been there before, because he too had been blown off his original course. So in this narrative, there were actually three groups traveling without knowing quite where they would end up: the Therans looking for the colonial site promised to them by Apollo at Delphi; Korobios, already blown off course once, then left behind and perhaps even abandoned by the Therans; and the Samians, who ultimately found their way to Tartessos. All of these problems lead the reader to sense the difficulty of long-distance travel and trade, and the remoteness of destinations such as Tartessos. Such difficulty was also, of course, the theme of the *nostoi* epics (such as the *Odyssey*) of the archaic period. The problem of communication related to overseas colonial expeditions also seems to be raised, as the Theran oikist was a man named Battos who may have had a stuttering problem. Battos was instructed by the Pythia to found Kyrene, even though his reason for his coming to the oracle seems to have been to find a cure (Hdt. 4.155; Malkin 1987, 62–65 with references). Similarly, Korobios tells his story twice but is left on his own both times (the Therans ultimately did return to found Kyrene, but we hear no more about Korobios); and the Samians do not seem to learn from Korobios's story, ending up far from their intended objective in an unknown land. Ultimately, however, both the Kyrenaians and the Samians profited from their expeditions, as the Theran colony was successful and the Samian sailors reaped enormous wealth from their trade with Tartessos.

Strabo, writing in a much later period, was impressed by the metal resources of the region: "Up to the present moment, in fact, neither gold, nor silver, nor yet copper, nor iron, has been found anywhere in the world, in a natural state, either in such quantity or of such good quality" (3.2.8, trans. Jones). He quoted Stesichoros (in fact, probably the very earliest source to survive on Tartessos) to describe the fertility and wealth of the Tartessian landscape, calling the springs "silver-rooted" (3.2.11, Schulten 1959, 74). The rich mineral wealth of this area is evident in the mining activity that has continued up to the present day, centered on the Río Tinto (so named for the red color given by the iron it carries within it). Among the other metals available in this area are copper, lead, zinc, gold, and silver (Jurado 2000, 138).[20] Furnace pits for refining metal, and slag from the refining process, have been found at Huelva and elsewhere

(Jurado 2002, 245–250). The production of metal, especially silver, seems to have declined at the end of the sixth century (Jurado 2002, 260, 262). Tartessians seem to have been unable to mine effectively at levels much below the surface, and the resources that they could mine thus ran out quickly; at the same time, new mines opened up in the eastern part of Andalusia, particularly around Jaén province (especially the hills around modern Linares, close by ancient Cástulo; Blázquez et al. 1984).

Foreign trade came to Tartessos in the guise of Phoenicians and, to a much lesser extent (it appears), Greeks. Some suggestions have been made relating the Greek name Tartessos with Levantine use of Tarshish (Isaiah 23:11–15, Schulten 1959, 98); the latter usage could have been a way for Phoenicians to mark the breadth of their maritime control from one end of the Mediterranean to the other (López-Ruiz 2009). The ethnonyms "Turdetani" and "Turduli," both found locally, are related to the same root, but may reflect ethnonyms used in later periods (Escacena Carrasco 1989).[21]

Archaeological evidence for indigenous life in southwestern Spain has shown strong signs of a radical social transformation in the Tartessian period (ca. 750–550). A significant development was the appearance of cemeteries. These necropolises featured two kinds of burials, tumuli or simple below-ground tombs, with either cremation or inhumation rituals used for the body of the deceased (Ruiz Delgado 1989). Such cemeteries existed neither in the preceding Final Bronze Age, nor in the succeeding Turdetanian period, and they seemed to present an arena in which hierarchies could be expressed and reinforced. Social hierarchies could not be determined by mere presence of the burial in a cemetery or even by burial type, however, as both kinds of burials were used for elites. Richer tombs were distinguished by the number and types of grave goods, including imported pottery, deposited with the body.[22]

The precise limits of Tartessos still remain to be determined, including how far inland it extended from the Atlantic coast, and whether it crossed over the Guadiana River to include some or all of southern Portugal. With regard to the latter issue, Ana Margarida Arruda (2000) has noted distinct differences between sites along the coast of Portugal (such as Castro Marim and Alcácer do Sal), and those in the interior, such as Ourique and Castro Verde. She does not see these differences as related to a cultural or ethnic division, however. Instead, they reflect the degree of interaction with foreigners and foreign goods that was available to coastal sites, which were "undeniably" a part of the circuit of trade regularly plied by Phoenician merchants (2000, 170, 176). Rather than one united social or political entity, spreading across southwestern Spain and southern Portugal, or two such distinct entities somehow corresponding to modern political boundaries, Arruda argues for a more subtle reading of the archaeological evidence. She sees strong similarities between the type and scope of activities found at coastal sites in both regions, such as Castro Marim and Huelva, and between interior sites in both regions, such as the sanctuaries of Cancho Roano and Castro Verde. In this way, the two regions were "profoundly connected . . . the use of artifacts which belong to the same technological and functional level does not simply demonstrate mastery of the same technology and the same centers for the importation of products, but similar social structures and economic resources" (Arruda 2000, 175–176; my translation). Even so, there were significant differences between and within the two regions that preclude them from being lumped together easily.

SUMMARY

In this chapter, the complicated history of Greek colonization, first in the central Mediterranean, and later in the western Mediterranean, has been outlined. While Greeks met only limited competition from Phoenicians and Etruscans in Sicily and south Italy, the situation was seemingly much more difficult for them along the coast of France and Spain. In addition, they encountered native groups from a wide range of cultural traditions. There seems to have been a great deal of mixing between native groups, particularly in Iberia, as well as mixing between natives and foreigners from elsewhere in the Mediterranean. The frequent mention in ancient literary sources of native leaders who sometimes offered assistance and sometimes led attacks on Greeks seems to reflect both the different kinds of reactions caused by the presence of foreigners, and the ability of natives to take control over relations.

Although Greeks were not able to settle many permanent towns in this region, they did trade widely, with their wares reaching not only the Straits of Gibraltar but the Atlantic coast, as well. Greek pottery also traveled up the Rhône valley into central and northern France, Switzerland, and even into Germany. The lack of Greek settlements of any kind, or even of Greek building techniques (apart from the early sixth-century fortifications at Heuneburg; see chapter 3) in native sites in the interior, suggests that Greek presence was limited at best. As a result, it should be expected that a wide range of consumption practices will be visible for Greek pottery in the archaeological record.

NOTES

1. This definition of an emporion is similar to the one made by Bresson (1992). For a full discussion of emporia and their definition (albeit focusing on the classical period), see now Demetriou (2012, esp. 16–21).
2. Mother-cities (metropoleis) did seem to expect political support from their colonies, as seen in the case of Korkyra and its metropolis Corinth at the outset of the Peloponnesian War (Thuc. 1.24–55), but there is no question

that governance of colonies was generally managed at the colonies them-selves. See also chapter 3 on the differences between ancient and modern colonialism.

3. There are signs that ancient authors were aware of these problems, and some presented solutions. Diodoros connected the Ausonians to the Sikels through a royal lineage (Liparos, son of Auson and leader of the Ausoni, settled the island of Lipari, where the wind-god Aiolos already lived (Diod. Sic. V.8.1–2); Aiolos married Liparos's daughter, and two of their sons, Pheraimon and Androkles, ruled over the Sikels and the Sikans). Dionysios of Halikarnassos (*Ant.* I.22.3), quoting Hellanikos of Lesbos, wrote that the king of the Ausoni was named Sikelos, and the group later changed their name to honor their ruler.

4. Dougherty (1993, 88–91 and 94–95) has shown how Greeks could attribute mythologies to non-Greek religious locations that justified Greek domination of those sites. Domínguez (2002) has also noted the "violence" done to indig-enous groups by the giving of new and incorrect or inappropriate names to them by colonizers.

5. The complications were created for the Megarian colonists by Greeks who had arrived in Sicily ahead of them, not by Sikels, according to Thucydides.

6. See also Pais 1933 (1894), 236, 560–564; Graham 1983, 177.

7. See also Domínguez 2001 (190).

8. In addition to the sources discussed below, see Thuc. I.13.6, Paus. 10.8, Livy, 5.34, Plut., *Solon,* 2.3. See also chapter 3 for a more detailed discussion of the archaeological record for Massalia's foundation.

9. After marriage, Gyptis changed her name to Aristoxene, or "Good Guest/ Host" (Olson's note in Athenaios 2007–2011 [2010 volume], 334).

10. According to Pompeius Trogus, the Celts learned from the Greeks, among other things, "how to live according to laws, and not violence."

11. Rhodes, according to Strabo, was founded by Rhodians from the Aegean and later taken over by Massaliotes (14.2.10), but elsewhere he attributes its foun-dation to the Emporitans (3.4.8). See also Domínguez (2013, 12–14).

12. One much later literary tradition pushed the foundation date for Gadir back to 1104 BCE (Velleius Paterculus *Roman History* 1.2.1–3).

13. At some point, an earthquake separated the peninsula from the mainland, making La Illeta dels Banyets an island. An effort to reconnect the island to the mainland in 1943 used dynamite, destroying much of the settlement's necropolis (http://www.marqalicante.com/Paginas/es/Illeta-dels-banyets-P21-M2.html, accessed in June 2013).

14. Other sites in this area include Portiragnes, Saint-Thíbery, Pézenas, and Méze, while Nissan-lez-Ensérune, which presented one of the largest col-lections of Greek pottery in this survey, lies just on the other side of Béziers from Agathe.

15. Not all Greek vases that have been discovered in these regions are included in the dataset; see chapter 5 for discussion.

16. Strabo (1.2.27) thought that "Celtiberian" was an incorrect group name.

17. Comparison of jewelry from the famous hoard at El Carambolo, adjacent to Seville, with bracelets from Hochdorf in southwest Germany has been used to suggest broad cultural connections over very long distances between Ibero-Tartessians and Hallstatt culture (Lenerz–de Wilde 1995, 544).

18. Despite the intervening mountains, Iberian Languedoc has historically main-tained strong connections to the south. Until 1659, part of this region belonged to the Principality of Catalonia, and even now much of the population contin-ues to speak Catalan in addition to French.

19. The provinces of Córdoba and Badajoz might also have been part of Tartessos.

20. Jurado (2000, 138, 2002, 242) has estimated that the Tartessians could have recovered more than 2 kilograms of silver and 70 grams of gold per metric ton of mined ore.
21. The evolution from Tartessos to Turdetanos could bear some resemblance to the transition from the Hallstatt facies to La Téne in the fifth century, with ethnic continuity but cultural change.
22. Other luxurious grave goods, though rarer, included scarabs, ostrich eggs, and carved ivories (Ruiz Delgado 1989, 277–280).

3   Comparison of Significant Sites

INTRODUCTION

In the previous chapter, some description of the groups who lived in the western Mediterranean and trans-Alpine Europe was given in the course of relating the history of Greek colonization, but little information was given about the diversity of settlements and especially the material cultures of these regions. In this chapter, further detail will be given about these areas and the populations living in them by means of a discussion of some of the most significant and best-studied sites. The sites are organized by culture—Greek, Hallstatt, Iberian—and offer summaries of their topography, history, and some of the important archaeological finds made at each.

GREEK SITES

Massalia

The city of Massalia was founded around 600 by colonists from Phokaia.[1] The date of the foundation was given by Timaios ("120 years before the battle of Salamis," in Skymnos *Periegesis* 209, *FGrHist* 566 F 71) and has generally been confirmed by the discovery of late seventh- and early sixth-century Greek pottery in the city. The choice of the site was clearly due to its excellent harbor and its proximity to the Rhône delta some 40 kilometers to the west. As previously noted, the foundation was only one step in a larger Phokaian effort to expand in the western Mediterranean. The new town was founded on the north side of the present central harbor of the city (though the sea level was significantly higher at that time, making the harbor much wider than today), from Fort St.-Jean and the Butte St.-Laurent, east through the Panier neighborhood, probably as far as the Butte des Moulins (Dietler 1997, 282; 2010, 308–316; Hermary et al. 1999, Hermary 2002b, 60–62) (Fig. 3.1).

Over the course of the following century, Massalia grew rapidly, probably as a result of Phokaians leaving their mother-city following its siege

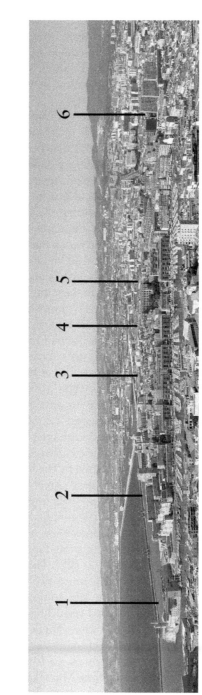

Figure 3.1 The Vieux Port at Marseille, where the colony of Massalia was founded ca. 600 BCE, looking north. (1) Fort St.-Jean, (2) Butte St.-Laurent, (3) Le Panier, (4) Butte des Molins, (5) Butte des Carmes, (6) Bourse

by the Persians in 540. Massalia extended farther east past the Butte des Carmes to the Bourse, where ancient fortifications have been found, the earliest dating to around 510. At the same time, a mole was constructed in the harbor to develop the port. Over the course of the archaic period, Massalia grew from about 10 hectares to 40 hectares (Dietler 2010, 312).[2] Even with its smaller size at the city's foundation, it was larger than any of the colonies that came after it in this survey.

Continuous occupation of the city has made excavation difficult. Only in limited areas is it possible to have a clear view of the ancient remains. First among these areas is the zone around the Bourse, where the demolition of housing blocks over the course of the 20th century allowed direct investigation to begin in 1967 (Euzennat 1980). This site preserves not only the late sixth-century fortifications just mentioned but also some of the interventions made by Massaliotes to improve the terrain during the sixth and fifth centuries, specifically filling in a swampy area at the easternmost extent of the harbor and reinforcing a natural causeway through a marsh in order to create the road that led into the city from the east. Unlike most Greek colonies in south Italy and Sicily, there was no single plan governing development of the urban space. Rather, a number of different plans were implemented at different times for new neighborhoods (Moliner 2001).[3] Limited evidence has also been found for other circuits of defensive walls built at successive moments to surround the city as it expanded, although none of these predate the wall represented at the Bourse excavations. Massalia's most famous monument was a sanctuary to Artemis that has not yet been discovered, but which seems to have served as a model for other Phokaian/Massaliote colonies.

In the earliest periods, Massalia's reliance on outsiders for many goods seems clear, highlighting the limited territory that it controlled. The description of the site by Strabo given in the previous chapter stressed how rocky and ill-suited for farming the area around the city was, and the surrounding territory, at least at first, was tightly constrained by the hills of the Huveaune River valley entering the harbor from the east (Arcelin 1986, Bats 1986, Sternberg and Tréziny 2005). Almost all wine was imported from Etruria, to judge from the amphora finds, through the middle of the sixth century, although from this period onward Massaliote wine not only took precedence over Etruscan wines at Massalia but also as far west as the Hérault and north into the interior (Dietler 2010, 197–199). The situation regarding its ability to grow its own grain has been more problematic to discern, but it seems clear that the land close to the city could not have supported the population, given what can be estimated regarding dietary needs, crop yields, and density of habitation in the city (Dietler 2010, 115–117). Substantial quantities of grain must therefore have been brought from elsewhere, either neighboring indigenous towns, or from Greek, Etruscan, or Phoenician settlements with surplus supplies. Massalia was a city designed primarily for trade, and lacking some of the resources needed to sustain itself fully, but it was also a large-scale settlement with significant industries (including pottery production) that sent out its own colonial expeditions. It thus seems to straddle the conceptual boundary between apoikia and emporion in ways that may have been unusual for Greek colonies generally, but which do seem to be reflected in certain respects at other Phokaian settlements (see, for example, Emporion, below; Lepore 1970).

Agathe

Sometime after the foundation of Massalia, colonization parties left to found new subcolonies to the east, west, and southwest. Initially, it was believed that the foundation of these new towns happened during the sixth century. Excavation since the 1980s, however, has shown that apart from the ones in Catalonia, these foundations were only initiated later, at the end of the fifth or even into the fourth century.[4] Agathe (modern Agde; Pliny, *Nat. Hist.* 3.5.1) is the only one of these that is included in this study; the others include Olbia, Antibes, and Nice, to the east in what was, in antiquity, Ligurian territory. It has been suggested that one putative Massaliote colony, Theline, could be associated with Arles, but the evidence is not strong (Dietler 2010, 118–119). Nickels (1983) has argued that prior to the foundation of Agathe, Phokaians lived around the mouth of the Hérault alongside natives from the first quarter of the sixth century, but there is not a great deal of Greek pottery at Agathe to support the idea that Greeks were present in significant numbers.[5]

It has not been possible to excavate Agathe thoroughly because it is occupied by modern and historic structures. It appears, however, that the new Greek settlement displaced (or enveloped) an indigenous town, taking over a hilltop almost at the mouth of Hérault River (Nickels 1982, 1995). Strabo described its function as a defensive outpost against the local population (4.1.5). The Hallstatt centers of Bessan and Nissan-lez-Ensérune (two of the largest consumers of Greek products) and the smaller towns of Béziers and Pézenas were all located nearby. The large number and wide range of types of Greek pots present in this area in the sixth and fifth centuries (i.e., before the refoundation of Agathe) presents a striking contrast to Massalia's apparent need for a permanent military presence. Massaliotes clearly felt it was necessary to improve their security, even in a zone that was highly receptive to their products, either as an act of expansionism or imperialism, or because they were facing competition from other traders.

Emporion

The most significant of the Massaliote settlements (and the best-studied by modern archaeologists) was Emporion, also known by its modern Catalan name Empúries (and formerly by its Spanish name, Ampurias), founded around the second quarter of the sixth century. The town's name would seem to state its function, at least originally, as a trading outpost rather than a full-scale apoikia. Strabo's description of the town (3.4.8) is complex and also extremely interesting, given the information it provides concerning the relationship between the Phokaian/Massaliote colonists and the indigenous Iberians, who reportedly belonged to a subgroup called the Indigetans. According to him:

> The Emporitans formerly lived on a little island off the shore, which is now called Old City (*palaia polis*), but they now live on the mainland. And their city is a double one, because, in former times, the city had for neighbors some of the Indigetans, who, although they maintained a government of their own, wished, for the sake of security, to have a common wall of circumvallation with the Greeks, with the enclosure in two parts—for it has been divided by a wall through the center; but in the course of time the two peoples united under the same constitution, which was a mixture of both Barbarian and Greek laws—a thing which has taken place in the case of many other peoples (trans. Jones).

The "doubled" nature of the city in the literary description is a fascinating suggestion, as it implies a level of cooperation not seen elsewhere, as well as some trust in the service of mutually recognized benefit. Yet there was also a desire on both sides to maintain their own traditions. It has not yet been possible, however, to discern evidence for conjoined settlements in the archaeological record.[6] Perhaps the evidence from Strabo can be taken to meant that Emporion began as other emporia did, in Spain and farther afield—even following the model established by Phoenicians in the south of Spain, where foreigners lived outside coastal settlements in the areas close to the water, and interacted from that position with the local population (see chapter 2).

What is clear, however, is that the first Greek settlement of Emporion, referred to as Palaiapolis, took over an area that had been settled by Iberians in the immediately preceding period (ca. 650–575). Hardly any Greek imports are known from the time before Greek settlement, but as Cabrera Bonet (1996, 46) has noted, even the few that were found at Emporion that date to the seventh century and first half of the sixth far outnumber those known from the rest of Catalonia. Whether the transfer of territory happened peacefully or through force is unknown. Palaiapolis was located on a small island separated from the mainland by only a few tens of meters (the distance between the two was so small that today, the island has become part of the mainland; a hill, in fact, crowned by a medieval fortified village named for the church there, Sant Martí d'Empúries, above the modern beach) (Fig. 3.2). To north and south a broad beach curved gently toward modern Empuriabrava and L'Escala, respectively, making an excellent place to pull ships ashore. Two rivers leading into the hinterland (today known as the Empordá) and up to the Pyrenees were each 10 kilometers distant: to the north, the mouth of the Fluvià River; to the south was the Ter River, which may have formed a territorial boundary with the indigenous center of Ullastret (for which, see below).

Figure 3.2   Sant Martí d'Empúries, location of the Palaiapolis settlement of Emporion, ca. 580–550 BCE

Figure 3.3   Excavations at the Neapolis settlement of Emporion

At some point shortly after the foundation of the Greek settlement at Palaiapolis, the Greeks moved down the coast to the south and onto the mainland, creating the town now known as Neapolis (Fig. 3.3). The circumstances underlying this change remain murky. By moving, however, the foundation of Emporion mirrored the history of the original western Greek settlement of Pithekoussai 200 years earlier: first, the establishment of an emporion focused on trade from a secure position offshore, followed by the creation of an apoikia on a larger scale and with some agricultural land to support it at Kyme. The effect could have been to yield greater (and perhaps more profitable) interactions with natives, or to establish firmer Greek control over territory for reasons of security or imperialism. At the same time, the town might have become more independent of Massalia (Sanmartí-Grego 1992). In any case, Emporion did not grow to a substantial size, possibly only having a population of 1500 and never occupying more than about one-tenth the area of Massalia (five hectares compared to 50; Sanmartí-Grego 1992, 28–29; Dietler 1997, 288).

The early phases of Greek settlement are particularly difficult to discern because the remains of later periods, especially the Hellenistic, lie over them. Strabo described worship of Artemis (3.4.8). A temple dedicated to her may have been located at Palaiapolis, but excavations have not yet revealed any trace of this structure. One especially striking set of remains from the late Classical or Hellenistic period come from a house close by the agora in Neapolis, where a rectangular room with an off-center doorway and cocciopesto-paved floor with mosaic decoration has been found. The white limestone or marble chips in the center of the pavement form a reticulate pattern with a meander border, while the border of the room is free of decoration (Fig. 3.4).

Figure 3.4   A room from a house near the agora of the Neapolis settlement

Figure 3.5   Detail of the room in Figure 3.4, showing a mosaic with the inscription "hēdukoitos" ("Sweet recline!")

There is also a panel at the entrance with an inscription reading "hēdu-koitos" (Almagro Basch 1952, 37–38 Fig. 3.5). Almagro Basch suggested that this inscription be translated "Sweet dreams!" but given the shape of the room (particularly its entrance) and the decorative elements of this fine paved floor, it does not seem necessary to identify the room exclusively as a bedroom. I would suggest that the room also served as an andron, and the meaning of the inscription is simply "Sweet recline!" or, less literally, "Enjoy the couch!" There is therefore evidence that sympotic activity similar to the type practiced in mainland Greece also existed on some scale at Emporion, albeit toward the end of the period under consideration here.

SOUTH HALLSTATT SITES

Saint-Blaise

One of the best-studied Celtic sites is Saint-Blaise, located on a hilltop just west of the modern town of Saint-Mitre-les-Remparts and about ten kilometers northwest of Martigues. Saint-Blaise was also only about 40 kilometers sailing distance from the harbor of Massalia and it overlooked both a series of saltwater ponds and the mouth of the Rhône River. It was therefore extremely well located to facilitate trade between Greeks, Etruscans, Phoenicians, and other indigenous groups along the coast and in the interior. The salt that was available in the ponds by the town would have formed one of the most valuable resources for trade (Bouloumié 1984). Saint-Blaise is most notable within this study because its pottery has been the subject of a particularly thorough publication by Bernard Bouloumié (1992), which included 4771 fragments or whole Greek vases (20% of the entire corpus analyzed here).

The town was refounded after a brief hiatus at the end of the seventh century or the beginning of the sixth century, perhaps precisely in reaction to the settlement of Massalia and the increased presence of traders. The character of the settlement seems highly influenced by Greek culture, and it has been argued that Greeks lived in the town, although the fact that Saint-Blaise also always had fortifications surrounding its hilltop position indicates some wariness of outsiders as well. Already by the first half of the sixth century, the inhabitants of Saint-Blaise incorporated new, Greek-style building techniques for houses, abandoning the longstanding Hallstatt tradition of wattle-and-daub construction for mudbrick on a stone socle (Py 1990, 638–642). This change happened much sooner at Saint-Blaise than at most other Hallstatt towns (Dietler 2010, 265–266). The design of the houses themselves, taking an apsidal rather than rectangular form, are less clearly Greek, since they may simply have been an adaptation of earlier domestic architecture (Dietler 2010, 276–277). The houses, at least in the period under consideration here (the Early Iron Age) were universally small, single-room structures where all domestic activities were collected. If Greeks did live here, then they did so as they did at other indigenous settlements: in the local style. This kind of adoption or adaptation by Greeks of indigenous practices is little recognized, but was probably common when exigency required it; compare, for example, the use of Greek and Sikel fine wares in the same assemblages at the mixed settlement of classical Morgantina, described in chapter 1 (Walsh 2011–2012).

NORTH HALLSTATT SITES

Vix

The site at Vix (also known as Mont Lassois, for the hill which was forti-fied in antiquity) is located near modern Châtillon-sur-Seine, in Burgundy. Descriptions of Vix and its importance often focus on its location as a kind of gateway from the Mediterranean to Hallstatt sites farther north and especially east (e.g., Chaume et al. 2012, 138). Such trade with sites in Germany and Switzerland likely followed the Saône river valley instead, which was approximately 100 kilometers to the southeast, toward Geneva, and onward to the Rhine (via the Aar valley). While Vix may well have been connected to Swiss and German Hallstatt sites, it was much better situated to mediate trade between the Mediterranean (accessed via the Saône, and from there to the coast by the Rhône) and the Atlantic, espe-cially the English Channel (via the Seine, whose headwaters flow just below the site). This trade likely consisted of one of the ancient supplies of tin for bronze, linking mines in Cornwall to the Mediterranean coast, Massalia, and beyond.[7]

The site of Vix is dominated by Mont Lassois, a hill that rises 100 meters above the surrounding countryside and the riverbed. As a result of its location and topographic features, Vix became one of the most important Late Hallstatt centers, on par with Heuneburg and Hohenasperg (see below). The top of Mont Lassois, a plateau called Mont Saint-Marcel, was already used as a sanctuary space and defensive emplacement in the Urnfield period, which preceded the Hallstatt period (ca. 930–810 BCE; Mötsch 2011, Chaume et al. 2012, 133ff.). After a break of roughly two centuries, the site was reoccupied around 620. The new town was carefully organized, with a north-south main street defined by the fences that laid out separate cultivated lots of land on either side. The houses had their internal spaces divided by a row of posts running down the middle that supported the ridgepoles of their pitched roofs. Dominating the settlement were two much bigger structures, built in the Hallstatt D2/D3 period (ca. 550–450), with their entrances facing east (Chaume et al. 2007). The larger of these build-ings was very grand, measuring 500 square meters in area. The buildings' exteriors were elaborated by a double row of wooden posts surrounding the outside wall and an apsidal end toward the street. Inside, the structures were divided into antechambers, main chambers, and rear (apse) chambers by rows of columns placed perpendicular to the buildings' long axes. The larger building even preserved some painting, red for the interior walls and yellow for the exterior—the earliest known examples of such decoration north of the Alps. These buildings may have been elite residences, or cultic in function; in either case, they also seem likely to have been the location of banquets, as many Greek sherds, including an Attic black-figure amphora, were found in them.

Although the site was excavated beginning in the 1930s, it first came to wide recognition upon the discovery of an extraordinary elite female burial by René Joffroy in 1952 (Joffroy 1954, 1957, 1960, 1979, Rolley ed. 2003). The woman was inhumed in a rectangular wooden chamber, together with a wagon, jewelry, and numerous vessels associated with banqueting. The most spectacular finds were a gold torc weighing 480 grams, decorated with winged horses similar to Greek representations of Pegasos, and the largest Greek krater that has ever been found—a bronze vessel 1.64 meters tall, weighing 208 kilograms, with a combination lid/sieve that added another 14 kilograms. A silver phiale and two Athenian stemmed cups (one decorated in the black-figure technique, the other in black gloss) were also found in the "Tomb of the Princess."

The meaning of the krater remains a puzzle (Joffroy 1979; Rolley ed. 2003). When filled, it could hold close to 1000 liters of liquid (Chaume et al. claim 1100 liters; 2012, 135; Megaw claims 1250 liters; 1966), but its great depth would have made it highly impractical for use as a container— how could liquid at the bottom, 1.5 meters from the rim, have been retrieved? And how many banqueters would this vessel imply? At the substantial (if not incapacitating) quantity of two liters of presumably alcoholic liquid per person, 400 to 500 people might be accommodated. If Shefton is correct that wine was not mixed with water in Hallstatt contexts (Böhr and Shefton 2000, 29–30; a later ancient source also suggests this; Diod. Sic. 5.26.2–3), the probable serving size per person would shrink significantly, yielding even more participants. Where would such an enormous feast have occurred, and under what circumstances? Relatively few transport amphorai have been discovered at Vix (even fewer than at other Hallstatt centers), implying that wine was scarce, however, or at least only an occasional drink. It might be more appropriate to expect beer or mead to be the beverage that the krater held at Vix, being available locally and probably in abundant quantities.[8]

The placement of the krater in a female burial also raises questions about its use and the woman's status (Arnold 2012b). Although some women at other Hallstatt sites also received rich deposits of grave goods (see Heuneburg for some examples, below), it was only at Vix that an import associated with such large-scale commensalism has been found in association with a woman. The association of women with status and possibly also power with the consumption of alcohol may be underlined by the story of Petta/Gyptis and Massalia, mentioned earlier; Bettina Arnold has drawn attention to the same phenomenon in the Celtic world during later periods (1999, 83). If the krater was not one of the woman's personal possessions during her lifetime, the placement of it in her tomb does seem indicative of a link of some kind between it and her prior to her death. Alternatively, it might also (or simply) have been part of the paraphernalia deployed by her family as part of the burial ritual—placed on view before the community, and perhaps used to dispense drinks to those assembled at the grave, endowing the woman's family with status through its display and disposal.

Cunliffe (1979, 36) has suggested that the krater was so big that it must have been shipped in pieces and assembled on site, an argument that might require the presence of Greek craftsmen at Vix, similar to the Heuneburg fortifications (see discussion of the fortifications at Heueneburg, below).[9] Arafat and Morgan (1994), by contrast, have pointed to the great distance between Vix and the nearest Greek settlement—some 600 kilometers downriver. They argued that Greeks would have been unlikely to travel so far in foreign territory, and envision that trade happened instead through many middlemen. There is, in fact, hardly any direct evidence for the presence of Greeks at sites more than a few tens of kilometers inland.

The krater's very individuality—with regard to both its size and its shape—suggests instead that there was no specific event for which it was intended, although events might have been created for its use once it had arrived at Vix. Even if we are comfortable accepting that the krater was used during banquets, it seems likely that its primary function at such meals must have been as a display piece. A theoretical perspective that incorporates the work of Homi Bhabha (see chapter 4) might allow the Vix krater to be regarded as an extraordinary example of a hybrid object: the vessel was made from a material that resulted from the trade enabled by the leader at Vix, but in an iconic form from the repertoire of those who needed access to that raw material. Perhaps, then, this was a gift in gratitude that recognized the interest of Hallstatt elites in Greek vases and, to a lesser extent, wine, as well as the Greeks' interest in the component elements of bronze.

In the early 1990s, a roughly square enclosure measuring about 20.5 meters on a side was excavated about 200 meters southwest of the "Tomb of the Princess" at a site called Les Herbues (Chaume et al. 2000, 2011, 2012). This space was fenced in antiquity, with a circular pit installation at its center. The pit, one meter deep and a little bit larger in diameter, was full of stones. Around the foundations for the fence were pottery sherds and animal bones, which help to date construction of the sanctuary to around 500. At the entrance to the enclosure were two life-size limestone statues, one male and one female (Chaume and Reinhard 2009). The male was represented as sitting on the ground with his legs pulled up to his chest and a shield in front of his legs. The woman was seated on a chair, and wore a torc with circular termini that has elicited comparison with the golden torc found in the "Tomb of the Princess." Indeed, it is difficult not to imagine that the statue either represents the woman in the tomb, or else a woman who preceded or succeeded her in the same position or role. The wealth and size of the female burial, together with the statue, seem strong signs that women could have powerful roles in the local community. Perhaps one or the other of the apsidal structures on the hilltop served as her residence. Both statues are missing their heads, suggesting that they were purposely broken at a later date, either during internal social strife or an attack by an external force, which might be associated with the transition between the Hallstatt and La Tène periods around 450.

Asperg

There are multiple late Hallstatt and early La Tène sites located around the modern town of Asperg (about 15 kilometers northwest of Stuttgart). These were centered on a hill now called Hohenasperg that seems to have been the location of a regional leader's residence between circa 650 and 400 BCE (Fig. 3.6), as well as many elite mound graves.

The hilltop has yielded only sporadic finds because it is currently the location of a castle that serves as a regional prison (Bolay et al. 2010), but the mound graves, especially one south of Hohenasperg, have turned up rich finds, including several imports associated with banqueting. One of these mounds was found 1.5 kilometers to Hohenasperg's east, at Grafenbühl. A central burial chamber, unfortunately partly robbed, but dating to around 500 or shortly thereafter (Zürn 1975, Krausse 2004), was found with a single occupant. At least 33 later burials were also found in and around the mound. The objects deposited with the main burial were not well preserved, but their types, at least, can be reconstructed. There were gold appliqués for fabric and a gold fibula. Various fragments of bone, ivory, and amber that formed inlaid designs such as Ionic volutes, palmettes, and a sunburst on the leg of a Greek-style couch were recovered (Spindler 1980, Fischer 1990, Jung 2007). The volutes, in particular, recall the terra-cotta couches that supported sculpted couples

Figure 3.6   The Hohenasperg citadel, Asperg

Figure 3.7   Tumulus mound at Kleinaspergle, Asperg (ca. 425–400 BCE)

banqueting, which were used as sarcophagi at Cerveteri in Etruria (today in the Villa Giulia and the Louvre, ca. 520–510 BCE). The Grafenbühl chamber also contained a stool or table with a lion's foot carved in ivory, and a lion-footed tripod in bronze, likely a support for a large bronze cauldron, similar to the dinos found at Hochdorf (discussed below). A smaller bronze cauldron sat on the ground beside the tripod. Finally, two spectacular finds were small carved bone sphinxes, one of which preserved an inlaid amber face.

Another mound, Kleinaspergle, was just to the south of Hohenasperg (Fig. 3.7; Kimmig ed. 1988). The main burial was robbed, but a secondary burial featured a group of bronze vessels: an Etruscan stamnos with satyr-head appliqués at the handle attachments, an Etruscan ribbed cylindrical vessel, and a large locally made bowl. There was also a locally made bronze situla that imitated Etruscan types, including a molded handle with an appliqué of a bearded man's head (possibly horned?), similar to a satyr. Two local drinking horns with gold attachments were also part of the assemblage; the points of the horns were decorated with rams' heads. Finally, there were two Athenian stemless cups with offset rims (Cástulo type; Böhr 1988). One of the Athenian cups was unpainted, while the other was decorated in the tondo with a red-figure image, attributed to the Amphitrite Painter, showing a scene of a draped woman between two sacrificial altars (Front cover). An ivy leaf motif was painted around the rim interior. These cups, dated to around 450, had been broken and repaired prior to the burial; at the time of their repair or sometime thereafter, they received gold foil decoration both inside and out in the form of abstracted leaves (Schaaf 1988). Like the bearded man on the imitation situla, this kind of decoration was typical of the early La Téne period (Schaaff 1988, 194–195), which can most clearly be seen in the metal decoration from a wooden bowl found at Schwarzenbach (Wells 2001). The added gold decoration must have been intended to increase the symbolic (as well as real) value of the cups, providing an important counterpoint to the argument that their foreignness was their most significant attribute. It is quite interesting that despite the clear regional importance of Hohenasperg, and the strong evidence for the ability of people there to procure imported goods, hardly any of the material that they acquired was Greek pottery.

Hochdorf

Hochdorf an der Enz was the site of a settlement (today mostly covered by the modern village) and several mound burials. It has been suggested that the Hallstatt settlement at Hochdorf was subordinate to the leader living at Hohenasperg, as it was within Hohenasperg's viewshed (Bolay et al. 2010, 50). The largest of the mound burials was excavated in the 1970s, revealing a low rectangular wooden chamber in the center (Fig. 3.8). This chamber, dated to the third quarter of the sixth century (Krausse 2004, 195), was richly outfitted with a wagon loaded with bronze bowls and cups, as well as an axe. On a low platform to one side with the wagon were harnesses for two horses, complete with bronze attachments. The deceased man was dressed in clothing with gold leaf accents on his shoes and wore a hammered gold torc and bracelets. Two daggers, one bronze

Figure 3.8 Reconstruction of the Hochdorf burial (Keltenmuseum, Hochdorf an der Enz, by permission of Dr. Simone Stork)

and one gold, were laid across the body in their scabbards. The man was wrapped in several layers of patterned cloth and lay supine on a bronze couch almost three meters long, with a high back and arms (unlike Greek-style *klinai* such as the one found at Grafenbühl). The couch had female figures as supports and was decorated with perforated designs of warriors fighting. On the wall at the head end of the couch, nine drinking horns (eight made from aurochs' horns, one completely in iron, all with gold attachments) were hung (Krausse et al. 1996). No Greek pottery appeared in this tomb, but at the foot end of the couch, in the corner of the tomb, there was a large bronze Greek dinos (0.80 meter tall) on a stand. The dinos was decorated with three lions around its rim. As with the stemless cups found at Kleinaspergle, the dinos was apparently damaged and repaired at some point prior to burial: one of the lions was replaced with a stylis-tically different local version. A gold cup was found on the rim of the dinos, with a cloth that covered the cauldron's opening. Testing of residues from inside the dinos revealed that it had been filled with mead at the time of interment. Although the man in the Hochdorf burial has usually been identified as a village elder or chief, Krausse has suggested that he may have been particularly associated with religious activity—a kind of high priest (1999).

Heuneburg

Heuneburg's fortified hilltop was the center of the largest known Hallstatt site, and it is also one of the best-investigated sites of this period (e.g., Bittel and Rieth 1951, Kimmig 1983b, Gersbach et al., 1995, Kimmig and Böhr 2000, Kurz et al., 2000, Van den Boom 2006, Kurz 2007). It overlooks the Danube River; its location close to the river's source in the Black Forest might explain Herodotos's placement of the Keltoi in this region (it may even be identified with Pyrene, the city that he names as being at the Danube's headwaters [2.33]). It was occupied throughout the Hallstatt period, beginning around 800, but the most important period was its last phase, Hallstatt D (620–450). By the first half of the sixth century, the settlement may have had an area of around 100 hectares and a population of 5000–10,000 (Krausse and Fernández-Götz 2012, 119–120), spreading west from the hill on the heights overlooking the river. Farmsteads outside the town were closely spaced and surrounded by wooden fences. The hilltop, measuring about three hectares in area, was first excavated in 1950. Around 600 BCE, the hill received an extraordinary new fortification, with a stone foundation three meters thick and four meters of mud bricks above, preserved for a length of at least 750 meters (Kimmig 1983b, 70–80, Van den Boom 2006, 13; Fig. 3.9–3.10).

On at least two sides, it had projecting towers. This wall has no comparanda from central Europe, but is rather in a distinctly Greek building style (Kimmig 1983b, 73). It seems to imply, at a minimum, the presence

Figure 3.9   Reconstruction of the "Greek-style" fortifications at Heuneburg

Figure 3.10   View of the Danube River and surrounding countryside from the reconstructed fortifications at Heuneburg

Figure 3.11   Reconstruction of houses at Heuneburg (600–550 BCE)

of an architect who had worked on Greek fortifications, and (perhaps more likely), an architect who was actually Greek. In 2004 and 2005, archaeologists also found a 16-meter-long stretch of stone foundation for a city gate at the outer earth bastion (the *Vorburg*), together with burnt fragments of mudbrick (Krausse and Fernández-Götz 2012, 119). Between the gate and the wall was a trench about six meters deep and 14 meters long, which would have been spanned by a wooden bridge.

The settlement outside the hill was scattered, but on top of the hill, houses were small, densely placed, and organized into rows (Fig. 3.11). The houses were wooden with walls of wattle-and-daub and pitched thatched roofs. The remains of a large building with several rooms dating to the first half of the sixth century has been found northwest of the Heuneburg hill, under the mound of a later necropolis. Its function has not been fully clarified, but its multiroom plan has been compared to Etruscan "palace" buildings at Murlo and Acquarossa (Krausse and Fernández-Götz 2012, 121 and fig. 129). The construction of tumuli to house elite graves, within larger necropolises that contained members of various social ranks, shows the stratification of Hallstatt society at Heuneburg. One of these tombs contained carved amber and ivory decoration similar to that found from the couch at Grafenbühl, which may represent the existence of a *kline* at Heuneburg (Van den Boom 2006, 14–16). The very recent discovery of major tombs for women, and especially of a child, at Bettelbühl, about 2.5 kilometers from Heuneburg, has been taken as evidence for the heritability of status and an attempt to lay claim to power by families, not only by individuals (Krausse and Fernández-Götz 2012, 121–122, Krausse and Ebinger-Rist 2012). These tombs, dated to the early sixth century by dendrochronology, were found in a mound. The primary burial, of a middle-aged woman, was made in a central rectangular wooden chamber, together with another, less well-adorned person who was perhaps interred at a later date. Both the child, whose age was placed at two to four years old based upon inspection of the dental remains, and the woman were buried with rich grave goods, including bronze rings, amber beads, and gold and gilded bronze jewelry (fibulae, earrings, and possibly a diadem as well) that were either imported from Etruria or made by a gold-smith trained in Etruscan techniques.

The Greek-style stone and mudbrick wall had a short life, being destroyed by fire around 540 and replaced with a wall built instead in the local style of "timber-laced earthworks" (Cunliffe 1979, 37, Kimmig 1983b, 81–83). It is unclear what the cause of the fire was: an external attack, internal strife, or some other problem. The orderly plan of the early sixth-century settlement inside the fortifications was replaced in the succeeding phase by buildings of various sizes and functions, including a few buildings of significantly larger size and development, possibly including a second story (one of these has been reconstructed on the site; Fig. 3.12). There is relatively little material dating after the middle of the sixth century in what had been the domestic zones located outside the fortified hill. Instead, at least one necropolis, reserved solely for elites, was created (as noted above) on the site of the large multiroom building of the previous period.

The end of major occupation of the Heuneburg hill seems to have come in the first half of the fifth century, just as it did at Mont Lassois. The collapse of the community appears to have been part of a general shift in power to regional centers farther north, such as Hohenasperg and the Ipf hill at Bopfingen, in this period. At the same time, the landscape surrounding the Heuneburg does not seem to have been completely abandoned; excavations directly below the site as part of an ecological effort to move the Danube

Figure 3.12 Reconstruction of large house at Heuneburg (550–450 BCE)

to a new course in 2009 and 2010 yielded the "surprising" finds of two late Hallstatt and two early La Tène fibulas (Krausse and Fernández-Götz 2012, 123). The presence of these objects, albeit possibly out of context (because they had been moved to their modern findspot by the river), indicates that there was still habitation somewhere in the vicinity after 450.

IBERIAN SITES

Cástulo

To my knowledge, no least-cost path analysis has been performed to identify the trade routes that were likely to have served the sites and regions under investigation here. Such a project is also beyond the scope of this study (although not, perhaps, beyond future work). The problem of trade routes does arise in some cases, however. For sites located on or near the coast, there is little trouble in identifying the routes that brought imported products. When sites are located inland and mountain ranges complicate paths, connections can be difficult to trace. Sometimes ancient texts offer clues to the trade networks that connected inland sites to the sea, but we remain ignorant about most links between sites. My methodology has favored riverine routes because transport over long distances in antiquity, just as today, was cheaper and often faster on water compared to moving goods over land (Laurence 1998, Garnsey 1999, 29–33; though see also Diod. Sic. 5.26 [quoted above, chapter 2]). In most cases, these routes were easy to identify, such as the one described earlier leading to Hallstatt centers from Massalia via the Rhône and Saône river valleys.[10]

One area has presented particular challenges, however: the Iberian settlements in the province of Jaén in eastern Andalusia, including the major town of Cástulo. The area belonging to the Bastetani, an Iberian group who inhabited the southeast coast around Alicante, was thought by Strabo to extend inland, perhaps as far as Jaén (3.4.1, 3.4.12, 3.4.14). The shortest possibility via water is either by the Segura River, a route that would also require passage over the hills of the Sierra del Segura, or else by the Almanzora River, which would allow travel over relatively flat territory, but in the latter case, more than 125 kilometers of the distance would be by land. From Almería, a land-based route could lead over mountains up to 1000 meters in height to one of the Guadalquivir tributaries, for a total distance to Cástulo of almost 250 kilometers. Finally, an entirely terrestrial path could be identified from Motril and Almuñecar on the coast, following the same route as that taken by the modern *autopista* (the A44-E902), via Granada toward Linares, for a distance of more than 150 kilometers. The most direct river route to this region, by contrast, would have required a journey of 350–400 kilometers along the Guadalquivir and Guadalimar (indeed, almost all the way to the river's headwaters), which on the face of it seems an unlikely choice for a site that is only

150 kilometers from the sea as the crow flies. Strabo (3.4.9), however, mentions a trading road that would have followed this route downstream in the Roman period to Córdoba and ultimately to Cádiz ("greatest of the trading places"). Slightly earlier, he says that the Guadalquivir was not navigable farther "towards Castalo" (i.e., upstream) than Córdoba (3.2.3). Of course, it is likely that trade to some sites—and perhaps especially the ones in Jaén province—occurred along more than one route; still, for most settlements included in this study, it seems clear that one route was primary and others of less or even no significance. As will be seen in chapter 6, however, the analysis of Greek imports might shed light on the issue of which route was preferred.

Cástulo itself, slightly south of modern Linares, was placed on a plateau overlooking a narrow valley to the south (Fig. 3.13). The Guadalimar River, a tributary of the Guadalquivir, runs through the valley below the site, meeting the larger river about 10 kilometers away. On both the north and south sides of the plateau were small stretches of flat arable land, though the cultivation of olives and (following contact with Greeks and Phoenicians) grapes must have also been important due to the prevalence of sloped land. The wealth of the area was perhaps primarily due to the prevalence of silver and lead (Strabo 3.2.10–11), which may even have led Tartessians to move here en masse once their own mines were no longer productive (Blázquez et al. 1984). Excavation of the settlement has concentrated primarily on its Roman period, especially in the middle and later empire, so unfortunately little is known of domestic life in earlier phases. The people of Cástulo buried their dead in several cemeteries located on the slopes of several hills surrounding the town; these preserve the vast majority of the information that has so far been recovered for the period between 700 and 350 BCE (Blázquez 1984, 1985, García-Gelabert Pérez and Blázquez 1988).

Figure 3.13   The plateau at Cástulo, looking south

What is clear is that Cástulo and its surrounding region were, in fact, quite well connected to sources of Greek pottery, as these appeared in significant numbers, especially in tombs—but there is also strong preliminary evidence that consumers at Cástulo had distinct preferences for certain types of Greek products over others. In particular, a type of stemless cup made at Athens, typically without figured decoration (although red-figured examples do certainly exist), appeared in enormous quantities relative to other types. The type, which was distinctive due to its heavy walls, concave rim, and sharp offset inside the rim, was so noticeable among the finds at Cástulo that it has become known as the "Cástulo cup," even when it has been found in significant numbers at other sites across Spain and the rest of the Mediterranean (Walsh and Antonaccio 2014). Brian Shefton (in Pellicer 1982) gave this shape its name in the 1970s, and later argued that it was intended by Athenian potters specifically for export (1996, 88).[11] Hundreds of Cástulo cups were found in the city's cemeteries (Blázquez 1984, 1985, García-Gelabert Pérez and Blázquez 1988, Shefton 1982, Shefton 1996). The Iberian tomb typology, as seen at Cástulo, shows a correlation between tomb type and size and the status of the deceased person in the burial. In all cases, cremation was practiced. The largest and most elaborate tombs were marked with structures built in the shape of towers, or with pillar-stelai erected over them. Other tombs, somewhat lower in status, were chamber-tombs cut into the bedrock of hill slopes, with built interiors of stone benches and paved floors.

Huelva

Archaeologists, intrigued by literary descriptions of Tartessos, have long sought specific evidence for its location and culture. As described in chapter 2, ancient geographies and the long-standing tradition of mining in the region of the Río Tinto have led to the area of southwestern Spain being identified with the name of Tartessos, although no site has yet been discovered that can be assuredly identified as the capital or regional center. From the late eighth century onwards, Huelva seems to have been one of the most important towns in the area (Domínguez 2001), but the lack of evidence for significant habitation at an earlier date makes its identification as Tartessos itself unlikely. The site's original ancient name is unknown, but at least by Roman times, it was known as Onuba.

Huelva is generally seen as having been the central point of exchange for metals, especially silver, from the Tartessian interior for foreign goods—first with Phoenicians, later with Greeks, too—during the period when the mining industry was at its height in Tartessos (Fernández-Miranda 1991, Cabrera Bonet 1994, 373). Its geographic location, at the confluence of the Odiel and Tinto rivers, protected from the Atlantic Ocean by small barrier islands, made it the ideal location for a port. The basis for current understanding of life at Huelva is largely due to recent excavations around an area of modern streets located between the high part of the city and the Odiel River. These investigations have led to the identification of an emporion-type zone outside the urban settlement, where there was space for traders to work and even to worship at their own shrines (Domínguez 2003b). There is also strong evidence for industrial activity in the form of furnaces for metalworking (Jurado 2000). Huelva was the site where the earliest example of Greek imported pottery has been found (an Athenian Middle Geometric krater).

In antiquity, the water level was somewhat higher than today, so the city's port was located farther inland, in the area around Calle Méndez Núñez and Calle Puerto. Areas of religious worship have been found there, including a building of cultic character with archaic Greek pottery (Osuna Ruiz et al. 2000). A poorly preserved Greek graffito found in an archaic context on a gray ware bowl in the same part of the city may read "gift to Hestia," while another gray ware bowl from the slopes of the city's central hill had a graffito probably referring to Nike (Garrido Roiz and Ortega 1994, Domínguez 2013). Domínguez (2013, 28) has noted the unusual choice of these gods for receiving offerings, suggesting that it is possible that they reflect Greek understandings of locally important deities, either Tartessian or Phoenician. Yet one more inscription from the lower city, on an Ionian cup to Herakles, who was identified with the Phoenician Melkart, further highlights the cultural mixing that existed at Huelva. As Domínguez notes, Strabo described an island offshore from Huelva that was sacred to Herakles (3.5.5); this island has been identified as Saltés, where an antefix depicting Herakles/Melkart was discovered (Garrido Roiz and Orta García 1966). Bronze figurines depicting Melkart or the Phoenician god Reshef in a striding pose were found in the water off the southern tip of Saltés. The inscriptions on the vases, in both Dorian and Ionian Greek, have been seen as clear signs of the presence of Greeks at Huelva in the first half of the sixth century. Unfortunately, evidence for indigenous life at Huelva has not been as clear or abundant, as those areas have been excavated only in a piecemeal fashion. Although the city continued into Roman times, as evidenced by Strabo's description, its period of significant trade was in the seventh and sixth centuries, in line with Tartessian fortunes generally.

Cancho Roano

Cancho Roano was the site of a large and (at least on present evidence) unusual complex that has frequently been described by its excavators as a "palace-temple" (e.g., Celestino-Pérez 1996 and Celestino-Pérez and Gracia Alonso 2003). It is located just north of the modern town of Zalamea de la Serena in southeastern Extremadura. The surrounding landscape consists of rolling plains and low hills. The major trade routes in the area are likely to have been defined by the Guadiana River, on whose banks the regional center of Medellín was located just 40 kilometers to the northwest. Although

Figure 3.14 Model of the palace-sanctuary at Cancho Roano (Cancho Roano Interpretive Center, Zalamea de la Serena, Extremadura, by permission of Dr. Sebastián Celestino Pérez)

the Odiel and Tinto river valleys and the Guadalquivir are not much farther away, and those rivers' mouths were the home of colonial or mixed-population trading centers in the form of Huelva and Cádiz (Phoenician Gadir), respectively, the high hills of the Sierra Morena in between would have made transit of people and goods much more complicated.[12]

The complex consisted of a large structure that received elaboration over a few centuries, beginning in the early sixth century and reaching its height in the fifth century. This chronology stands in contrast to much of the other archaeological data from southwestern Spain, which shows the decline of Tartessian culture around 550, and it thus raises questions about the extent of connections between the deep interior and coastal Tartessos. The structure was built on a rectangular plan in mudbrick on a stone socle and, in its last phase, surrounded by a moat (Fig. 3.14).

As one of the primary excavators, Celestino-Pérez has noted (2009, 244) that the complex was placed in a low-lying plain near a stream, not on a hilltop where it might attract greater attention. There was a courtyard at the entrance to the building on the east, preceded by two towers or bastions (one on either side of the entrance, serving to monumentalize it and narrow the access route). Beyond the courtyard, the structure rose up on a platform, with a long room oriented on a transverse axis at the front, and several smaller groups of rooms behind. Surrounding this central structure was a series of 24 rooms, six on each side. In the courtyard was a pit with a drain to the moat where offerings could be made, while the rear central room had a hole in the floor, built into an unusual structure in the shape of a circle with an isosceles triangle at the bottom (Fig. 3.15).[13] In a later period this structure was replaced by an altar. On either side of the rear central room were groups of small chambers—four on the north side and three on the south. The entire complex was ultimately destroyed by fire and covered with soil around 400–350.

Figure 3.15   The "Tanit" altar in the palace-sanctuary at Cancho Roano

Large quantities of drinking equipment, almost exclusively Athenian stemless cups, were found at this site; however, they were rarely found in clear use contexts. Instead, the majority of Greek vessels, especially in the central structure, were found in fill levels (though not, apparently, *under* the building) or in the soil covering the site after its destruction, with joining parts of some vessels found in different areas (Celestino-Pérez and Gracia Alonso 2003, 25–27). Several theories have been offered to explain this phenomenon, including the intrusion of a medieval trench that might have displaced the sherds in some spaces, or the purposeful breakage and scattering of vases (as is known from southeastern Iberia). The excavators have argued, however, that the chaotic nature of deposition was not the result of these factors but instead due to the collapse of an upper floor.

Celestino-Pérez has argued strenuously that while the Cancho Roano complex was primarily intended for ritual use, other functions were also prominent (2009, 242–245). He has suggested that political and economic activities took place here during the fifth century, the period of the building's greatest elaboration.

Ullastret

Ullastret was the most important Iberian town in northern Catalonia. Two archaeological sites, Puig de Sant Andreu and L'Illa d'en Reixac, located about 400 meters apart, have been discovered and partly excavated. About one kilometer farther north, at Serra de Daro, was a necropolis that was associated with the settlements. The two inhabited zones seem to have formed a single community. The town was not on the coast, but instead occupied a central position in the flat territory of eastern Girona province, close by a tributary of the Ter River, which flowed into the Mediterranean, 10 kilometers distant. Ullastret was also just 30 kilometers south of Emporion and Rosas, and formed the primary indigenous trading partner with those Greek towns. The earliest significant settlement was made at L'Illa d'en Reixac, which was located on a small island in the center of a lake that has been drained in modern times. This site has been the subject of intensive archaeological investigation (Martín Ortega et al. 1999). Occupation of the site began around the end of the seventh century and continued uninterrupted until the arrival of Romans in the second century, flourishing particularly in the second half of the fifth century through the first half of the fourth. Archaeologists have been able to uncover several blocks of buildings and part of the fortifications at the east side and the south end of the island. The defenses consisted primarily of a wall several meters thick on a rampart. The wall was built of stones and mudbrick; the date of its construction is unknown, but it certainly existed by the fourth century and probably by the end of the fifth (Martín Ortega et al. 1999, 25, 29). As far as the plan of L'Illa d'en Reixac can be determined, it was not orthogonal, but rather determined by the circular or ovoid shape of the island, with a major street that seems to have run parallel to the wall. Spaces were left between blocks to create side streets, possibly public or semipublic areas, as well. Earlier buildings dating to the sixth through fourth centuries were located closer to the center of the island, with later ones taking up the outer space. The earliest phases (ca. 625–550) are not well preserved, with storage pits and scarce traces of walls the most visible remains. In the fifth century, with the introduction of construction techniques using a stone socle and mudbrick, houses were small and rectangular, measuring no more than about 10 meters on their longer side. They had one or two rooms inside. These changes in technique may have been associated with contact and interaction with the new settlement of Greeks at Palaiapolis. In at least one area (Insula 7), there are signs of expansion in the middle of the fourth century from one of these typical structures to a multiroom building with functions spread over more than twice the surface area and six distinct interior spaces. There has been little other sign of architectural distinctions that might indicate social or political hierarchies. A final note should be made of the osteological remains, which consisted primarily of infant burials under the floors of houses. Occasionally, the skulls of adults were also found, both here and at Puig de Sant Andreu, which might represent part of the burial ritual, or else might show the practice of displaying the heads of defeated enemies (a practice also known in Ibero-Languedoc and South Hallstatt sites; Dietler 2010, 324–332, with references).

The site at Puig de Sant Andreu was also founded around the last quarter of the seventh century, overlooking L'Illa d'en Reixac and the surrounding plain, and it, too, was occupied until being abandoned in the second century (Oliva Prat 1950, 1953, 1954, 1962, 1976) (Fig. 3.16). It occupied a hill that has been described by one of the excavators as having the form of an isosceles triangle, with a sharp drop-off on the south side, but a gentle slope approaching from the west (Martín Ortega 2000, 107). Puig de Sant Andreu has been regarded as an early example of a settlement type that became widespread in later settlements, especially in France, the *oppidum,*

Figure 3.16   The excavated area of Puig de Sant Andreu, Ullastret

Figure 3.17   Fortifications at Puig de Sant Andreu, Ullastret (600–400 BCE)

or fortified citadel. Almost from the beginning of the hill's settlement, there were massive fortifications surrounding it, several meters high, with round and square towers and a major gate at the southwest corner (Fig. 3.17).

As with L'Illa d'en Reixac, the plan of the settlement seems to have been irregular but also included a major road that ran parallel to the fortifications. By the end of the fifth century, the wall was expanded to triple the size of the enclosed site, using the original wall as a foundation, and adding at least one new large gateway at the northwest. The gateways were monumental, with passages measuring more than five meters across. The typical house of the sixth and fifth centuries was similar to those found at L'Illa d'en Reixac, square or rectangular with one or two rooms and a small courtyard or patio in front (Fig. 3.18). Groups of storage pits or silos for storing grain were found in houses throughout the town, as were cisterns up to three meters deep. Evidence has also been discovered for metallurgy taking place within houses (Martín Ortega 2000, 117). Terracing walls were built in several locations inside the citadel to allow for leveling of the terrain.

In the fourth century, a large space on the west side of the settlement, abutting the interior of the fortifications, was taken over by a house of exceptional size. The entire house lot measured over 1000 square meters, divided in half for the living quarters on the north and a large courtyard for industrial activity to the south. The scale of this house suggests that it was home to one of the wealthiest and most important families in Ullastret. As at L'Illa d'en Reixac, a pit was found in this house's courtyard, containing the lower jaws of four adult men and fragments of a skull. Their significance is unknown, even though Martín Ortega notes that such discoveries are not unusual in Iberia or the south of France (2000, 120). Suggested

Figure 3.18   View of the countryside surrounding Puig de Sant Andreu, Ullastret

explanations for this deposit of human remains include the veneration of ancestors, the burial place of people executed for some reason, or a deposit of body parts taken from defeated enemies in war. The house was outfitted with paved stone floors and drains to bring water and waste out of the house into the street to the east. A room opening onto the street has been interpreted as a possible shop. The house continued to be elaborated over time, with more rooms being constructed on the east side of the courtyard and a staircase built up to the fortifications, which were given a small opening at this location.

The two parts of Ullastret together form the largest and most complex Iberian site in Catalonia, even as they display features in common with other sites—for example, the choice of defensible locations inland from the coast, the use of large-scale fortifications with monumental gates, and the lack of a grid plan. Widespread innovations introduced during this period included the use of iron in metallurgy, the use of the fast-turning potter's wheel for ceramic production, and the construction of architecture with rectilinear plans and using a stone foundation with mudbrick above.

SUMMARY

This survey of major sites in ancient western Europe has aimed to show both the diversities and the commonalities shared between and among cultures in a period of extensive colonization and trade. At almost all of these sites, monumental architecture was discovered, although in some regions, such as the North Hallstatt area, these followed local traditions, while in others, such as in Iberia, certain cues were taken from colonizing groups. Rectilinear plans were a feature of both Greek and Phoenician architecture, so it is often difficult to determine precisely where influence originated for this style. Another similarity across almost all these sites is the clear delineation of status within communities. Such delineations could take the form of a social or political hierarchy, as at Ullastret, Vix, or Heuneburg, or it could be a cultural distinction, with some groups marginalized to the exterior or fringes of a settlement, as at Huelva or other emporia (including, very likely, both Agathe and Emporion in their early phases). The latter distinction seems particularly important as we consider the extent of Greek colonists' and traders' impact on the native groups they encountered. Even as indigenes were open to new ideas and practices in architecture or technology, and to Greek products—especially pottery— the overall plans of settlements, political systems, religious life, and other aspects of local culture evidently remained largely unaffected by the presence of Greeks.

NOTES

1. Hermary (2002b) has questioned whether all the colonists were Phokaian, suggesting that an initial wave of Ionians from various cities was supplanted by a later group of Phokaians.
2. Tréziny (2001) has argued that the Butte des Moulins was part of the original foundation, making it about 25 hectares in size at the beginning.
3. The classical site where such a phenomenon of multiple plans reflecting growth of the city over time is most clear is Pompeii, although it can be seen in many other towns as well, including the Greek colony of Megara Hyblaia and the mixed town of Morgantina (particularly in the area known as Papa Hill).
4. The phenomenon of founding those colonies that were located farthest away first, especially as a means of marking out territory or a sphere of influence, was not new to Massalia and Emporion. The placement of Pithekoussai north of the Bay of Naples, and the foundation of Katane and Leontinoi at the northern and southern ends of the Plain of Catania, show that this was a common Greek strategy when planning colonial efforts.
5. La Monédière, near Agde, had a few houses similar in form to others found in Massalia, which therefore might reflect a small implantation of Greeks within an indigenous settlement (Nickels 1989, Dietler 2010, 119).
6. The city's doubled nature might also have been reflected in the fact that its name in Latin was "Emporiae," though it is also possible that the plural could refer to Palaiapolis and Neapolis, or between the Greek settlement and the much-expanded Roman one, rather than a Greek town and an indigenous one.
7. Dietler (2004) has questioned whether there was any significant trade in tin at all, noting the lack of tin ingots at Hallstatt sites and Northover's observation of the limited exploitation of Cornish tin mines in this period (1984).
8. Due to the large amount of sugar in the honey used to make mead, the alcohol content would be almost as high as wine—perhaps even higher—resulting

in similar difficulties in understanding the use of the krater at a banqueting event.

9. There seem to have been markings on the krater which could have assisted a craftsman in reconstructing it (Megaw 1966).

10. Etruscan trade routes to northern Hallstatt sites went overland across the Alps, but it appears that these routes did not come into use until the fifth century, when Greek pottery consumption in that area was on the decline.

11. See also discussion in chapter 5 regarding how shapes with flaring concave rims and sharp offsets were designed to resemble metal vessels in order to have greater appeal to consumers.

12. It is possible, for example, that traders could have crossed the Sierra Morena by means of the Viar River from Carmona and the Guadalquivir, or by means of the Guadiato from Córdoba, but these routes seem significantly longer and more arduous than the Guadiana from the Mediterranean at Castro Marim.

13. The structure is perhaps similar to a "sign of Tanit," except that the circle is much larger relative to the triangle, and there are no arms projecting from the point where the circle and triangle join. Whether the structure is actually related to the "sign of Tanit" is perhaps an unresolvable issue on current evidence (Celestino Pérez and López-Ruiz 2003).

4 Developing a Theoretical Basis for Understanding Consumption

INTRODUCTION

The previous two chapters have shown the complexity of the cultures that inhabited the ancient western Mediterranean and trans-Alpine Europe and which consumed Greek pottery over a period of several centuries. This study hopes to explain the place and role of those imported objects in new cultural contexts, which requires developing appropriate theoretical approaches to the material, conditioned by previous scholarship on the region and elsewhere. It must also contend with past and contemporary cultural values related to the subject material, in this case especially the heavy weight of associations drawn by modern Western elites between their own cultures and those of ancient Greece and Rome (Dietler 2010, 15–24, 27–43). This chapter will present the methodology and theoretical approach underpinning the statistical analysis that follows it.

In brief, the subject of this book is to attempt to understand how the consumption of luxurious imported goods—in this case, Greek pottery, especially fine wares—was carried out by consumers in ways that allowed them to present a specific identity to their surrounding community. Likewise, the community that witnessed displays of luxurious goods would also come to their own conclusions regarding aspects of the identity of the goods' owner—conclusions that might or might not have aligned with those desired by the person making the display. It will therefore also be necessary to explore how anthropologists have begun to understand the malleable relationship between objects and their functions and meanings, the connection between the choices made by consumers and status competitions, and even the task of defining "identity."

THE INTELLECTUAL HISTORY OF INTERCULTURAL
CONTACT STUDIES

Identity

Identity and the means used by ancient people to send signals to one another regarding their identity are at the core of this study. The term "identity" is taken here simply to mean perceived or actual membership in a group. Identity groups are defined by descent, gender, political or social class, occupation or community role, age, or many other variables.[1] The attribution of identity can be made by a person regarding themselves or regarding others, often based on markers such as dress, role, or association with certain kinds of objects. Identities can be consciously created by an individual to serve a purpose, or they can be created subconsciously in a manner that makes them seem, even to the individual themselves, to be fundamentally associated with that person. Where the former kind of identity might be called "constructed," the latter appears to be "essential." The existence of constructed identities draws attention to the fact that people can and do change their identity, often in response to different social contexts or in order to achieve short- or long-term goals.

Most recent studies of identity in the ancient Mediterranean, especially in colonial situations, have concentrated on ethnicity as a kind of identity, just as Greek and Roman authors did (Hall 2000, 2005, Antonaccio 2001, 2005, 2009, Owen 2005, Hodos 2009).[2] Herodotos defined Greeks as a unified group by virtue of their shared blood, language, religious life, and customs (8.144). Ethnicity was often seen by scholars in the 20th century as having strong biological aspects, relating to genetics, lineage and familial relationships (Antonaccio 2009, 33). Jonathan Hall's recent and influential list of characteristics that define ethnic identity emphasizes more symbolic features, which he refers to as criteria. These consist of a sense of shared kinship, whether real or invented, an ancestral territory, and shared subscription to a foundational myth. Athenians, for example, believed that they were related to one another, and that they had been born autochthonously from the territory of Attika. These beliefs defined them as a group. Their identity was central to their claim on the land—it was theirs because they had literally emerged from it—and to the construction of the bonds that united their community. Hall's concept has been fundamental for classical historians, even as it has been criticized by archaeologists for not also including shared material cultural traits. Culture historians of the early 20th century noted that objects can, through examination of the ways in which they were produced, used, and discarded, give evidence of the boundaries between groups in ancient society. Several scholars have argued that the introduction of new types of tools can lead to innovative practices, and vice versa; those tools and practices might thus become associated with membership in a group (even an ethnic one; Jones 1997, 116–119 and Ruby 2006, 54–59).[3] This study is interested in all of the kinds of identity that were held by ancient individuals—not only ethnic or cultural identity, but also status, gender, occupational identity, or any other kind. It is also interested in the various ways in which those identities were constructed, especially through the activity of exchange of goods.

Trade and Exchange

A rich body of anthropological literature on trade and exchange has developed over the last hundred years, to the extent that it might fairly be argued that anthropologists consider exchange to be a fundamental type of human relationship (Thomas 1991, 7). As Wells has stated (1995, 213), while trade can be seen as consisting of any kind of peaceful transfer of goods or raw materials in return for other goods or raw materials, exchange carried with it social or political implications, as in the case of gift-giving or tribute payment. It might be possible to push Wells's categories further, to distinguish between trade or exchange that happened between individuals or small groups on a more or less spontaneous basis, and trade or exchange that formed part of long-standing relationships, especially if managed by polities rather than individuals.[4] Regardless of the specific circumstances in any given transaction, it is clear that in the absence of money, trade in the Mediterranean and trans-Alpine Europe was carried out over long distances, across cultural and linguistic boundaries, and through multiple middlemen. Trade involved raw agricultural produce such as grain, meat, or honey; manufactured foods such as wine or cheese; mineral resources such as metals, amber, or salt; and durable goods such as textiles, pottery, or other items. Metal seems to have been particularly important as an exchange product in Andalusia and perhaps also in the North Hallstatt region. In the south of France and Catalonia, agricultural goods were likely of primary importance. This study must therefore be properly situated with respect to earlier evaluations of exchange, especially in the Mediterranean, so that its debts will be clear, its attempted innovations can be explained, and its conclusions can be properly evaluated. At the same time, modern scholarship on Greek pottery, in Greece or in foreign contexts, has a history largely determined by the interests of classical philologists, historians, and archaeologists, rather than by anthropologists specializing in other cultures. The classicists, whose work primarily concerns the cultures of ancient Greece and Rome, have studied the western Mediterranean, especially where evidence for the presence of Greeks and Romans exists—and they have brought the biases and approaches of their field with them.[5] Great interest has been focused on the west because the emergence of Greek culture, including the rise of the *polis* form of state, urbanism, and other such phenomena, seems easier to identify in an arena where it was imposed de novo, so to speak, rather than developing over time out of older cultural forms. Study of Greek culture in a context where it was surrounded by non-Greek cultures is also aided by the ability to make comparisons with their neighbors. Although classical archaeologists were always interested in problems associated with exchange, they largely followed their own path, ignoring developments in the rest of anthropology until very recently.

In addition, classicists have tended to focus largely on Greeks as actors who determined the course of history, and on other populations either as passive spectators (or victims) of the events that unfolded, or as imitators who changed, uniformly and rapidly, to make themselves more like the Greeks. There are a number of reasons why classical archaeologists often privileged Greek activity over that of those the Greeks they met. First, and perhaps most obvious, is the fact, already noted, that we only have written accounts from Greek writers (and, later on, from Roman ones), so their view of events is the one most accessible to us. But the bias of modern scholarship is also due to other factors. In the Renaissance, classical culture began to be regarded as a model for appropriate intellectual and artistic activity. Fluency in the Greek and Latin languages, and deep familiarity with the extant texts, became both a prerequisite for elite status and a marker of it. As ancient objects began to emerge from the soil of nations across Europe, these, too, were prized, assigned high economic value, and formed into collections in the homes of nobility and the wealthy bourgeoisie. Indeed, the pottery that forms the evidence under consideration in this study underwent a radical transformation from its original meaning as a special (if relatively quotidian) commodity in the ancient world, to esteemed artworks assigned a value in the thousands or even millions of dollars today.[6]

Colonialist Approaches

In the late 19th and early 20th century, the perception on the part of modern Western nation-states that they had deep cultural connections with classical Greece and Rome, together with the seeming superiority of the achievements of those earlier societies over their contemporaries (mirrored by the accepted superiority of Western nations over the cultures they had colonized), encouraged scholars to view colonizing Greeks and Romans as behaving in ways similar to their own colonial expeditions. These perspectives did not only serve historians' purposes. By linking themselves to ancient colonizers rather than indigenous populations, the ruling elite of Spain, Portugal, France, and other states could legitimize their own ambitions and activities (Dietler 2010, 33–39), even if there were important differences between ancient and modern colonialism.

The colonialist attitudes of scholars working on classical Mediterranean subjects in the 19th and 20th centuries are evident at several levels, both in specific statements and in the scope and approach of their research. The British scholar E.H. Freeman, for example, made a thorough study of

Sicilian history at the end of the 19th century. Typical of this period's strong interest in the classical world, he directed much of his attention to the period of Greek colonization of the island. In one of his many descriptions of the Sikels, Freeman wrote,

> The Greek settler in Sicily came across men far beneath him in all political and social advancement, but who were still Europeans like himself, kinsfolk who had simply lagged behind. The Sikel needed not to die out before the Greek; he could himself in time become a Greek, and could contribute new elements to the Greek life of Sicily (1891 [Vol. 2], 22–23).

On its face, Freeman's statement clearly defined the colonized group as inferior to its colonizers (Shepherd 2005). Some natives could be civilized, however, and even rise to the point where they would ultimately become indistinguishable from their colonizers. Sikels could help to develop Greek culture, but only after they had become sufficiently Greek themselves. In addition, with this passage's racist undertones—implying, among other things, that in colonial contexts where the indigenous population was not of European descent, the success of an expedition might actually depend on natives "dying out"—Freeman's attitude betrays a 19th-century elite Briton's views of contemporary Italians as Europeans who were therefore redeemable, and non-Westerners who were not, much more than it does the realities of ancient Greek colonization.

Freeman's perspective was typical of many in his time and place. By assuming some equivalence between ancient and modern types of colonization, he suggested that ancient metropoleis sent out colonial expeditions that would allow them to control foreign lands and access to resources. As T. J. Dunbabin noted some 50 years later about his own fundamental work on Sicily and south Italy (1948, vii), and as Franco De Angelis has further elucidated (1998), the British colonial experience, especially in Australia (where Dunbabin himself was from) and New Zealand, was explicitly taken as a model for Greek colonization.[7] In reality, there were significant differences between ancient and modern colonization. From the time of the European discovery of the New World, modern colonization was carried out with a view not only to controlling far-off territory in response to the actions of rivals but also (and perhaps more importantly) in order to lay claim to resources that could be shipped home, enriching the colonizers at the expense of indigenous populations. The comparative independence of Greek colonies, on the other hand, has already been described. They were expected to show loyalty to their mother-cities, and even give support and aid (like the Doric Greek cities in Sicily did for the Peloponnesian League in the 420s and 410s BCE), but they did not participate in the war themselves until they were attacked by Athens. Likewise, although the colonies in the far western Mediterranean were all founded at least partly by Phokaians, it is not clear that the purpose of these foundations was to exclude other Greeks from access to resources. Samians and others were known to ply the same waters. Instead, the Phokaian foundations were a reaction to competition with Phoenicians and Etruscans, as well as a reaction to events taking place at the metropolis in Ionia.

The superiority of Greek culture was an evident fact to early scholars of this period, and it must, they imagined, have been equally obvious to those who encountered it in antiquity. Contact with native populations therefore could and eventually did yield new Greeks, or at least people who acted like Greeks and spoke their language, forgetting their former ways of life entirely and merging with their colonizers' culture. Sikels, in this model, recognized what their civilized visitors (or rulers) had to offer, and, almost bewitched by the potential for sophistication afforded by becoming like Greeks, would discard their own traditions wholesale (e.g., Boardman 1999, 180).[8]

Hellenization and Romanization

It is clear today that early scholars like Freeman had recognized the existence of an important phenomenon—at least in Italy, which was the prime area of interest for Anglophone and German-speaking scholars of Greek contact and colonization.[9] In Sicilian and south Italian contexts, if not in areas farther west, such as the coast of southern France, or Spain, indigenous groups eventually did become indistinguishable from colonizers in both the literary and archaeological records. From the end of the fourth century BCE and later, it is impossible to determine whether sites are occupied by Sikels or Greeks, or perhaps both together (Antonaccio 2001). The subsequent expansion of Roman dominion led to a similar transformation, but over a much larger scale—from Britain to North Africa, many distinctions between native groups and Romans were ultimately erased as Latin became a lingua franca (at least in the West) and Roman customs and governance were widely adopted.[10]

These processes of simple homogenization have fallen under the rubrics of "Hellenization" and "Romanization," respectively.[11] These terms are local variations on the anthropological theme of "acculturation," which broadly describes the changes that happen in a colonized culture under the influence of colonization. Until only 20 years ago, such labels likely would have been called simply "descriptions" of processes of cultural change. As social-science methodologies have been adopted by classical archaeologists in growing numbers, however, and especially as the implications of postmodernist critiques of objectivity became more widely known within the field, it now seems more appropriate to call these descriptions "models" instead. The use of such terminology recognizes that even approaches that ignore or are unaware of modern theory-building, as well as those that explicitly reject "theoretical" models (or claim to be somehow "objective"), in fact espouse and display their own kinds of theoretical bias. For example, as just described, Hellenization was at one point taken as an appropriate model for understanding contact between Greeks and natives in colonial situations in the west. To scholars who used that term to describe historical and cultural processes, Hellenization did not simply include the fact that indigenous populations ultimately become indistinguishable from their colonizers, but often also implied a kind of inevitability to that transformation. Dunbabin, for example, stated that Greeks learned little, if anything, from their contact with non-Greeks in the west (1948, vi).[12]

World-Systems Theory and Network Theory

One reaction to Hellenization models was the attempt by some scholars who concentrated on Hallstatt Europe to put more control over the creation of the material record in the hands of some local participants in trade (see, for example, Brun 1987, 1992, 1995, Cunliffe 1988). In this paradigm, local leaders in colonized or near-colonial zones ("princes" or "princesses," "chiefs" or "big men") actively mediated exchanges between centers of production in the colonies and colonizers' homelands, and peripheral regions, thereby producing differential, status-based access to prestigious imported goods. World-systems theory was developed by Wallerstein (1974, 1991), primarily as an attempt to understand trade in modern capitalism (Dietler 1997, 480, 2010, 48–50). The elite mediation of trade described by world-systems theorists may well have happened, for example, if those leaders used the public presentation of rare imports as a way to reward loyal underlings. But there are also many important criticisms to be made of the deployment of world-systems theory to the ancient world, including its emphasis on macroscale economic exchange, rather than on individual transactions and distributions; the mechanistic quality of the described process; and the fact that, like Hellenization, world-systems theory was designed explicitly with modern colonialisms, rather than colonization generally, in mind (Arafat and Morgan 1994, Dietler 1997, 480–483).

Most problematic, however, is world-systems theory's definition of colonizing powers as the "center" and colonized zones as the "periphery," even if all that is meant by "center" is "center of production." Colonized areas were also producers of goods that were highly desired by people in the regions where colonial expeditions originated, even if those goods might not always have been durable, like pottery. Dietler (2010, 49) has correctly criticized the idea as essentially binary, and therefore unable to capture shades of "in-betweenness" adequately. The assumptions underlying the concept of center and periphery fail to acknowledge the full range of power relationships and perceptions found in colonization, whatever the period or location (Thomas 1991, 83–93). They fail in another way, too: since our perception of the world is individual and personal—we cannot see through someone else's eyes or hear through someone else's ears—we must take the fact that our view of the world necessarily tends to revolve around our own selves as a fundamental truth.[13] In other words, it is highly likely that Iberians, Hallstatt people, and all of the other people involved in exchange in ancient western Europe each considered their own lives and their locations to be central, and the rest of humanity and the world beyond their direct experience to be peripheral. At Vix, for example, the local leader almost certainly did not think of his or her home as a frontier on the edge of a Greek world, but rather considered himself or herself the sole arbiter who decided whether trade of tin would occur between one region peripheral to his or her own (Cornwall) and another one, equally peripheral (Massalia).

This last observation also shows some of the shortcomings of a much newer (and increasingly popular) development in classical history and archaeology: the deployment of a network paradigm to understand trade and encounters across the Mediterranean (e.g., Malkin 2011, Knappett 2011, Brughmans et al. 2012, Tartaron 2013). The "network theory" perspective, derived from social science studies going back to the 1960s, sees regions or sites in different locations that participate in linked activities as nodes placed at various points within a network. The network might be hub-oriented, radiating out from a central node, or distributed with interconnections between and among many different places. Although network theory's proponents have called it a useful heuristic tool, in fact it is merely descriptive and ultimately fails to explain why networks form. Carl Knappett (2011, 49–50) briefly acknowledged this shortcoming, but has argued that by tracking changes in the structures of networks over time, the reasons for those changes will become evident. Such an approach is unconvincing in my opinion because, lacking recourse to external variables, it risks circularity of argument (the network changed because it changed). Network theory can therefore be useful for telling us what happened, but not why.

In one example of this problem, Irad Malkin discussed the Greek diaspora during the archaic and classical periods, depicting the spread of colonies as a distributed network along which goods and ideas could pass. He focused particularly on the idea of a singular "Greek" identity, which, he noted, developed at precisely the same time that Greeks themselves were becoming more dispersed. Malkin's "small Greek world" had "edges" where Greeks encountered people from other cultural groups; exchanges happened in the "middle ground" at those edges. The middle ground is envisioned as a space where groups meet and interact with one another in ways that are shaped by their perceptions and misperceptions of one another (Malkin 2011, 46). There is little criticism to be made of the middle ground between diverse cultural groups as a descriptive concept, but it ultimately does little to explain intercultural encounters. Additionally, Malkin's idea of Greek colonies as a network unto themselves is a purely Hellenocentric formulation that fails to recognize how, in reality, the process of colonization and trade necessarily and deeply involved other groups. The "edges" in his network of Greek foundations likewise seem to imply that colonization happened in a vacuum, when the ancient world is better visualized as a network that was practically infinite in its extent. Lattes, Massalia, Vix, Huelva, Athens, Cástulo, Gravisca, Carthage, Syracuse, Heuneburg, Phokaia, and each of the other similarly linked sites in Europe and around the Mediterranean ultimately formed part of one highly complex network, linked to one another by trade, conflict, intermarriage, settlement, and many other kinds of events and relations. When Greeks came to the far western Mediterranean, they were looking for territory to claim, but they were also looking to initiate or reinforce interactions with other groups for a variety of other reasons.[14] In any event, the actions of Greeks and non-Greeks cannot be understood without taking the interests and perceptions of all sides into account. Finally, even my own account of a network of practically infinite extent is simply a description of a phenomenon. What we really need to try to understand is *why* the interactions for which we have evidence occurred the way that they did.

NEW POSSIBILITIES

Critical Reactions to Colonialist Scholarship

Beginning in the late 1980s, especially in regional and chronological studies of cultural anthropology outside the ancient Mediterranean, some scholars began to look at objects brought to new places by traders and colonists in different ways. These researchers became interested less in how native groups were transformed into "civilized" societies by the process of colonization, and more in how natives actively incorporated foreign objects into their behaviors and existing traditions. Two important new areas of research drove this discussion. In the first area, critics such as Edward Said and Homi Bhabha reevaluated how cultures that had once been regarded as subordinate were studied. Said's *Orientalism* (1978) demonstrated the effect of stereotypes that enabled the modern West to exploit non-Western societies. Portrayal of Arab countries, for example, as backward and barbaric allowed Western cultures to gloss over their own crimes, incivilities, inequalities, violence, and other shortcomings, and to claim that they were conducting a mission to civilize the uncivilized (Dietler 2010, 38–39). It also served to justify their domination of Arab nations and their control of those nations' valuable resources, especially petroleum. Applied to antiquity, Said's approach revealed the chauvinism of Greeks toward the uncivilized *barbaroi* they encountered, but also the parallel attitudes of modern scholarship concerning non-Greeks in descriptions of the ancient world. Bhabha (1994) built upon Said's work by introducing the notion of hybridity, a model which suggested that when two cultures meet and interact—including the exchange of ideas and goods—both cultures are changed by the experience. For as much as modern Indian culture, for instance, has been influenced by Great Britain, from its system of governance to public passion for the game of cricket, British culture has also been affected by its contact with India, with the introduction of curries to popular cuisine, consumption of mass quantities of tea, and the importance of polo to elite leisured lifestyles. At the same time, none of the examples just listed made the transition across cultural boundaries unaltered—local changes were made to the meaning and practice of each as they were adopted. New hybrid cultural creations also sprang into being, such as the gin-and-tonic, a drink that was created in the nineteenth century by English soldiers and sailors in India to ease the administration of the antimalarial compound quinine (itself a colonial product manufactured from the bark of the South American cinchona tree) by combining it with England's most popular spirit (Jacobs Solmonson 2012, 65). British citizens who had enjoyed gin-and-tonics in India and other tropical colonies brought the drink back home, where it became common despite the fact that its medicinal qualities were now superfluous in the home nation's malaria-free environment.

Bhabha's work has had an important, though perhaps limited, impact in studies of the classical Mediterranean—that is to say, while the term "hybridity" has become increasingly visible, few scholars have done detailed and rigorous investigations of hybridized culture. Peter van Dommelen and Carla Antonaccio are two researchers who have examined hybridity in the western Mediterranean carefully, focusing on Sardinia and Sicily, respectively. Van Dommelen applied the concept of hybridity to Punic colonization, noting that in previous studies of Carthaginian activity in Sardinia, rather than discussion of cross-cultural interactions, there was instead a "virtual absence of any reference to local inhabitants or a colonized population" (1997, 313). Yet there are signs in the archaeological record, not only of the continued survival of a native Sardinian population following colonization, but also of their adoption of some aspects of Punic culture. For example, terra-cotta objects were placed in Punic sanctuaries following the colonists' tradition, but some of these objects differed from Carthaginian ones both stylistically—they were sometimes simply limbs, as was typical of Italic offerings, rather than the whole figures found in most Punic sanctuaries—and in the manner of their manufacture (1997, 317–318). In other cases, Punic items were offered at sanctuaries that were clearly associated with indigenous deities (1997, 314).

Antonaccio's work on the interactions between Sikels and Greeks in the archaic period, especially at the site of Morgantina, examined several phenomena. First was the emergence of Greek-style religious architecture in a Sikel context, where both the forms of buildings and the style of their construction was foreign, but at least some of the offerings were local fine ware pottery (Sjöqvist 1962, 58–59; Antonaccio 1997, 172–179). Antonaccio also investigated the production of local pottery styles that were influenced by Greek imports as evidence for hybridity. The matt-painted ware known as Siculo-Geometric appeared in the eighth and seventh centuries, adopting the decorative style, if not the precise techniques, of Greek Geometric imports.[15] While Greek vase painters developed new techniques over the succeeding centuries, and moved from being largely concerned with abstract motifs to figural scenes, their Sikel counterparts continued to produce essentially the same decorations until at least the end of the fifth century. Siculo-Geometric was, in other words, an example of a borrowing from a foreign tradition, followed immediately by a loss of interest in copying foreign methods and motifs. Siculo-Geometric may have become identified as a local style quickly. Finally, Antonaccio and others examined the possibilities for Sikels using Greek pottery while dining, either with or without Greeks also being present (Antonaccio 1997, 2003, Lyons 1996a, 1996b).

Hybridity has been a useful lens through which to view Greek adoptions of foreign cultural traits as well. For example, in the late sixth century, the city of Thasos in the northern Aegean chose to adorn its gates with sculptures depicting figures entering or leaving, following Persian artistic practice (as seen in the contemporary palace complex at Persepolis, among other examples; Walsh 2009, 182–183). In the fourth century, by contrast, images of Zeus and Hera that decorated a Thasian gate were composed in a manner similar to Athenian funeral stelai, with the figures placed within *naiskos*-frames, and gods seated and interacting with their servants (the messengers Hermes and Iris). These images reflected the currents of political and cultural influence at Thasos, which was dominated by Persia and Athens at the respective moments when the artworks were executed, but was not controlled by them. Margaret Miller has likewise described Greek adoption, adaptation, and derivation of vessel shapes from Achaemenid Persia (1997).

Objects and Meaning

Apart from the role of natives in constructing new kinds of culture in response to outside influences, the other new and important kind of anthropological investigation of colonialism concerned the problem of how objects become associated (or invested) with meaning at all. When this question is analyzed closely, it becomes clear first that just as no person maintains only one identity, no object has a single meaning. Instead, there are many kinds of meaning associated with any given object simultaneously. For example, a knife might have a utilitarian meaning derived from its usefulness for accomplishing the task of cutting (e.g., having a large blade or a small one, being sharp or dull), a formal meaning based on the materials and skills that went into its manufacture (being of unusual design or material in order to enhance its visual appeal, having an exotic jeweled handle or a quotidian wooden one), a symbolic meaning reflecting nonutilitarian functional concerns (reserved for rituals such as animal sacrifice or used for everyday meal preparation), and an economic meaning derived from its ability to be exchanged, and especially its value in exchange for something else (monetary price or bartered goods). There are certainly other types of meaning that could also be added to this list. Moreover, none of these variables can be considered to be independent from the others. An object that is symbolically significant may, of necessity, have spectacular formal qualities, and in any case it is highly likely to be considered economically "priceless" (i.e., not fungible). Indeed, the relationships between different kinds of meaning are likely to be reflexive, whether in the same direction or inversely; a change in one type of meaning would be reflected in the others.

At the same time that objects are recognized to be imbued with multiple and often intersecting levels of meaning, though, a new scholarly consensus, led in many ways by Arjun Appadurai (esp. 1986), sharply criticized the notion that such meanings are in any sense inherent to objects. The meanings associated with objects or their qualities—or to put it slightly differently, the meanings embodied by them—are attributed to them solely by the humans who use them, regard them, think about them, or otherwise interact with them (even if they do not consciously ponder the question of the object's meaning). Appadurai's focus was on the object as "commodity"; he specifically linked its social meaning to exchange. In this way, his evaluation was grounded particularly, though perhaps not exclusively, in the contemporary globalized world and its predominant economic schema, industrialized free-market capitalism.

Perhaps the most useful theoretical concept to emerge in recent decades regarding how people interact with objects is entanglement. This word emphasizes the deep two-way relationships that exist between people and their activities, on one side, and objects and their meanings or functions, on the other side, as suggested by the work of Antonaccio mentioned earlier (2005, 2009), as well as by Nicholas Thomas (1991). In a recent formulation, entanglement has been defined as "the sum of human dependence on things, thing dependence on things, thing dependence on humans, and human dependence on humans" (Hodder 2012).[16] Hodder placed special emphasis on the distinction that could be made between dependence, or reliance (but also contingency), on a thing or person, and dependency, meaning constraint or limitation by a thing or person and their abilities, and suggested that the entanglement could be found in the dialectic between dependence and dependency. In order to understand entanglement, dependence, and dependency, he started from first principles regarding how people relate to things. In an initial moment, we encounter things (such as a pebble on a beach) by sensing them and their physical qualities by looking at them, smelling them, hearing them, tasting them, or touching them (Hodder 2012, 23–24). The sensations we feel are experienced in the context of the time and the environment in which it happens, and are conditioned by our previous experiences, which together help us to build associations between the thing and ourselves. In the next stage, we might take hold of the thing, and, if it is portable like a pebble on a beach, take it with us, building a history of experience with it. We can also note other associations between people and things—some people use cooking bowls, some people wear unusual hats, some people wear swords, some people consume certain kinds of food, some people live in big houses. In these ways, people become entangled with (form dependences with and dependencies on) things. Things also become entangled with other things, for example, in the ways that they are used together or exchanged for one another, while things become entangled with humans in the ways that they grow or are transformed by people (Hodder 2012, 43, 64–70). Finally, the relationships between humans are themselves entangling, as our actions are made possible by others, or are contingent upon others, or are constrained by others.

Related Postcolonialist Responses

Marshall Sahlins, whose work mostly concentrated on Western contact with Polynesian societies, has offered valuable insights about how to understand the ways in which meaning is attributed to objects as well as events across premodern historical periods and in non-Western contexts. Sahlins argued in several venues that "culture is history"—in other words, that culture forms the structure within which meaning is created, and thus is the lens through which events are interpreted, and action considered and taken (1987, 1996, 2004). Culture consists of communally determined values, meanings, and associations, including social and political hierarchies, kinship and nonfamilial relationships, gender roles, the economy, and belief systems concerning the surrounding world (including, but not limited to, religion). Since objects are attributed meaning by groups as well as individuals, they, too, can fall under the rubric of culture—in this case, "material culture." Although Sahlins' work long predates Hodder's formulation of entanglement, Sahlins' idea of the lens through which humans view the world which is created by cultural structures is a useful addition to it. He is able to show precisely how meaning can be associated with the dependences and dependencies between entangled humans and objects. The cooking pot might be connected to gender roles, for example, or the hat to political status, or the sword to occupation, or the food to ritual activity, or the big house to wealth.

One example used by Sahlins (1987) to show how culture helps to define interpretations of events or actions concerns the death of Captain James Cook at the hands of Hawaiian islanders in 1779. Upon his arrival on Oahu, Cook's role as the leader of his ship was recognized by the islanders. At that moment, the Hawaiians happened to be celebrating an annual festival in which their god Lono was expected to arrive in order to bless the community. For the islanders, Cook took on the role of Lono, and they initially welcomed him with great fanfare. After a brief stay, Cook left Oahu, but he was forced to return in order to make repairs to his ship. Cook's now-inappropriate reappearance, outside of the festival season and after he had previously been recognized as Lono, now led to hostility from the islanders, the theft of some of Cook's small boats, and ultimately to an attack that ended with the deaths of Cook and four of his men. Sahlins has argued that the Hawaiians' actions, and Cook's crew's surprise at the turn of events, together showed how the different cultures to which each side belonged determined how they perceived each other and the events that had transpired.[17] Further, this example demonstrated that just as Westerners had to find a way to fit native groups into their worldview (in order to justify dominating, colonizing, exploiting, displacing, and enslaving them) so, too, did native populations have to interpret the new presence of explorers, traders, and colonists within their own preexisting set of beliefs and understandings of the world.

A satirical postcolonialist commentary on the importance of cultural structures in determining perceptions of the colonization process can be found in the Australian television mock-documentary *BabaKiueria* (1986), which depicted an inverted colonization set in the present day. The film's first scene shows an armed naval detachment of Aboriginal people in Western-style military uniforms arriving on a beach where white families are relaxing and holding a party. When asked by the colonizers what the place where they have landed is called, one of the white men answers, "This? It's a barbecue area." The colonists plant their flag and claim the country, which they now refer to as "BabaKiueria" ("A nice native name, colorful," remarks the leader of the colonization party condescendingly), as their own territory. Later scenes show Aboriginal people in dominant roles (journalist, government minister), discussing in a paternalistic fashion the endemic social and economic problems now faced by the colonized white underclass.[18]

Another modern example of the way in which objects' meanings can be culturally determined as they cross borders is the Western artistic movement of *Japonisme*. The style emerged in the middle of the 19th century just as Japanese products began to appear for the first time in large numbers in Europe. Japonisme was particularly influenced by the woodblock prints called *ukiyo-e*, which tended to show rural landscapes, historical and dramatic narratives, and aspects of quotidian (rather than courtly) Japanese life. Due to their "low" subjects and their status as prints rather than unique works, ukiyo-e were not an elite form of art in Japan. As they were collected and examined by European painters, however, their foreign qualities, such as asymmetry and a flattened pictorial plane, began to appear in Western fine art. Well-known examples include lithograph posters by Henri de Toulouse-Lautrec in the late 1880s and early 1890s, or Vincent van Gogh's *Portrait of Père Tanguy* (1887, today in the Musée Rodin). The validation of Japanese prints by local arbiters of artistic quality, combined with the rarity of the original works in the West, also raised their aesthetic and economic value, which in turn created a fashion for collecting Japanese objects. The effect of Japanese art on Western art production demonstrates another example of reflexivity, in which objects— by virtue of their design, decoration, function, and availability, and through their use—can have an impact on culture. Innovation, whether related to existing objects or to the introduction of new ones, can create new meanings or allow new traditions to develop.[19]

Consumption

Michael Dietler has worked for two decades to direct these approaches toward the import of Greek objects and behaviors in the western Mediterranean (1990, 1997, 1998, 1999, 2001, 2005, 2010). His most significant contribution, in my estimation, has been the use of the term "consumption" to describe how imports were not only purchased by natives but given new and different meanings by them. Dietler was certainly not the first scholar to employ this term—it has been widely used in studies of the ancient economy. Most recently, the consumption of Greek imports, especially luxurious ones, has been the focus of researchers like Foxhall (1998) and Hodos (2006, 8–9). These writers have not explicitly defined the term, however, leading to some potential confusion about what precise activity they mean to describe. From the contexts in which they mention consumption, it appears that the concept is, like Appadurai's notion of the object as "commodity," related to the largely modern and economic version of consumption, which is connected to contemporary "consumer culture." Following the spread of Western-style free-market capitalism in the 20th century, people around the globe now consciously participate in markets as agents who are motivated by the acquisition of goods, especially those associated with luxury. Moreover, economists (and the lay public, as well) conceptualize the purchase and use of products as "consumption" or "consumerism."[20] As Foxhall aptly put it, luxury goods from far-off locales, both in antiquity and today, become "cargoes of the heart's desire" (1998). We will return to the relevance of this kind of consumption momentarily.

Dietler's consumption is quite different, however, and is clearly influenced by the work of Sahlins and Thomas. He concentrated on the transformation of the object's meaning as it crosses cultural boundaries (1999). For example, Greek pottery that was traded to people outside of Greek communities seems to have been used in different ways from the ways it was used by Greeks. Even if Greeks were present, either in the form of traders bringing the imports or in some other capacity, they may not have explained how different kinds of vases were used in their home context, and it is currently far from clear that buyers would have been interested in such explanations even if they were available. In any case, for Dietler, the act of using a new foreign object (consuming it) requires the user to integrate it into preexisting social and cultural structures. Consumption thus pushes scholarly attention to native rather than Greek perspectives: what did these objects mean for their buyers and users? The decoration, shape, size, and place of origin of foreign goods, as well as the materials used in their construction, all rich in meaning in their home context, were interpreted by buyers according to locally developed systems of meaning.

A relevant example of the reinterpretation of Greek vases can be found in a comparison of their use in late archaic Greece and Etruria. In Greece, shapes such as the krater and table-amphora were intended for specific commensal activities, especially the banquet known as the *symposion*. These shapes, in Greek wares, were also used in settings of public and private entertainment in Etruria. But they were also commonly used as prestigious grave goods in Etruria, while in Greece, vases were only occasionally placed in tombs, and the range of shapes used for this purpose was sharply circumscribed (particularly small oil containers like lekythoi and wine containers such as askoi), more rarely including vases used for serving at table. Dietler has also offered a modern example: the meaning of Coca-Cola in western societies, where it is a quotidian and low-status beverage, as compared to sub-Saharan Africa, where it is associated with high status and used for welcoming esteemed guests into the home (Dietler 1999, 485–487, 2010, 61–63).

The Importance of Acquisition

As the Coca-Cola example above suggests, a common kind of meaning that can be associated with objects is related to class or status boundaries within a society. One of the most influential studies on the association between objects and class has been that of Pierre Bourdieu, particularly in his book *Distinction* (1984). Bourdieu was attempting to discover evidence for what he referred to as the "habitus," which he defined as "the relationship between . . . the capacity to produce classifiable practices and works, and the capacity to differentiate and appreciate these practices and products (taste)" (170). The habitus thus concerns both the things people say and do, and how they interpret the things that others say and do in relation to themselves and their place in society. The dual nature of the habitus—this "structured and structuring structure" (171), in Bourdieu's words—will be a critical component of my theoretical approach to understanding the decisions made by consumers, because identity, too, has a dual nature, being created by one's self and by external observers. The habitus is manifest in consumption because, as Cook et al. (1996, 54) have cogently written regarding Bourdieu's work, "goods are part of a social reality of signs and classificatory systems closely related to social position." In a wide-ranging investigation of the taste preferences of mid-20th century French people from all levels of society, Bourdieu identified how members of the same social class very frequently espoused similar taste with regard to fine art, music, dance, cuisine, sports, and fashion, among other categories. Indeed, appreciation of the same kinds of things—and rejection of the same kinds of other things—has become an outward expression of a value system that was linked to membership in a particular class. The kinds of films one goes to see (artistic or avant-garde as opposed to mass-market entertainments), or the kinds of clothes one wears, or knowing which fork to use at an elaborate meal, or drinking wine or champagne instead of beer or soda (and knowing which shape of glass to use for which beverage) are all clear examples of the ways in which taste can be used as a way to lay claim to an identity—in these cases, an identity connected to high status. Knowing and following "the rules" associated with the lifestyle of a group can be tantamount to membership in that group. Just as clearly, the judgment of others for their taste in film, clothes, table manners, or choice of beverage and means of consuming it constitutes a primary means for attributing an identity to others.

In the arena of historical archaeology (defined as archaeology concerned with societies since 1500 CE), several authors have begun to examine not only the kinds of things bought but also the process of shopping itself. Interest in shopping, a trend that emerged in the 1990s in a field known as consumer behavior studies (Cook et al. 1996), has been particularly linked to the growth of investigation in human agency and the ways it might be reflected in the archaeological record.[21] Research on exchange and shopping in the South Pacific and in the North American Pacific Northwest has showed how native groups often were not interested in the goods Western traders offered for exchange, and requested other objects instead, and how natives could and did often determine what kinds of goods and how many of they would offer in exchange for European products based on local value systems (Thomas 1991, Marshall and Maas 1997). The preferences of natives could change depending on local developments (for example, initially rejecting most European ceramics, only later to consume them in significant quantities following the use of some larger vessels as display items during potlatches). As Cook et al. (1996, 52) have noted, consumption is not merely an economic process of buying and "using up" goods, but must be understood as "linked to individual, intentional, communicative acts." Moreover, the act of shopping—regarding products available for exchange, identifying the ones that are appealing, negotiating with the seller, and completing the exchange transaction (or failing to)—is itself laden with meanings and significance, and can take on the quality of ritual behavior, particularly when it happens in a public space, where other members of the community can witness it. In other words, study of consumption as a human behavior must also be concerned with the signals people send to one another through the objects with which they associate themselves. But how exactly does the consumption of imported luxury items (as I have defined Greek pottery in this study; see the following chapter) send positive signals about the purchaser to other people in a different culture? While it is now clear that imported goods can take on meanings associated with status, we are still not sure how do they do so.

Recent sociological research on modern consumption can be useful in helping to understand the relationship between shopping, the meanings of goods to their purchaser, and identity formation. Through consumption, people help to create their identities by making purchases that define or reinforce their social relationships with other individuals and groups. The extent to which people explicitly and consciously define themselves through consumption of course varies by individual, by time, and by place, but in a community where even one person believes that the items they surround themselves with reflects some intangible characteristic associated with them, all members of the community will be judged according to their consumption habits (if only by the person or people who sees consumption as related to identity). In a study of consumption in the modern Western world, where people have perhaps been most sensitive to how shopping reflects identity, Robert Dunn has explicated important aspects of that relationship. Again, I want to be clear that there is no doubt that the modern model of capitalism as it is described by neoclassical economics, with its emphasis on supply and demand, cost and price, maximization of utility, and market efficiencies, is a very different system from the one that existed in antiquity, and contemporary economic modes of analyzing data can tell us little or nothing at all about how consumers in antiquity behaved (Walsh 2013, esp. 232–235). The level of consumer consciousness that exists in contemporary Western society regarding the ways in which adoption of luxury goods can send messages to others about the adopter is difficult to observe directly in ancient western Europe. Even so, we have already seen repeatedly how ethnographic analogy can be employed as a constructive means of understanding and interpreting ancient behaviors. In the Greek world, many authors (e.g., Athenaios 1.27d-1.28d) composed lists of spectacular imported things, including cups, from across the Mediterranean. Other poets, including Homer and Pindar, made frequent reference to the origins of things as a sign of their value or workmanship. Exposure to the luxuries of Persia may have been an important catalyst for Greek adoption, adaptation, and derivation of rich foreign banqueting equipment (Miller 1993, 1997, esp. ch. 6; see also Strong 1966, 75–77, and Sparkes and Talcott 1970, 15 n. 29). These facts are no guarantee that other Mediterranean groups behaved similarly, of course. But even if we remain ignorant of mechanisms of supply or the specific routes traveled by people and goods, we know that Greek vases were sent very long distances and willingly acquired by people. Presumably these consumers acquired as much as they wanted to, within the constraints of their resources, since traders would have traveled to bring them more if it had been desired. The Phoenician sailor Hanno the Navigator, for example, claimed to have sailed along the west coast of Africa as far as the Gulf of Guinea in the fifth century BCE in the search for new markets (Blomqvist 1979, Lacroix 1998), and some Greek merchants probably sailed into the Atlantic, even beyond Huelva, as well. The consumers also must have had something traders wanted, since they were able to negotiate trades for the vases and other goods.

Dunn stresses how consumption is tied both to the construction of self-identity and to the attribution of identities to a person by external observers—and that our perceptions of our own identity are colored by how we believe others see us, including the goods we own (2008, 174). The construction of monumental domestic architecture or tombs, as appeared across the survey zone for this study, is a strong sign that intracommunity communication occurred via costly expenditures. I would suggest that the extensive consumption of luxury goods by ancient people is a sign that they participated in a process of identification that might have been different in degree or type, but not in fundamental nature. The deployment of imported goods in domestic, funerary, and religious settings likewise presents signs of the importance these items could have by being displayed.

Dunn also parsed the internal identification dialectic concerned with evaluating and prioritizing the different qualities embodied by various goods for shoppers—between what he called "codified identifications" and "individuated identifications" (Dunn 2008, 176–177)—and, as we will see, these ideas can inspire new ways to view the ancient world. The codified mode of identification refers to the association of the self with goods that have a specific, widely known, and accepted meaning, particularly because of their relationship to a certain "style" (in the contemporary sense, synonymous with "fashion") or "brand" (2008, 179–182). By associating with such goods, one lays claim to the meanings they have already been given within society. In other words, the goods become a code or shorthand for the identity one wants to display. Codified identification is strongly related to claimed membership in a group—such as "fashionistas," the modern group of people who pay attention to seasonal changes in haute couture and shop for clothes from established designers on the basis of those changes. This group forms a kind of social elite (even if not all members of our society accept them as such) because membership in the group presupposes great wealth, specialized knowledge, and leisured lifestyles that allow members time to stay abreast of the latest trends on a global scale. The individuated mode of identification, by contrast, appears when a consumer acquires an object and uses it in ways that express their individuality, rather than their membership in a group. The object has a personal rather than a social significance (2008, 183). For both modes, identification is rendered through considerations both of the good's appearance and the goals it can be used to accomplish (2008, 184).

Simultaneously, buyers can react strongly to the good's aesthetic or functional qualities (How attractive is it? How good is it for accomplishing the required task?)—what Dunn called the "expressive" and "instrumental" aspects of consumption, respectively. To frame this process in terms of ancient consumption, a buyer might have sought a large vessel to hold the alcohol for a big party he planned to hold for some friends or other associates. In deciding which vessel to purchase, he might have considered a bronze krater, an Athenian black gloss krater, or an undecorated large bowl. Each choice might offer the same functional utility (instrumentality) but score differently on the other three components. The consideration of the meaning of each choice for the buyer's identity will be a factor in his selection—what will his choice say about him? What message can he send, and to whom? How much will his guests care? How much does he worry about what his guests will think of him?

Costly Signaling

A tension exists within recent scholarship regarding the place of logic and rationality in human decision-making, especially how people perceive and discern between costs and benefits connected with certain actions, including consumption. At the risk of being too reductive, there are those who see human activity as ultimately focused on a single goal: success as measured by survival and propagation of genes into succeeding generations. This kind of rationality, being theoretically instinctive and universal in humans, as in all animals, would avoid the dilemma of being associated with a single culture's version of logic. On the other hand, there are human behaviors that seem to be illogical or irrational from the perspective of evolutionary fitness. The wasteful expenditure of resources on luxuries like a Prada dress in the United States in 2013, or Greek pottery in the ancient western Mediterranean, would seem to be prime examples of such illogical activity. Several archaeologists have seen a way to deploy Darwinian evolutionary theory, specifically dealing with what is termed "costly signaling," to understand these behaviors.[22] Fraser Neiman (1997) studied the competitive creation of public monuments by Mayan elites, and suggested that the enormous expense associated with their construction—what might be termed a kind of "conspicuous consumption"—is, in fact, an example of "wasteful advertising." The latter term, coined by evolutionary biologists, is used to describe traits that, due to their costs, appear unhelpful or even to cause deficits to an individual's likelihood of survival, but which in fact do somehow improve access to greater resources, more (or better) mates, or both of these advantages. A peacock's tail would be a spectacular example from the natural world of this kind of wasteful advertising, since it costs the bird the biological effort of growing it, and the tail both draws attention from potential predators and is a hindrance to swift movement away from threats. The enormous tail is important for attracting female mates, however, because it sends a signal about the fitness of its owner and his genes. It is thus critical to the success of the peacock in mating, justifying its high cost.

There are three main factors governing how effective wasteful advertising can be for those trying to send signals: the competitive ability of the worst advertiser (since that person's ability to participate sets the bottom end of the scale for all advertisers); the amount of variance in competitive ability (because the more "space" to be marked out between competitors, the more advertising will have to be done); and the value to be gained from advertising (the larger the audience, and more competitors, the greater the payoff for sending signals by advertising wastefully) (Neiman 1997, 270). In the case of stone monuments built by Mayan elites, Neiman was able to identify how understanding wasteful advertising could clarify the reasons behind their placement around the landscape. These monuments were explicitly designed to publicize the political and religious status of specific individuals whose names were carved on them. Increasing evidence shows that during the Late Classic Period (ca. 600–900 CE), ecological disaster (in the form of soil erosion) was likely the result of deforestation of lowlands for agriculture. Up until the end of the Late Classic Period, when population collapsed (shrinking 40–85%at some sites), monuments continued to be built, but the locations for constructing new monuments changed, moving from the lowland valley up into the surrounding hills, which received greater rainfall (Neiman 1997, 281). The increase in the number of monuments was a direct result of increased competition for resources (higher-yield farmland). Neiman was able to show that spatial patterning of monuments over time did correlate highly with mean rainfall levels, which increased with altitude. High levels of rainfall are also associated with greater soil erosion, though. In other words, the distribution of stone monuments across the landscape over time charts a cycle of competition among Mayan elites for dwindling resources. The cessation of monument construction, Neiman argued, was ultimately a result of the population collapse—not, however, because there was no social stratification, or an inability to procure stone or artists to carve the monuments. Instead, with few competitors, and a low level of competition threatened by the weakest remaining members of post-Classic Mayan society, there was little need to continue to advertise in such a wasteful manner.

Neiman's anthropological formulation of wasteful advertising provides an attractive explanation for human interest in luxury goods. Although luxuries are by definition not a necessity for human life, displaying a preference for their consumption over less costly alternatives allows individuals to increase their access to resources and mates by creating a public arena for status competitions, where those who have the resources to spend can claim status or reinforce such claims. This explanation therefore also has the virtue of concentrating on local transmission and reception of signals. Those who are less fit (i.e., who do not have the same level of resources to spend) might also buy luxury goods in order to send similar messages, but the competition usually ensures that the signals are accurate representations of fitness, since fitter individuals buy more or higher quality versions of the luxury goods. As Neiman wrote:

> Senders should send accurate signals. There is little point in investing energy in a deterrent that can be counterfeited by inferior competitors. Hence there is a continual selective pressure to invest in wasteful signals at a level that just exceeds the level that inferior competitors can afford. Conversely too large an investment in wasteful signaling guarantees that you will have nothing left for direct investment in yourself and your offspring (1997, 270).

James Boone (2000) expanded on Neiman's approach, focusing attention on effective strategies for defining status within groups, and confirming access on the part of high-ranking individuals to limited resources. Chief among these strategies was the creation of opportunities for wasteful display: for example, the preparation and carrying-out of Hopi religious rituals and dances in the American Southwest, and Kwakiutl potlatch ceremonies in the Pacific Northwest of North America. Among the Hopi, farmland is distributed according to clan membership, and the hierarchy of clans determines who is eligible to receive land of different qualities. Members of the dominant clan receive the best land, while those from lower-ranked clans receive marginal land or no land at all. Those who are unable to support themselves are threatened by the possibility of being forced to leave the community, or even with not surviving times of hardship at all. Periodic rituals and dances, which are seen as bringing rain, causing agricultural fecundity, or marking transitions at certain points in life such as the passage to adulthood, require great effort above and beyond normal farm labor to feed dancers and other participants (even the growth of cotton for ritual garments on land that could otherwise be used for food production) (Boone 2000, 104). Hosting elaborate festivals is therefore a primary way of signaling strength; by contrast, low social ranking is associated with an inability to perform necessary rituals properly. As Boone notes, "approximately half the clans listed in Hopi origin myths [now] appear to be 'extinct' or at least 'vacated,'" a process that is likely due to ever-increasing pressure on those least able to perform—that is, to advertise themselves in a wasteful fashion.

Kwakiutl potlatches were one of the most widely studied forms of non-Western ritualized activity. At a potlatch, a high-ranking individual collected and then distributed vast quantities of various goods to invited guests. The function of a potlatch was at least partly to demonstrate control over hereditary lands for hunting and fishing and over titles passed down from generation to generation. The more material that was given away, and the greater the number of potlatches held by a given individual, the greater the status associated with that individual. Boone (2000, 106–107) notes the seeming paradox between the decline of the Kwakiutl population following contact with Europeans in the 18th century and the ever-rising amount of goods distributed at potlatches through the end of the 19th century. This phenomenon, he argues, was actually an example of an increase in the range and scope of competition between elites. Pacification of the region by Europeans brought a wider array of Kwakiutl groups into contact with one another, so that elites at local centers were no longer competing only with their close neighbors but with elites from far away as well. Density of population is only one way in which competition can intensify—range of effective signal is another.

Brenda Bowser's work on pottery in the Ecuadorian lowland rain forest town of Conambo (2000) particularly highlights the ways in which domestic objects can communicate signals about their owners. Pottery is homemade by women in the town; its decoration is highly individualized and intended to represent its maker. At the same time,

> [p]olitical decisions are reached through the painstaking process of consensus, involving extensive visiting and discussions among adults in different households to define and resolve issues, sometimes culminating in a large group meeting in which an influential person sanctions a decision reached by consensus (2000, 224–225).

As a result of this system, private domestic spaces become venues for public display, giving the makers of pottery an opportunity to have their work seen (particularly since the serving of sweet manioc beer [*chicha*] in ceramic vessels is part of the hospitality offered to guests). Through study of the component design elements in the vase paintings, Bowser has been able to show that these superficially similar vessels actually represent ethnic identities that themselves are associated with the town's primary political factions.[23] Further, Conambo women were able, when asked, to recognize one another's pottery as belonging to one or the other ethnicity merely by its appearance. Thus, the pottery can be seen as displaying "clear alliance" between a household's members (especially the women in the household) and a specific political point of view in a setting where political decisions are made (2000, 242). Ultimately, the style of one's household equipment can have significant effects on a guest who views it.

The other side of the debate between rationality and irrationality is espoused by scholars who have specifically resisted "logocentrism," that is, the need to suggest a rational explanation for all human behaviors. Most prominent with regard to human choices relating to consumption is the anthropologist Anne Stahl, who has noted that while the specific way in which some luxuries are chosen over others is derived from the cultural meanings attributed to them, these meanings are constantly changing. The manner of their changes does not always conform to Western expectations (which are, as already noted, culturally constructed; see note 17 on Obeyesekere), and may even resist explanation of any kind. Stahl's study of women in African societies and changes in the use of different colors of decorative beads over time specifically avoided any attempt to understand change as a logical process. She argued that "fashion" or "taste" shifts frequently, even unexpectedly, in both modern and premodern cultures.[24] It may be possible to chart the variables involved in taste-making, but the nature of these variables themselves can shift, as well. To summarize: the practice of wasteful advertising can be universally explained as endowing participants with a means of sending an important signal to their community regarding status, but the precise system of signals—that is, the items on which resources are "wastefully" spent—remains locally determined and infinitely changeable.

Acquisition and the *Chaîne Opératoire*

It seems to me, following the discussion of acquisition above, and in accordance with the clear importance of the ancient consumer's agency to make choices about which products to select and which to reject from an array of possibilities, that Dietlerian consumption ought to be integrated with the economic concept of consumption, as represented by Foxhall, Hodos, and others (Walsh 2013 and forthcoming). André Leroi-Gourhan's concept of the *chaîne opératoire* ("operational sequence," or "life history") may offer a way to make this connection by considering the variables that contribute to an object's meaning. The chaîne opératoire of an object directs attention to all phases of the object's existence, from the collection of raw materials, to manufacture, transport, sale, incorporation into the buyer's set of possessions, use, possible resale and reuse, breakage, and deposition (Van der Leeuw 1999).[25] The chaîne opératoire seems useful because the two different kinds of consumption are related to fundamentally different moments in the life of the same object. Dietler's ideas about consumption, on the one hand, seem to focus primarily on the period of an object's use, because that is where the meanings attributed to the object used by its owner tend to be most evident. Archaeologists usually lack direct access to the meanings and functions of objects, but those meanings can be revealed in the archaeological record by the way they are grouped with other objects or installations, or in the location of their deposition—for example, objects found in a house likely had a domestic meaning (and function), while those found in a sanctuary were religious and those in a tomb were related to death. Objects that had to pass through many hands before arriving at the location of their use will have different meanings from those that were designed to be used by their maker alone.[26] While economic consumption also is related to the use or utility of the object, it concentrates primarily on the moment of sale, in which various considerations concerning price, fashion, and other factors are contemplated in relation to other available commodities. Evidence for these considerations can be found in the chaîne opératoire—through the kind of materials used and the effort used to collect them, the quality and effort of workmanship, the distance traveled by the object from its place of manufacture, the identity of the buyers and sellers (and their status), the places and times when the object was used, and the places and times when the object was transferred or discarded. Every step in the chaîne opératoire may, to varying degrees, create an impact on the conscious (and perhaps even unconscious) meanings of the object to its consumer within their own culturally conditioned perspective.

SUMMARY OF THEORETICAL APPROACH

A very wide array of theoretical approaches and ethnographic analogies has been described in the previous pages. What remains is to integrate them into a single formal structure that will describe our expectations about how ancient consumers might have behaved when presented with an array of local and foreign goods to incorporate into their lives.

The perspectives outlined above are unanimous in claiming that human beings consume the goods that they do not merely because of their functional utility for sustaining life, but because those goods have symbolic meanings for their consumers. Those meanings are not inherent but rather attributed as a result of the relationships that emerge between humans and objects when they become entangled with one another. Meanings are especially attributed on the basis of existing regional and local cultural structures. Marshall Sahlins has demonstrated the importance of culture for helping to define human interpretations of the world around us. At the same time, since culture itself is not static, the meanings attributed to objects are potentially subject to constant change as circumstances or fashions change.

While it is not possible (or even desirable) to map the modern capitalist economic system directly onto ancient contexts, certain apparent similarities suggest that some ethnographic analogy with the modern world may be suitable for understanding consumers' decision-making processes. Consumers at various points of exchange possessed the agency to choose among these options according to their biologically determined needs, culturally constructed interests, and ability to offer something in return. Each side must have offered something considered to be valuable by the other, although the thing offered in exchange may not necessarily have been tangible; a local leader could have granted a trader access to territory or his community in return for foreign goods, for example. The value of the object was ultimately determined by the buyer's identification of various attributes relating to different aspects of the object's design, manufacture, materials, origin, and potential utility (as discernible in the chaîne opératoire). Consumers sometimes decided to sustain the greater cost that was associated with selecting foreign goods like Greek pottery over locally manufactured alternatives—even local copies of foreign products—however that cost was reckoned. It is likely that they did so because at least part of the value of a foreign good was connected to the role it could play in local or regional status competitions. This probability can be deduced from Bourdieu's work showing how objects, ideas, and interests can be linked to membership in different status groups (or, indeed, how objects themselves can actually define the boundaries between those groups), as well as from Neiman's and Boone's research suggesting that wasteful expenditures of resources on displays of wealth can be an effective way of increasing status or distinguishing between individuals or groups of different status. The new ways in which foreign products were used and displayed—Dietler's "consumption"—and the ways in which they related to status must have varied from place to place, but in all cases, the foreign goods served as transmitters of signals from their purchasers about positive qualities with which they wanted to be associated. The extent to which they were acquired reflects the success the goods were perceived to have had in sending signals that were accurately received by the appropriate audience. The incorporation of Greek goods into non-Greek societies and western Greek colonies alike could create divergent and hybridized cultures, according to specific local interests and events, since, for example, Greek colonies were not Greek in the same way as Greek cities in the homeland were (or even in the same way as each other; Antonaccio 2009).

NOTES

1. Vives-Ferrándiz (2010, 206, perhaps influenced by the Lacanian construct of the other/Other) has suggested that difference, rather than similarity, is at the core of how identity is articulated through material culture, but I think this can only be true when we attribute to others identities that are different from the ones we claim for ourselves. Difference is not important when we attribute identities to those we see as being members of the group to which we claim identity. Moreover, when we claim identity, we are saying that we are similar to members of some larger group—even if the reason for that group's existence is to claim difference from some other group.
2. Less frequently, cultural identity has also been a point of interest (see, for example, the papers in Gruen 2011).
3. There are connections here with what has been called Actor-Network Theory, where "both people and things can be 'actants' in social relations" (Knappett 2011, 8). See also Antonaccio 2005 and 2009.
4. Cf. Morel 1983b, 69–70, and Johnston 1991a, 204–205.
5. I do not intend to suggest that the only archaeologists who have studied the ancient western Mediterranean are those whose background is in the classical world—archaeologists of prehistoric France, Spain, Portugal, Switzerland, and Germany have been leaders in this area. The deployment of explicitly theoretical approaches to exchange by European prehistorians has, however, only rarely been more widespread than for classical specialists (see, for example, the adaptation of "world-systems" models, below).

6. This phenomenon was correctly identified by Vickers and Gill (esp. 1994), even if their conclusions regarding the phenomenon's implications for the ancient value of Greek pottery exports are likely flawed (Walsh and Antonaccio 2014, with references). See also below for an extended discussion of Vickers and Gill and responses to their work.

7. See also Hurst and Owen, eds., 2005.

8. Boardman's writing cited here probably dates back to his book's first edition in 1964, but such perspectives have persisted even into recent decades. Shefton, for example, referred on multiple occasions to the use of Greek pottery at "uncivilized" barbarian banquets in Spain and Sicily, and the importance of the vases' durability for the apparently inevitable moments when brawls would break out (1982, 403 and 1996, 88). Traces of this attitude can be found in more recent scholarship, too. For example, Adolfo Domínguez, a scholar who has frequently given critical and nuanced postcolonialist attention to certain aspects of Greek-Iberian interactions, in one work seems to offer instead a view of Iberians as subordinate to (and passive recipients of) Greek activity (2002). He begins by saying: "For much of antiquity the Iberian Peninsula represented a peripheral and marginal region with respect to the major centers of the ancient Mediterranean." Iberia may have seemed peripheral or marginal to the Greeks—it certainly seemed distant (see Strabo 3.2.12 for his view on what Homer thought about Tartessos)—but perhaps it did not seem so to the Phoenicians who settled many sites there, nor much less still to the Iberians themselves, who likely considered their own settlements to be "major centers." See also my description of criticism of "world-systems" approaches below.

9. Northern European scholars' tendency to be interested in Greek colonization of Italy, but not elsewhere (except for French scholars working on Greek activity in France), was undoubtedly because Italy had been the locus for the intermixing of Greek and Roman cultures, which they took to be the source of their culture—indeed, the Romans' earliest contact with Greek cities was through their interaction with (and later conquest of) colonies in the Mezzogiorno and Sicily.

10. As already noted, the spread of "Roman-ness" across Europe in antiquity was the source of the ability for dominant Western nations to assert that their culture derived from classical sources (Dietler 2010, 27–43).

11. More recently, the supposed aspirational instinct of indigenous groups to emulate other cultures in the classical period has been referred to by Morris (2003), Hodos (2006), and Schweizer (2012) as "Mediterraneanizing," although this formulation clearly becomes problematic for non-Greek and non-Roman groups living around the Mediterranean.

12. Likewise, the extent of Greek debt to eastern Mediterranean cultures for much of what is today recognized as "Greek"—such as their alphabet, artistic styles and types of artworks, certain pottery shapes, their habit of holding banquets where participants reclined on couches, many of their myths, etc.—was often minimized, if not ignored, until the 1990s (Miller 1997).

13. The novelist David Foster Wallace aptly expressed this idea in a speech given in 2005 (published posthumously in 2009) in which he cautioned against the solipsism that he identified here: "Everything in my own immediate experience supports my deep belief that I am the absolute center of the universe; the realest, most vivid and important person in existence. We rarely think about this sort of natural, basic self-centeredness because it's so socially repulsive. But it's pretty much the same for all of us. It is our default setting, hard-wired into our boards at birth. Think about it: there is no experience you have had

that you are not the absolute center of. The world as you experience it is there in front of YOU or behind YOU, to the left or right of YOU, on YOUR TV or YOUR monitor. And so on. Other people's thoughts and feelings have to be communicated to you somehow, but your own are so immediate, urgent, real." The development and use of gesture and language by humans to communicate are empirical signs that we lack an innate ability to understand precisely what others feel, perceive, or think without those means of communication. At the same time, we frequently take the meanings encoded in those forms of communication for granted (see, for example, Searle 1995). See also Hodder on the ways in which we often take both objects and their meanings for granted, too (2012, 5–7, 18–20, 101–103).

14. These interactions were not always to both sides' benefit—there could certainly be "winners" and "losers" (Morris 2003).

15. See Lyons (1996a) for a detailed description of Siculo-Geometric pottery in the Morgantina necropoleis.

16. Hodder's work is consciously linked to the ongoing discussion within anthropology and archaeology of the social significance of objects, now referred to as "materiality," which in some respects found its genesis in the work of Appadurai and Thomas. See also Olsen 2013.

17. It is worth noting that Sahlins's interpretation of Cook's death was forcefully disputed by Gananath Obeyesekere (1997), who accused Sahlins of condescending to the native Hawaiians by imagining that they were so naïve as to be unable to tell the difference between Cook and Lono. Sahlins responded with equal force (1996), arguing that Obeyesekere—who had claimed the islanders ought not to be considered less "practical" and "rational" than the British—in fact was refusing to contend with the ways Hawaiians understood the world, as it had been defined within their culture. Indeed, as Sahlins showed, even the notions of "practicality" and "rationality" are themselves culturally constructed, for an action that seems practical or rational to one group will often seem entirely impractical or irrational to another.

18. The program is available to be watched in its entirety on YouTube (as of July 2013). I thank Devon Richtmeyer for bringing this satire to my attention.

19. An ambivalent reaction to new technology and its effect on people was vividly described in Booth Tarkington's classic novel about industrialization in America, *The Magnificent Ambersons* (1918). In this story, Eugene Morgan is an inventor working to build an automobile-manufacturing business at the turn of the 20th century. George Minafer, the old-fashioned son of Morgan's romantic interest, criticizes automobiles as "a useless nuisance." Morgan responds, "I'm not sure George is wrong about automobiles. With all their speed forward, they may be a step backward in civilization. . . . It may be that they will not add to the beauty of the world, nor the life of men's souls. I am not sure. But automobiles have come and they bring a greater change in our life than most of us suspect. They are here, and almost all outwards things are going to be different because of what they bring. They are going to alter war and they are going to alter peace. *And I think men's minds are going to be changed in subtle ways because of automobiles; just how, though, I could hardly guess. But you can't have the immense outward changes that they will cause without some inward ones.* . . . Perhaps in ten or twenty years from now, if we can see the inward change in men by that time, I shouldn't be able to defend the gasoline engine but would have to agree with him that automobiles had no business to be invented" (emphasis added).

20. This kind of consumption creates an analogy between the physical use of resources and of finished products—as resources are used, their quantity decreases until it disappears, while finished products almost inevitably will be

broken somehow, or lost, and require replacement. There may therefore also be a connection between this type of consumption with the contemporary notion of "planned obsolescence," in which products are designed with their use to completion and replacement in mind.

21. Domínguez (2002, 70) was among the first to use the word "agency" to describe human interactions in Mediterranean colonial settings.

22. The biological underpinnings of the theory, which are derived from Zahavi's "handicap principle" (1975 and 1977), can be found in Grafen 1990a and 1990b. See also Smith et al. 2001; Bliege, Bird, and Smith 2005.

23. As Bowser writes: "In the sample of 40 chicha bowls, I have recorded more than 80 design elements, and no motif appears on more than one bowl in the sample. One design element occurs with sufficient frequency to analyze comparably with the other nominal variables: a dot, usually made with the finger. . . . Political affiliation correlates significantly with the use of dots in the upper design field on the interior of chicha bowls ($\chi^2 = 5.914$, df = 1, p = .015). Quichua-allied women incorporate dots into the upper design field more often than Achuar-allied women" (2000, 235).

24. Likewise, Smalls has suggested a simple difference in local taste as an explanation for the lesser quantities of Athenian imported vases at Veii relative to other Etruscan sites (1994, 55–56).

25. The chaîne opératoire obviously bears strong resemblances to the kind of descriptive object histories that appear in some examples of entanglement theory (see, for example, Hodder 2012, 44–48).

26. See also Hodder (2012, 106–107) for an almost identical description of how an object can be "more entangled" or "less entangled."

5 Greek Pottery at Home and in the West

STUDYING POTTERY

Up to this point, very little discussion has been made of the material that makes up the primary evidence for this study: Greek pottery. This chapter seeks to describe the importance of pottery within Greece and the Greek world more generally, as an export commodity, and as an archaeological datum. Research on Greek pottery, like research on Greek colonization, has followed a pattern related to the colonialist bias of Western culture generally. This often unspoken agenda continues, in some respects, to limit the kinds of research that can be done using Greek pottery, since it has favored investigation and publication of painted vases from historically important pottery production centers over other types, and investigation and publication of intact vases over fragmentary ones. It has also emphasized interest in vases used for the drinking banquet known as the symposion, almost to the exclusion of other Greek behaviors. The discussion that follows will briefly describe the history of the Greek pottery manufacturing industry and trade before moving on to consideration of historical trends in scholarship, evidence for the symposion as well as other activities involving Greek pottery, and what information besides pottery might exist for understanding how vases were used by non-Greeks in western Europe.

The Greek Pottery Industry and Exports

As in many other parts of the world, the technology of pottery production emerged in Greece during the Neolithic period. By the Late Bronze Age (roughly 1600–1200 BCE), pottery was just one of the many types of objects that moved around the Mediterranean as part of larger trading patterns. Minoan and Mycenaean pottery has been found in Sicily, Spain, the Levant, and Egypt (Voza 1973a, 1973b, García Martin 2003)—in the New Kingdom tomb of the vizier Senemut at Deir el-Bahri, attendants are even depicted bringing Senemut products from the Aegean, including a bull's head rhyton and a (probably ceramic) cup painted with a spiral design very similar to gold cups found in the Late Helladic I Mycenaean tholos Tomb 3 at Peristeria in Messenia (Smith 1998, Korres 1976 and 1984).

Following the resurgence of Greek communities in the eighth century, pottery began to move over long distances again. Different cities' wares appeared in different proportions depending on the period in question. In the eighth century, Euboian, Corinthian and Athenian pottery was most widespread, followed by Argive and Theban wares. In the seventh century, Corinthian pottery seems to have been most prolific, perhaps as a result of the development of the black-figure painting technique, but beginning around 600, Athens became the primary exporter of pottery from the Greek mainland. One scholar has suggested that 50,000 painted vases were manufactured for local and export consumption each year in Athens, together with several times that number of unpainted vessels (Boardman 2001). It is difficult to delineate precisely the extent to which pottery was exported as an important product in its own right, both in the Bronze Age and later, as a corollary to other products, or whether it was included in long-distance trade merely as an easily stackable good that could serve as ballast to round out a load of cargo. Analysis of shipwrecks from the classical period in the western Mediterranean seems to show that table wares formed a primary component of ships' cargo, along with metal in the form of ingots and liquid products carried in transport amphorai, but the value of these vases is difficult to pin down (Long 1987, 1990; Pomey and Long 1992; Long et al. 1992, 2002, 2006; Hesnard 1992; Dietler 2010, 134).

ART HISTORICAL STUDY OF POTTERY

From the moment that excavators began to dig at archaeological sites such as Pompeii and Herculaneum in the first half of the 18th century, pottery was seen as worthy of interest—at least, certain kinds of pottery. Even more than the Roman wares found around the Bay of Naples, the intact painted Greek vases found in tombs of the archaic and classical periods at Nola, Paestum, and Capua attracted attention. These vessels, with their glossy surfaces and rich imagery, were initially thought to have been either local Campanian or Etruscan products, although both Johann Joachim Winckelmann and William Hamilton raised doubts, arguing that they were in fact Greek (Lyons 2007, 239–241). Once their Greek origins, and thus their connections to the height of classicism, were established, vases from Athens and elsewhere became prized possessions. They served as evidence for myth, for daily life, and even for an entire genre of art (major painting) which was now almost completely absent and otherwise known primarily only from the writings of ancient authors such as Pliny the Elder.[1] Interest in Greek vases as artworks continues up to the present day, with collectors paying enormous amounts of money for them. Vessels are placed prominently on display in fine art museums beside not only ancient sculptures, mosaics, and other genres, but also major paintings and sculptures from other periods.[2] Like other kinds of art, painted Greek vases were analyzed for the development of their imagery and the artists' techniques over time. Early antiquarians considered the findspots of vases of little consequence relative to the places of their manufacture, since Athens, Corinth, Sparta, and other centers figured greatly in the histories recounted by ancient authors. Winckelmann began the process of dividing Greek art into styles that were explicitly related to chronological periods; these eras were developed and refined by the early 20th century into the nomenclature of archaic, classical, and so on, which is familiar to us today. Studies concentrated not only on the way vases were painted but also on the subjects and themes of images, which often could be related to literary versions of mythological stories or even to specific pieces of literature, such as plays from fifth-century Athens. The paintings were used to confirm written sources, or else to provide counterpoints to them.

In the first half of the 20th century, one scholar, J.D. Beazley, defined the study of Greek vases and especially the decoration of vases with imagery in a new way (Boardman 2001, 129–138; Rouet 2001). Beazley's close observation of Greek vases and the signatures of potters and painters on some of them led him to wonder whether it might be possible to study ateliers of painters, such as had been done for painters in other periods, especially the Renaissance and baroque (1956, 1963, 1971). Organizing vases by their artists had already been undertaken by other scholars, most notably Adolf Furtwängler, Karl Reichhold, and Alois Huber (1924). Beazley's innovation was to adapt the methodology of a 19th-century scholar of Italian Renaissance painting, Giovanni Morelli, to Greek vases. Morelli had argued, among other points, that painters tended to spend little time and effort on details that viewers did not examine closely, such as hands, feet, ears, and eyes (Morelli and Frizzoni 1890). Artists therefore painted these parts of their works quickly, without great attention, and, most importantly, in the same manner every time. Using these details, Morelli felt able to attribute (or reattribute) unsigned works to artists with known oeuvres. Beazley followed Morelli's principles, attributing thousands of vases to artists, including many whose names remain unknown (such as the Berlin Painter, the Kleophrades Painter, or the Painter of the Louvre Centauromachy, for example), on the basis of similarities he detected in minor details. The result of Beazley's work was to identify not only the hands of individual artists, but also to reconstruct the histories of workshops where certain artists worked side by side or learned from one another, apprentice from master. Other scholars have carried out similar studies for artists from other centers, especially Corinth (Amyx 1988, Amyx and Lawrence 1996) and Sparta (Stibbe 1972, 2004). Today, a digital archive named for Beazley, located at Oxford University, has collected records on tens of thousands of Greek vases located in public and private collections around the world, building on his and others' lists of vases and artists (Smith 2005).[3]

Beginning in the 1980s, however, several scholars—particularly Michael Vickers and David Gill—criticized modern art historians, archaeologists, and collectors for the attention that had been paid to painted ceramic vases. These critics believed that pottery had been overprivileged relative to its ancient significance (among others: Gill 1988a, 1988b, 1990, and 1991; Vickers 1999; Vickers and Gill 1994 and 1995; Vickers et al. 1986). Vickers and Gill pointed out that metal vessels, especially gold and silver ones, were vastly more expensive (on the order of a hundred times or more) in antiquity than clay vessels. Literary sources and price dipintos on ceramic vases seem to support this relationship (Johnston 1979), even though very few metal vessels are preserved in the archaeological record (most seem to have been melted down to make the metal available for other uses). Vickers and Gill suggested that pottery was actually worthless, placed on merchants' vessels merely as ballast to accompany what they regarded as the true objects of exchange: perfumed oil, silver, gold, and ivory (Gill 1988a, 9); in the western Mediterranean, wine could also be added. Vickers and Gill also suggested that the colors that appeared on Athenian ceramic vases were a sign that they were intended to slavishly copy the appearance of gold and silver, with the glossy black slip looking like silver (especially if that silver was tarnished), and the orange-red of the vases' clay bodies looking like gold. They pointed to a few examples of silver cups with figured decorations in gold as evidence for this hypothesis (e.g., a kantharos, phiale, and stemmed cup from a tumulus in Duvanli, Bulgaria, today in the Plovdiv Archaeological Museum; Vickers et al. 1986, plate 4).

It is impossible to know how many metal vessels were available or how many of them different classes of people could afford. Thucydides's description of a visit by Athenian ambassadors to the Elymian town of Segesta in western Sicily (6.46), for example, hinges on a trick played by the Segestaians in order to win military support from Athens. The people of Segesta gathered all of the gold and silver vessels they could, not only from their own homes, but borrowing from neighboring Phoenician and Greek towns as well. They then used all of these vessels each night at a different house for banquets held in the Athenians' honor, leading the visitors to believe falsely that great wealth was widespread in Segesta, and that every house had a full table service in precious metal. The provocative arguments of Vickers and Gill were met with a strong response (Robertson 1985, Cook 1987, Johnston 1991a, 1991b). Boardman (1987) has pointed out that while it is clear that vessels made of precious metals were associated with prestige, it is equally clear that Greeks did not allow their silver to tarnish, preferring it to remain gleaming white instead—indeed, its brilliance was the reason it was highly prized. There is therefore no reason to believe that black gloss surface treatments on pottery had any connection to silver. It is worth noting that black gloss, while shiny, is not especially reflective. If it were intended to resemble metal, the target would more likely be bronze, which produces a similarly dim reflection (Walsh and Antonaccio 2014). Other formal features of clay vessels, such as carinations, vertical strap handles (especially when they are high-swung, as on kantharoi), offset ridges on the interior of cups, and rims with a concave or flaring profile, also seem to have made reference to metallic prototypes (Antonaccio 2009). In the western Mediterranean, these features appear most frequently on drinking cups, such as the ubiquitous "Ionian" stemmed cups, the Athenian stemless variety known by its type-site, Cástulo in Spain, and the related cup-skyphos shape that we have identified at Morgantina in Sicily. These shapes seem to have been popular, not just because they were Greek in origin, or because they mimicked metal vases, but because they mimicked *local* traditions in metal vases—traditions that dated back into the Early Bronze Age, in some cases—while adding features that made them locally rare (e.g., shiny black surfaces).[4] Indeed, it is highly important to mention that the vast majority of ancient Greek metal vases have not been found in Greek contexts at all; in addition to the silver vessels found in Bulgaria mentioned earlier, one can point to equally spectacular examples such as the Vix krater (see chapter 3).

As for the purported worthlessness of ceramic vases, several factors argue for them having had at least some economic value. First (and perhaps most important for this study), the broad distribution of Greek wares indicates that there was interest in it on the part of consumers as a good worthy of exchange over long periods of time and in a variety of places. Second, the presence of often-complex imagery, and even of shiny slips, was an investment of time on the part of producers that must have had some payoff beyond what could have been gained for selling undecorated pottery. That the black gloss slip used at Athens had value is clear from the presence of imitations now known to be made in Sicily and southern Italy. The signatures found on many painted vases form a further argument in this direction—in Athens, at least, the names of artists must have had meaning and value. It is not yet possible to make the argument that signatures or images necessarily added value in non-Greek contexts, but again, the fact that Greek vases were acquired despite their higher cost shows that value was attributed to them, even far from Greece. They were luxury items—perhaps not treated as an "ultimate" luxury similar to precious metal, but rather as a luxury *relative to pottery produced locally.*[5]

ANTHROPOLOGICAL STUDY OF POTTERY

Archaeologists outside the classical world recognized early in the 20th century how pot sherds could be analyzed as significant traces of past peoples' lives. At first, they were used as a tool for identifying cultures—decorative motifs, fabric, and shapes were seen as essentialized. This perspective developed in the 19th century, when scholarship and nationalism became intertwined in the European academic world. Franz Boas, working on the prehistoric United States, emphasized the uniqueness of cultures and historical particularism, while Oscar Montelius, following other Scandinavian anthropologists, developed the first typologies of artifacts based on formal and stylistic features (Trigger 2006, 219, 224–228). These two approaches were combined by Gustaf Kosinna in his identification of prehistoric Germanic cultural groups by their material culture. Kosinna's culture groups were explicitly tied to ancient and modern racial characteristics and thus to predetermined notions of superiority or inferiority (Trigger 2006, 237). He also identified cultural groups with geographic territories, an effort that was later used to support German claims to a larger homeland (Trigger 2006, 238–241). Finally, however, V. Gordon Childe discarded the racist tendencies of Kosinna's "culture-history" and argued for the adoption of empirical approaches to identifying cultural groups and to build chronologies through the archaeological record (Trigger 2006, 244–245).

Pottery finds became seen as particularly useful for establishing chronologies not only of vases and decorative styles, but also of sites. In a study of sites in the American Southwest, Alfred Kroeber (1916) noticed a difference between the colors of sherds associated with sites with well-preserved architecture and local names, and those that were associated with no visible architecture and whose names were practically forgotten. He concluded that the well-preserved remains (and therefore the accompanying sherds) were more recent than those which had disappeared. Although sherds of both colors were found at some sites, red ones appeared in greater numbers at others that appeared to be "older" and black ones at sites that were "younger." At some older sites there were no black sherds, and at some younger ones there were no red ones. Thus, Kroeber felt justified in claiming that the use of red and black wares overlapped, and that red ware pottery was older but was eventually superseded by black ware.[6]

The most important aspect of Kroeber's new understanding, as it applied to the formation of the discipline of culture history, was the chronological phenomenon of an artifact type's growth in popularity, its subsequent overlapping with a new type of the same kind of artifact, and finally the waning popularity of the original and the subsequent waxing of the new type. Excavation of sites and new understandings of stratification allowed archaeologists to plot types of artifacts, including pottery, over time. These charts, called seriations, frequently demonstrated the growth, plateau, and decline of types, featuring "battleship"-shaped profiles (Ford 1938). In classical archaeology, interest in creating typologies and chronologies for pottery focused on painted types and the ways in which pottery could be useful for providing dates for stratigraphic contexts.

QUANTIFYING POTTERY

In any study where archaeologists are trying to understand the character of pottery assemblages, one of the very first questions that will be asked is, "What types of pottery were there, and how many of each type were preserved?" This question is actually far more complex than it might appear to be at first. The primary issue that creates complications is the fragmentary nature of most archaeological pottery (Orton et al. 1993). Apart from vessels that were purposely buried intact—which is normally the case only in grave contexts, although even these sometimes break between deposition and recovery, or even during recovery—ancient pottery users, just like their modern counterparts, tended to use pots until they broke. The various fragments of a given pot normally become separated from one another during the breakage and discard process. In addition, it is extremely difficult to know how much of a given pot is represented by the fragments that do survive and are correctly identified by the excavator as belonging to the same original individual. There is no direct relationship between the size of a vessel, its shape, the thickness of its walls, the specific fabric of the clay, or any other variable and the number of fragments into which it might break—any vase might break into two parts, 10 parts, or some other number of fragments. The quantity of pottery found at most archaeological sites makes any attempt to guess what proportion of an original vessel is represented by each sherd unfeasible. Simply counting sherds does not provide numbers that have any demonstrable relationship to the population of vessels used at an archaeological site in antiquity, beyond, perhaps, a large number of sherds representing "many" vases, and a small number representing "few" vases.

Archaeologists have tried to solve the problem of "brokenness" through a variety of approaches. These have included counting and measuring only what are referred to as "diagnostic" sherds (rims, feet, and handles), which allow for the easy identification of the vases' shapes. The number represented by these counts is called the "minimum number of vessels" (MNV). There are several problems with MNVs; most important, they underrepresent certain types of pottery, and they bias counts against pots whose body sherds are better preserved than their diagnostic fragments (Rice 2005, Voss and Allen 2010, 1–2). Another approach is to weigh all of the sherds of the same fabric from the same context, which would provide a good sense for the proportions of types. Unfortunately, weighing pottery usually does not take shapes into account, making this a fairly coarse method for estimating the makeup of pottery assemblages.[7] Another significant problem is that different fabrics cannot be compared easily, especially when the vessels in one fabric tend to have thicker walls (and thus be heavier) than another fabric. Ultimately, weighing pottery might tell an investigator how much pottery there was, but not how many pots there were.

Clive Orton, a specialist in medieval ceramics and quantitative archaeology, made important efforts in the 1980s to develop a statistically useful way of quantifying pottery found through excavation and making it possible to compare complex assemblages (Orton et al. 1993, 166–173). He employed measurements of the diameters of vessel rims and feet, and of the percentage of each rim and foot that was preserved, in order to create what he referred to as "estimated vessel equivalents" (EVEs). These EVEs could be transformed into "pottery information equivalents" (PIEs) using a computer program called Pie-slice, designed by Orton together with Paul Tyers for the UNIX and MS-DOS operating systems. These PIEs, while not representing actual counts of vessels, could be treated like counts for statistical purposes. This method remains the only one that currently exists that can cope adequately with the brokenness problem. Regrettably, the software (last modified in 1993) never became widely distributed, and it will become increasingly difficult to find computers (in the Windows environment, at least) that are capable of running it, since it has no graphical user interface, it does not work in the DOS emulator of current 64-bit Windows operating systems, and most archaeologists do not use text-based UNIX systems.

It would have been highly desirable to use Orton and Tyers's software to help analyze the dataset.[8] Unfortunately, none of the publications consulted gave information that would have been necessary to assign EVEs. While diameters are typically given in comprehensive final publications of pottery from individual sites, few ceramicists, if any, publish the preserved percentage of individual rims and feet.[9] So what strategy remains in order to understand how Greek pottery was distributed in foreign contexts? One possible approach, which is more reliable (albeit subject to the same caveats regarding thorough excavation and publication), ignores quantities entirely. It focuses attention instead on the presence or absence of categories such as functional types, wares, and shapes. A wide array of shapes may show a strong interest in Greek pottery, and also perhaps that Greek vases were intended for a variety of uses. The appearance of only a few different shapes, conversely, shows a limited interest in Greek pottery, and perhaps that activities or opportunities for using Greek vases were sharply circumscribed.

The original design of this project envisioned the use of multivariate statistical modeling of a type known as correspondence analysis. This method allows for the comparison of counts or the presence or absence of types from whole assemblages associated with multiple sites, and for the identification of the most significant factors determining the similarities and differences between assemblages (Shennan 1997, 308). Unfortunately, the assemblages from almost all the sites were far too sparse to make correspondence analysis viable. There were many vessel shapes—115 as categorized in this dataset—but only a handful of sites, particularly Saint-Blaise and Massalia, did not show null values for the vast majority of shapes. The same problem of sparsity makes chi-square testing, which would show the significance of the variance within site assemblages, impossible. In consultation with a professional statistician, I therefore decided to abandon this design in favor of other kinds of analysis.[10]

Three primary approaches will be taken for the analysis of the dataset in order to understand the distribution of pottery over time and in diverse locations. The first method will examine the presence and absence of various types, as just mentioned. It is possible to divide the pottery by its intended function into five types: drinking, eating, household, storage, and transport (this last group consists exclusively of transport amphorai). By only making reference to the number of types represented at each site, it is possible to avoid the problem associated with sherd and vessel counts. Each type can be broken down further into subtypes, such as the different shapes of vessels used for drinking, to determine how broad a range of vessels was being consumed at a given site. A site might have only drinking vessels, but those vases might be represented in 10 or 12 shapes. It would thus score low on the distribution of types of Greek pottery while showing that the interest in Greek-style drinking vessels was, in fact, strong. Measures of presence-absence can be considered relatively robust, statistically speaking, because they are unaffected by extreme outlying values for counts of sherds.

The other approaches to understanding distribution are somewhat more problematic, since they rely partly or entirely on the previously discredited method of sherd and vessel counts. In spite of the very real problems associated with brokenness described above, it may be useful to examine whether accepting the counts as having some (again, undemonstrated and unclear) relationship to the quantity of vessels that existed in the past can give us some potentially useful picture. Since the dataset allows for counts of the fragments and vessels to be made, they can be used to form tentative conclusions—with the understanding that these counts do not (and cannot) reflect actual numbers of vessels. Larger numbers will be taken to indicate greater presence of Greek wares, generally speaking, and smaller numbers to indicate lesser presence. For example, of the three sites with the highest counts in the dataset, two (Massalia and Emporion) were Greek colonies. This pattern seems to follow common sense: Greek colonies would likely have the most Greek pottery. Similarly, many of the sites with very low counts were those located farthest away from Greek colonies, such as Somme-Bionne (only about 50 kilometers from the Belgian border in northern France), Palenzuela (in northeast Spain), or many of the sites in Portugal. For these reasons, analysis will be carried out on the quantities of sherds published from the various sites, and how that distribution might reflect some aspects of the consumption of Greek pottery (in actual practice, in fact, presence-absence analysis will be used to confirm or reject conclusions regarding distribution that have been arrived at using artifact counts). It must be remembered, however, that large numbers might also be the result of more thorough excavation or publication (as seen for example, in the thousands of Athenian red-figure vessels published from Emporion (Miró i Alaix 2011).

Concomitantly, a third approach will use a statistic originally developed for ecological studies, Simpson's D (Simpson 1949). Simpson's D was designed to measure diversity as a function both of the number of different species of animals present in a habitat as well as the number of individuals in each species.[11] The formula is as follows:

$$D = \frac{\sum n(n-1)}{N(N-1)}$$

where *n* is the number of individuals in a particular species and *N* is the number of all individuals in the sample. The quantity is computed for each type or species and the results are added together. The measurement provided by the formula typically falls between zero and one, with a lower number signifying greater diversity. This inverse relationship is counterintuitive, so a variation on Simpson's D has been selected for this study. Simpson's Index of Diversity, is instead equal to 1-*D*, making higher numbers equivalent to higher diversity , and thus providing a more desirable result.[12] Where Simpson's D represents the probability that two individuals randomly selected from the same sample belong to the same type, Simpson's Index of Diversity represents the probability that two individuals randomly selected belong to different types.

A habitat is considered diverse according to Simpson's Index of Diversity if individuals are evenly distributed across the species present in the habitat. A habitat with a high number of species is not considered diverse if there are many species represented in a sample, but most of the individuals are only from one or two species. In fact, Simpson's Index of Diversity does not tell us anything about which types were represented, how many types were represented, or how many individuals were counted. Simpson's Index of Diversity only measures how evenly individuals (in this case, sherds) are distributed across taxa (typological designations). As with analysis of the presence and absence of pottery, use of Simpson's Index of Diversity will depend on the identification of functional types, first on the macro scale (drinking, eating, etc.), and separately, on subtypes within the larger types. Pottery types and subtypes take the place of species in the index's formula here, while sherd and vessel counts represent individuals. Simpson's Index of Diversity scores can only be computed for sites with three or more individuals represented, since sites with just one or two individuals or types resulted in Diversity Index scores of zero (no diversity), one (infinite diversity), or an undefined number, which were not meaningful.

Using this multiplicity of perspectives, it will be possible to examine the archaeological record in complex ways. In addition, examination of the distribution of types present, sherd counts, and Simpson's Index of Diversity according to the type of context (especially tomb, settlement, or sanctuary) and the cultural group that inhabited each site will be of critical importance for determining the effects of consumer choice in the purchase and use of Greek vases.

THE DATASET

Greek pottery was chosen as the subject material for this study for a number of reasons. As a luxury good (in export contexts), it is a useful indicator of how ancient consumers' choice of goods reflected their efforts to construct public identities. Consumers, then as now, were free to make selections from among the available array of products. Absent the modern concept of "loss leaders" (the practice of selling some merchandise below cost in order to attract buyers who might then also decide to purchase higher-priced and higher-margin products, thereby boosting overall revenues) among ancient merchants, it can be assumed, from the similarity of the raw materials, and the expense and effort associated with transporting imports to a new place, that Greek wares were more costly than those that were locally produced. The fact that they were selected in spite of their higher cost—and the fact that rather than creating less-expensive local equivalents, Greek originals were consumed over several centuries—demonstrates the importance attached to them by consumers. Imitations of Greek pottery are widely known from archaeological contexts in Italy, where they are often attributed to colonial production, although little clay sourcing has been done to confirm this designation (the author is involved in a current effort to perform this analysis for pottery found at Morgantina in Sicily). Imitations are rarer, however, in the regions under study here. One significant example is an unslipped local copy of an Athenian stemless cup of the Cástulo type that was found among the numerous authentic ones deposited at the Iberian sanctuary of Cancho Roano (Fig. 5.1). Other scholars have noted Iberian imitations beginning from the middle of the sixth century and continuing through the fourth century (Pereira Sieso 1987; Pereira Sieso 1988, 962; Domínguez 1999, 313–317). Such imitations can give signs of which features were of specific interest to local consumers;

Figure 5.1 Imitation Cástulo cup found at Cancho Roano (Museo Arqueológico Provincial de Badajoz, by permission of Dr. Sebastián Celestino Pérez)

in the case of the Cástulo imitation, the form seems to have been more important than the black slip found on authentic Athenian versions. The imitations should not be considered counterfeits—not only do they not copy Greek vases slavishly, they are easily identifiable from visual cues as being imitations rather than authentic.

Greek pottery is easily identified in the archaeological record because of its distinctive formal characteristics (with regard both to shapes and decorations). It also tends to attract attention from scholars when they write final publications of site excavations, both because of the existing (though admittedly diminishing) bias in scholarship toward the Greeks and their activities over indigenous groups, and because of Greek pottery's just-mentioned visibility. It is therefore likely that when Greek pottery is found at a site, it will be published, and often in greater detail than local wares (although figured wares are also often favored over undecorated ones, and fine wares over coarse wares). In the particular geographic area under investigation here, Greek pottery was widely distributed: the database includes 23,928 whole vases or fragments from 233 sites where at least one fragment was published (the site with the most pottery, Saint-Blaise, had 4,771 entries). The sites are located in 57 provincial-level administrative divisions across five countries (Portugal, Spain, France, Switzerland, and Germany). Even so, the database makes no claim to being completely comprehensive with regard either to the number of sites included or to containing data from all of the relevant publications—the number of published Greek vases is so great that such comprehensiveness would not have been feasible within the available time and resources.

For each entry in the database, the following information was recorded, insofar as it was published: the country, province, site, and subsite (for example, a specific cemetery or sanctuary) where the vessel was found; the country and city where the piece is currently held; the fabric, shape, subtype, and dates of the vessel; the context in which the vessel was found (settlement, sanctuary, cemetery); and the relevant bibliography. Information was also added to the database concerning the geographic location of each site, and a functional designation for each vessel based on its shape.

Two works that compiled finds from sites across Spain and France were particularly useful sources: Adolfo Domínguez and Carmen Sánchez Fernández's *Greek Pottery from the Iberian Peninsula* (2001), which collected the published Greek pottery from all of the Iberian Peninsula for the archaic period, and from eastern Andalucía for the classical period; and Jean-Jacques Jully's multivolume *Céramiques Grecques ou de Type Grec et Autres Céramiques en Languedoc Méditerranéen, Roussillon & Catalogne : VIIᵉ-IVᵉ s. avant Notre ère, et Leur Contexte Socio-Culturel* (1982), which lists the finds from Greek and indigenous sites of all sizes in the region. Although Jully's book does not include pottery found more recently, the very large number of vases and sites represented in it are appropriately comprehensive for a useful analysis.[13] Final excavation reports were used to fill in gaps during the classical period in Spain and southern France, especially for Catalonia.[14] Preliminary reports were used for some sites where no final report has been made, such as Agathe and Vix. The relatively few Greek vases from Germany, Switzerland, and Portugal have been collected in a few museum exhibition catalogues and in both final and preliminary excavation reports. Since it was not always possible to know whether later archaeological site reports included data that had already been published in one of the compendia, the decision was made to include only the material in the later reports. For example, since a full publication of the Athenian red-figured (ARF) pottery found at Emporion was made by the excavators (Miró i Alaix 2011), the ARF that appeared in Domínguez's and Sánchez's earlier collection was not included. The attempt to avoid duplicating entries also reflects how an unavoidable bias has been introduced into the dataset due to the uneven publication of sites and of different material from the same site. Earlier synoptic works such as Gloria Trías de Arribas's *Cerámicas griegas de la Península Ibérica* (1967–1968) and Pierre Rouillard's *Les Grecs et la Péninsule Ibérique du VIIIᵉ au IVᵉ siècle Siècle av. J.-C.* (1991) were not used, because these had largely been superseded by later works such as the ones mentioned above. Despite these selections, and within the limits imposed by scholarly bias as mentioned above, the dataset can be considered to be relatively representative of the ancient situation due to its large size. After all, the archaeological record is itself an incomplete sample of an original set whose size is unknown. Most importantly, the statistical methods employed in the analysis reveal the degree of confidence that can be placed in the final results.

Some further limitations need to mentioned, however. In the vast majority of the publications where the data originated, only coarse-grained contextual information is given for the pottery (at best). In other words, it is not generally possible to be more specific about the findspot for any given vessel or fragment other than to say that it came from a settlement, sanctuary, or tomb context. The database therefore cannot be used to reconstruct assemblages from specific houses, civic spaces, votive deposits, or graves—or, for that matter, to investigate the relationships between assemblages that come from these more specific contexts.

In addition, the paucity of historical information regarding the trade of Greek goods limits our ability to draw conclusions. Unlike in historical archaeology (see, for example, several of the papers in Spencer-Wood 1987), we do not know the names or identities of the people involved in the specific trades represented by the material in the catalogue. The only exceptions are the relatively rare cases of some Athenian black- and red-figure vases that have been attributed through signature or stylistic comparison to named artists. Even in those examples, the names we know are those of the people who were least proximate to the ultimate purchase and use of the vases. In all likelihood, knowledge (or lack of knowledge) of the potter's or painter's identity had little impact on the decision of a consumer located in Massalia, more than 1500 kilometers away from Athens, about whether or not to buy a specific vase. For someone even farther removed, either by culture or geographic location, the names of artists would have had even less significance.

Perhaps just as important as knowing precisely who was selling and buying Greek pottery in the western Mediterranean and trans-Alpine Europe would be a detailed understanding of the cost of the pottery in these regions. Exchange in most of these areas would not, in this period, have been based on coinage, but on barter of goods, resources, and produce, and so it is to be imagined that prices would have been quite flexible, depending on the time of year, the location, and the interests of both merchant and buyer. Rather than seeking an equivalent value between a vase and some quantity of other items, we would probably be satisfied in knowing merely the relative costs of Greek imports compared to local vessels—but here, too, we are in almost total ignorance. The only thing that can be stated with some degree of confidence is that imports were generally more costly than local vessels.

GREEK VASE SHAPES AND FUNCTIONS

As stated in the previous chapter, it is clear that the meanings Greek vases had in Greek communities were attributed rather than inherent; in addition, it seems very likely even before analyzing the dataset that non-Greeks gave new meanings to the Greek pottery that they purchased. In order to understand how meanings might have shifted, however, it will be useful to review the ways Greek vases were used in Greek contexts. The nomenclature used here and in the dataset follows the one established by Sparkes and Talcott (1970). In certain instances, it was necessary to adjust the names used in publications to align with the one used here; Jully (1982), for instance, seems to have used the term "cup-kotyle" to refer to the shape known in the rest of this corpus as a "cup-skyphos." In the list below, the vessels have been organized by their primary function (drinking, eating, storage, household equipment, and transport) and then by shape.

Vessels associated with drinking are both the most common in the Greek world and the easiest to identify. Many descriptions of drinking parties, such as the *Symposia* of Plato and Xenophon, survive from antiquity. These works give names and instructions for the use of different types of vases at particular times during a party. Still more useful are the scenes of drinking that appear on many contemporary vessels. Pictures showing reclining men drinking from various vases, pouring from others, and mixing wine in still others demonstrate the uses of those vessels. Narrative scenes are occasionally supplemented by bands framing the bottom of the scene that depict an even wider range of cups and pitchers and relate them to the activity occurring above. Information about eating vessels and practices comes less frequently, though in a similar fashion. We have even less information about cooking or storage vessels, or those with household uses such as lamps or oil flasks. These types appeared infrequently in vase paintings, and they were even more rarely mentioned in literature. Inventories of objects listed in inscriptions also give an idea of the roles of different kinds of vases. The most important inscriptions for vase names are the Attic Stelai, which list the possessions of those convicted for defacing the herms in 415 (Amyx 1998). Lewis has studied temple inventories for similar evidence (1986). Archaeologists have instead assigned extant vessels to the categories of cooking, storage, or household by studying their shapes, fabrics, sizes, decoration, and other attributes. It is assumed in this study that Greek potters designed their products adaptively for the uses to which they would be put in their home contexts (i.e., vessels used for distributing liquid would be designed for pouring; vessels for eating would have shapes useful for holding local cuisine; and so forth). Identification of functions in Greece is aided by the depiction of the use of vases in images, which most often survive in paintings on the vases themselves (Gericke 1970). As a result, examination of all of the various types of evidence relating to vessel functions has made it possible to draw educated inferences about cuisine from pottery. These inferences may not reach the threshold of informing precisely which foods and drinks were placed in which containers, but they are valuable nonetheless.

Vessels for Drinking

Greeks drank wine and water (or the two mixed together) almost exclusively. Dietler (2006) has thoroughly explained the importance of wine, not only for its psychotropic qualities, but also because it is the only fermented beverage made in this period that could keep for more than a few days at room temperature—beer, mead, and other kinds of drink that were available at the time all turn bad much more quickly. The Greek repertoire of vessels used for drinking, like that found in modern Western nations, was elaborate and included many shapes that were not specifically for holding liquid and raising it to one's lips to drink. To be sure, there was a wide array of cups, ranging from narrow-mouthed and deep (skyphoi, kotylai, mugs, mastoid cups) to wide-mouthed and shallow (stemmed cups, stemless cups, bolsals) to wide-mouthed and deep (kantharoi, cup-kantharoi, cup-skyphoi). In addition, there were jugs for pouring, also in several different shapes (oinochai, olpai, askoi), and one large type of vessel, the krater. The krater—essentially a large bowl with very high walls—was used for mixing wine with water, a practice that was considered by Greeks to be a fundamental component of commensal drinking. This point will be discussed in further detail in relation with the symposion below.

Vessels for Eating

Greek cuisine consisted primarily of grains, fruits (especially olives), and vegetables, supplemented with fish and, less frequently, meat from cows, pigs, sheep, goats, and wild game. Honey was probably important, since no other sweeteners were known in the ancient Mediterranean until the fourth century BCE (Curtis 2001, 322 and n. 127). Knowledge of sugar came to Greece from India, although sugar itself did not come to the Mediterranean until sometime later. Although Greeks made ceramic beehives such as the ones found at the house at Vari in Attika (Jones et al. 1973, Jones 1976), in contemporary central Europe there was no such technology, and honey would have had to be procured from wild beehives (Arnold 1999, 75). We have descriptions of recipes from Arkhestratos of Gela's *Hedupatheia* ("Life of Luxury"; Olson and Sens 2000), and from Athenaios's *Deipnosophistai* ("The Learned Banqueters"), although as the titles of those works imply, the recipes tended to be extravagant and sumptuous, intended for the tables of the very wealthy and using ingredients sourced from many parts of the Mediterranean.

The shapes of vessels associated with eating include vases for the table such as bowls and plates (including fish plates, easily identifiable from the depression in the center for holding a sauce, and because the figured versions have paintings of fish on them), and condiment containers. Eating, of course, also implies cooking and food preparation. Greek cooks used large casserole dishes, bowls with lids, and ovens for heating food. They could grind and mix ingredients in shallow, thick-walled mortaria.

Vessels for Household Uses

Pottery vessels also served important functions unrelated to dining. Small oil flasks could be used for cosmetic or hygienic purposes (aryballoi, alabastra), or for funerary functions (lekythoi). Containers for perfumed oil were designed with overturned rims so that their expensive contents could not spill out (kotha, plemochoai, or exaleiptra).[15] Pyxides were used as containers for valuables such as cosmetics or jewelry. Finally, miniature versions of vases from other categories, especially cups and kraters, were made for religious purposes, and were often left at shrines as offerings to deities.

Vessels for Storage

The storage of liquids and grains was accomplished through the use of large closed vessels, some of which were finely decorated or even painted with imagery and used at table. These included amphorai and the related shape of pelikai, which were used for holding large quantities of wine or oil, and hydriai, used for holding water. Much larger vases in coarse ware called pithoi, which could hold hundreds of liters, were used for stockpiling unprocessed food. These vases were so large that they required enormous kilns that used large quantities of wood to fire. They were thus extraordinarily costly; Cahill (2002) has noted inscriptions showing that they could cost as much as a house. These would have been traded over long distances only extremely rarely due to the difficulty of transporting them, but people were known to move them from an old house to a new one because they were so expensive to replace.

Vessels for Transport

The vessel shape used for transport was the transport amphora. These vessels were mass-produced in shapes that were generally unique to the place of their manufacture, so the origin of the goods they contained can often be identified. These vessels primarily carried wine or oil, though they could also hold grain or other perishable food products. They typically lacked a foot and were stacked in rows on their side in the holds of boats; their shapes allowed them to be placed in interlocking patterns, which kept them stable in rough weather and allowed merchants to maximize the space available in the boat for goods.

THE SYMPOSION

Pottery and Banqueting

While Greek vases could obviously be used when dining alone (Wilkins and Hill 2006, 63), their features related to display—shiny surface treatment, elaborate shapes, or decoration with imagery—seem to associate them strongly with commensality and display to others. Such group dining could include family meals, feasts at religious festivals, or nonreligious civic banquets (Schmitt-Pantel 1990, 1992).[16] One Greek commensal activity has attracted far more attention and study than any other: the symposion, or drinking banquet. The word literally means "drinking together." However, the symposion went much deeper than a group of people drinking at the same time and place. It was enmeshed in male aristocratic values, practices, and privileges. It fostered social associations between friends and lovers. It served as a place to enact the competitions (*agōnes*) so important to proving and winning honor (*timē*) in Greek society. It created an arena in which people could deal as a group with the various effects of alcohol on the human body. The reasons for such strong interest in the practice of the symposion stem from the wide array of evidence for it, and for the fact that it represented one of the primary ways in which Greek men could reinforce social bonds with other men to whom they were unrelated by blood.

There are many references to the symposion in ancient literature—as a setting for action in philosophical dialogues, as the subject of lyric poetry, and perhaps especially from stories about banqueting such as those collected in Athenaios's *Deipnosophistai*. Images from vase painting in the archaic and classical periods frequently depict symposia, giving strong evidence for various aspects of sympotic drinking, such as the accommodations (furniture and vessel types) provided for participants, and the activities that might occur at a symposion. Architectural spaces with specific characteristics have been identified as locales for symposia; these appear in both public and private contexts.

Symposia were, in their way, ritualistic events. We know from literature that a typical symposium probably involved a proper meal followed by a short break, prayers and offerings made to the gods on a small altar or thymiaterion, the placement of small tables with finger foods such as eggs, olives, and cakes before each participant, the mixing of wine in measured proportion with water, the distribution of drinks by slaves, and the consumption of drinks in prescribed quantities, along with conversation interspersed with hired entertainment (Wilkins and Hill 2006, 176, 179–182). Symposia could include music, dance, storytelling, recitation (or composition) of poetry, and games such as *kottabos* where wine dregs were hurled at a target (Pellizer 1990, Kritias in DK 1–2); discussion of politics, philosophy, gossip, and current events; and sexual encounters with prostitutes or other party-goers. Following a symposium, drunken revelers might spill out into the streets in search of another symposium to join (*kōmos*).

The practice of the symposium seems, from literary sources, to have developed in Ionia during the seventh century. This fact is perhaps of significance for understanding developments in the western Mediterranean, since Phokaia, the metropolis for the far western colonies, was located in Ionia. It seems clear that the practice of gathering to drink while reclining on couches was brought to the Greek world from the Near East; a famous image of the Assyrian king Ashurbanipal, found in the North Palace at Nineveh (ca. 650 BCE), now in the British Museum, shows him raising a cup to his lips while reclining on a couch in a garden (Matthäus 1998).[17] His queen sits on an upright chair below the couch and also drinks. Increasing contacts between Mesopotamia and Ionia seem to have grown, first through the expansion of Phoenician trade, and later, in the sixth century, through the military conquest of Ionia by the Persians.

The participants in symposia seem to have been primarily male. The people by and for whom symposia were held were certainly adult men. Older youths might be brought to parties by mature companions following the *erastēs/erōmenos* model of introducing the younger generation to adult roles and responsibilities. There is no direct evidence that women of high status would have been present at banquets attended by men who were not related to them by blood (Isaios 3.14; Dalby 1993, 170; Corner 2012). When women (or girls) did attend, they were hired entertainers: trained courtesans, sex workers, musicians, or acrobats. Children of both sexes could also be present as slaves to serve the guests.

Symposia have long been seen as primarily (or originally) aristocratic events, perhaps even as a phenomenon that was believed to reify specifically antidemocratic values (Kurke 1999, Morris 1996 and 2000; for a critical response, see Hammer 2004). However, some public dining at Athens could take the form of a symposion, as seen from the design of spaces in public buildings such as South Stoa I in the late fifth century; by contrast, if public dining happened in the Tholos, it almost certainly did not involve couches (Cooper and Morris 1990). It is hard to tell how frequently private parties were celebrated in a sympotic style, by whom, and when. Part of the problem comes from the difficulty of identifying the boundaries of sympotic behavior—was it, for example, an absolute necessity that participants recline on couches, or that wine be mixed with water, for an event to be considered a symposium? Topper (2009) has argued that there is strong evidence from Athenian vase painting that not all sympotic activity required couches— Greeks could and did recline on cushions placed on floors instead. Her conclusion from these facts was that sympotic behavior might have been widely spread, rather than the exclusive domain of aristocrats.

Equipment and Spaces

The spaces where symposia took place had to accommodate the activities that occurred as well as the furniture and equipment associated with banqueting (Bergquist 1990, Boardman 1990). Rooms found in classical Greek structures that seem to have been purpose-built for feasting have been labeled androns, or "men's rooms," highlighting the apparently segregated nature of the symposium.[18] This nomenclature reflects the ancient Greek literary descriptions of homes (e.g., Lysias 1, Xenophon *Oikonomikos*) as having been divided into men's spaces (*andronitis*) and women's spaces (*gunaikonitis*); there have been numerous recent scholarly critiques of these texts suggesting that such segregation cannot be found in the extant material evidence (Jameson 1990, Nevett 1999, Antonaccio 2000, Cahill 2002, 191–193). Androns are typically identified by the presence of a square plan and an off-center doorway, which together would accommodate the placement of couches for between five and 11 participants around the edge of the room. Other features sometimes associated with androns include a slightly raised (ca. 1–3 centimeters) platform around the rooms' edges for the couches, paved floors (occasionally with mosaic decoration), drains to assist with cleaning up spilled liquids, and an antechamber that provided a transitional space or buffer zone between the house's courtyard and the andron itself.

Rooms with some or all of these features have been found in nondomestic contexts, as well, showing that banqueting in the style of symposia was not confined to the private sphere (Garnsey 1999, 131–134). The original version of the South Stoa in the Athenian agora (built ca. 425–400) included a row of 16 rooms at the back of the building. Fifteen of these rooms had the same plan as a standard andron; the 16th room served as an antechamber for one of the other 15. The use of this building for public dining in a sympotic style may be connected with the need for the Athenian democracy to provide food for prytaneis who were on duty at the nearby Tholos. In the late archaic and early classical colonial Sicilian setting of the upper plateau of the Cittadella hill at Morgantina, a building preserving four square chambers on a lower level may reflect the existence of androns on the now-missing upper level (Antonaccio 1997, 2001, Walsh and Antonaccio 2014). The preserved lower rooms were used for the storage of sympotic equipment, including Greek cups and even an Athenian red-figure krater painted with a scene of a symposium by Euthymides (ca. 510 BCE; Neils 1995).

More perplexing is the occasional appearance of groups of andron-type rooms at extramural sanctuaries dedicated to female deities, including the sanctuary of Hera at Perachora (Tomlinson 1990), the sanctuary of Demeter and Kore at Corinth (Bookidis 1993, Bookidis and Stroud 1997), and the sanctuary of Artemis at Brauron (the last of these being the location of a coming-of-age festival specifically for Athenian girls, the Arkteia; Themelis 2002). To what extent did practices in these spaces mirror banquets for men back in the urban centers (Burton 1998)?

With regard to pottery equipment, Lissarrague has offered the traditional view, stating that "the krater is an indispensable element of the symposion: it is in the krater that the mixing of the wine takes place without which there is no proper art of drinking" (1990a, 197). Study of Olynthos, the site with the best-published and largest number of excavated Greek residences, provides a powerful counterpoint to claims such as Lissarrague's, however. There were only 44 kraters found at the site, from the 108 houses that were excavated (Cahill 2002, 181). In addition, only 34 androns were found, in just 31 of the houses (Cahill 2002, 186). Only five houses with androns were found to contain any kraters, accounting for seven examples in total. Boardman (2001, 251) noted that depictions on vases suggest that kraters were stored near or in the andron—yet only two kraters were found in androns at Olynthos (Cahill 2002, 186). Various conclusions might be drawn from these results—such as the possibility that the paucity of kraters (and, indeed, other drinking paraphernalia) at Olynthos might reflect the overwhelming use of now-missing metal vases, rather than ceramic ones.

Pictorial Evidence for Symposia

As noted above, some of the best examples of sympotic behavior and equipment come from paintings. In major painting, however, the only known example comes from the interior of the sarcophagus from the Tomb of the Diver at Poseidonia (modern Paestum; Napoli 1970, Holloway 2006). Couches, each supporting two reclining men, surround a krater (pictured at one end of the sarcophagus), while new participants enter the room at one end, heralded by a flute player. The men sing and play music as they drink and are served by a young boy. The colonial context of this example is worth remembering, since the symposion was here placed firmly in a relationship with death. Many other sarcophagi at Poseidonia received fresco paintings, which have also been found as adornments for tombs in earlier periods at Italic communities, such as Etruscan Tarquinia in the sixth century. The scene from the Tomb of the Diver therefore raises questions about hybridity and interactions between different cultural groups related to the symposion.

There appears to have been a wide disparity in the display of symposia in vase painting produced in various centers around the Greek world. At first glance, in fact, it might appear that sympotic imagery is the exclusive purview of Athenian vase painters. For example, of 2560 Corinthian vessels in the Beazley Archive database, none show depictions of symposia (according to the definitions of the database). This pattern is also true of Lakonian, East Greek, and every other fabric except Athenian, as represented in the database, although production centers other than Athens or Corinth are represented by a much more limited number of examples. By contrast, 2518 of the 81,698 Athenian vessels in the Beazley Archive have depictions of symposia (a sign not only of Athenian pottery's prominence in the archaeological record, but also of the bias in traditional scholarship toward Athenian wares). The very earliest depiction of diners reclining, however, appears on a Corinthian krater (Louvre E635, ca. 600 BCE), which shows Herakles feasting (Amyx 1988, 147, Topper 2009, 5). There are examples of reclining diners on Corinthian and Lakonian vases and on at least one Boiotian skyphos (Smith 2000, 315–316).

Other imagery that may relate to symposia depicts kraters without diners, but often with dancers wearing padded costumes (Smith 2000, 2010). These dancers have often been called "komasts," signifying a connection to *kōmoi*, which were processions of revelers through the city from one sympotic banquet to another. Fehr (1990) identified the dancers as *aklētoi* ("the unbidden guests"), lower-class citizens who were unable to afford the luxuries of banqueting, who hoped for some food and drink in return for performing (possibly ribald) dances.

Paintings on vases can be read as revealing some of the preoccupations of Greeks with regard to the effects of alcohol. The development of eye-cups, stemmed cups with giant eyes on the exterior of the cup's bowl, could serve a double function at a symposion. The vase protectively watched the drinkers when its owner was not in the process of drinking, acting in the manner of the "evil eye." On the other hand, as the drinker raised the vase to his mouth, the entire vase formed a mask, with the painted eyes and the stem forming a nose/mouth. Similarly, molded rhytons with animal heads (rams, donkeys, dogs) could take the place of the drinker's face as a mask, showing the transformative (and potentially uncivilizing) effects of alcohol. In this way, vases can be related to dramatic masks worn by actors in another realm controlled by Dionysos (see Lissarrague). Images on vases, such as the pictures found in cup tondi as the drinker tipped the cup toward him, often seem to warn drinkers of the dangers of the dangers "hidden" in wine. They depict gorgons' heads, slowly revealed as the drinker consumes the wine. Other vases exploited the description by Homer of the "wine-dark sea," adding an element of visual punning to painted scenes and perhaps making reference to the voyage taken by the symposion itself, as seen on Exekias's famous cup showing Dionysos's transformation of sailors into dolphins that appear to jump out of the wine (Munich 2044). The rims of dinoi and kraters frequently were decorated with ships that would have appeared to float on wine when the vase was full. Still others depict mythological scenes that foster conversation, such as the mid-sixth-century Lakonian porthole compositions, which raise artistic questions on the part of the viewer by refusing to reveal the entirety of a unified scene (Stibbe 1972, Hurwit 1977). Images such as the horrifying Cerberus by the Hunt Painter would serve a similar function to the gorgoneia just mentioned, but with the added impact of insinuating the presences of Hermes and Herakles, provoking surprise, thought, and conversation as the realization of the entirety of the scene became clear.

On other kinds of painted sympotic vases, mythical scenes dominate the representations, especially in black-figure. For the most part these scenes are taken from Homeric epics or other heroic endeavors. Again, these are primarily understood as conversation starters or icebreakers, allowing discussions to range over related political or cultural issues (Topper 2012, Schmitt-Pantel 1992, Lissarrague 1990b). With the development of red-figure symposia themselves became major subjects of paintings on vases such as cups, hydriai, kraters, or psykters (Topper 2012). The Pioneer Group and others depicted many symposia on large vessels, sometimes including other painters in the parties, as we can tell from labels identifying figures (Topper 2012, 147–153 with references). Following the Pioneer Group, symposia continued to be of interest to Douris, Oltos, and other painters, who took considerable liberties with the scenes (many of which are pornographic) but by the middle of the fifth century, the fashion had gone out of style, and mythical scenes took over almost exclusively. Overall, the important mythical scenes reinforced masculine virtues such as courage in battle, beauty, and athleticism.

GREEK POTTERY IN FOREIGN CONTEXTS

Although it is relatively clear how different shapes were intended to be used in Athens, Corinth, or Ionia, direct evidence for how Greek pottery was used in foreign contexts is unfortunately lacking, except when vases are found deposited in sanctuaries or in tombs as an offering. When fragments of Greek pottery are found in domestic contexts, one cannot be certain precisely how the original vessels were used—bowls or jugs may well have been used for drinking, for example, or not for consumption of food or liquid but merely for display. The latter possibility seems most likely when evidence for only one Greek vase exists in a given house or site. As the number of imported vases rises, so too does the likelihood that some sort of utility other than display alone was found for them—but there is still no guarantee that they were used the way Greeks used them. An important question that needs to be addressed, then, is just how did non-Greeks use the pottery they imported? Did they follow Greek traditions closely, somewhat, or not at all? Etruscans, for example, fell into the "somewhat" category, since they used Greek vessels, including kraters, at banquets where they reclined on couches, but the depiction of high-status women reclining with their husbands in paintings and sculpture marks a notable difference from Greek practice (Reusser 2002, Avramidou 2006). Likewise, I have already noted the common use of vessels normally associated by Greeks with drinking as prestigious grave goods in Etruscan tombs.

The patterns revealed by analysis of the database will go some way toward helping to resolve this question for native populations farther north and west. Before beginning that analysis, however, it will be worthwhile to consider the few Greek literary descriptions of Iberian or Hallstatt daily life, whether banquets, funerals, or worship. The fragments that exist generally date significantly later than the fourth century, when this study's data ends. Even so, they offer tantalizing evidence for non-Greek customs. Unfortunately, none of them mention Greek vases, nor do any ancient images show members of western Mediterranean or northern European indigenous groups using Greek pottery.

Celtic Banquets

Extant sources on drinking in Celtic societies concentrate on the differences from Greek habit rather than similarities (Arnold 1999, 72–75). It is difficult to know how far these sources can be trusted, for many of the reasons described in Chapter 2. Moreover, there is no evidence that any of these writers had traveled to the regions that they were describing. In a rare fourth-century description of non-Greek drinking practices, Plato also made brief reference to the feasting of both Celts and Iberians. This commentary described various groups (including Greeks apart from the Spartans, who had outlawed drinking clubs), attributing to them the practice of drinking in order to become inebriated:

> But, my dear sirs, our argument now is not concerned with the rest of mankind but with the goodness or badness of the lawgivers themselves. So let us deal more fully with the subject of drunkenness in general for it is a practice of no slight importance, and it requires no mean legislator to understand it. I am now referring not to the drinking or non-drinking of wine generally, but to drunkenness pure and simple,

and the question is—ought we to deal with it as the Scythians and Persians do and the Carthaginians also, and Celts, Iberians and Thracians, who are all warlike races, or as you Spartans do; for you, as you say, abstain from it altogether, whereas the Scythians and Thracians, both men and women, take their wine neat and let it pour down over their clothes, and regard this practice of theirs as a noble and splendid practice; and the Persians indulge greatly in these and other luxurious habits which you reject, albeit in a more orderly fashion than the others (Plato *Laws* 637d-e, trans. Bury).

Unfortunately for our purposes, the Celts' and the Iberians' practices are not mentioned in as great detail as those of other groups, but the negative implication of the text is nonetheless clear that these groups drank to excess, and drank specifically with the intent to become drunk.

Later writers gave somewhat more information about non-Greek drinking habits. Diodorus Siculus, writing in the first century BCE, describes Celts of his own day (during the Late La Téne period, not the Hallstatt period) in the following way:

Since temperateness of climate is destroyed by the excessive cold [in Gaul], the land produces neither wine nor oil, and as a consequence those Gauls who are deprived of these fruits make a drink out of barley which they call *zythos* or beer, and they also drink the water with which they cleanse their honeycombs. The Gauls are exceedingly addicted to the use of wine and fill themselves with the wine which is brought into their country by merchants, drinking it unmixed, and since they partake of this drink without moderation by reason of their craving for it, when they are drunken they fall into a stupor or a state of madness (5.26).

Such dining is clearly far from what has been described of sympotic behavior: wine was not the only beverage consumed at banquets, and when wine was consumed, it was not mixed with water. Diodorus, too, subscribed to the notion that excessive drunkenness marked Celtic banquets. According to him, wine was highly prized among the Celtic populations, perhaps because of its rarity, but as Arnold has noted (1999, 75), it never completely replaced beer or mead. Analysis of residue found in the bronze dinos from the burial at Hochdorf showed that it had been filled with mead at the time when the tomb was closed (Krausse and Längerer 1996). The drunken behavior cited by Diodorus is not necessarily a difference from Greek drinking, however, as is clear from vase paintings in the sixth and fifth centuries.

Athenaios, whose *Deipnosophistai* (dating to the end of the second and beginning of the third century CE) includes quotations from a wide variety of earlier authors on the subject of banqueting, forms the primary source on non-Greek dining practices. The authors quoted by Athenaios referred to Celts as both Keltoi and Galatoi, but it is not clear whether the use of a particular name implies the location of the Celtic group being described. In the first passage, Athenaios quotes Phylarkhos, a historian of the third century BCE whose works are no longer extant:

> Among the Celts (*Galatoi*), according to Phylarkhos in Book VI (*FGrH* 81 F 9), many loaves of bread are broken into pieces and placed on the tables in a heap along with chunks of meat from the cauldrons; but no one tastes anything until he sees that the king has touched the food he was served. In Book III the same Phylarkhos (*FGrH* 81 F 2) says that Ariamnes the Celt, who was extremely wealthy, announced that he would feast all the Celts for a year, and did this by making the following arrangements. He set stations along the most convenient roads in various parts of the country and installed shelters in them made of poles and willow branches and large enough to hold 400 men or more, so that the places would be sufficiently spacious to accommodate the crowds likely to stream there from the cities and villages. He installed large cauldrons full of meat of every kind in them; he summoned craftsmen from other cities the previous year, in advance of when he intended to do this, and had them forged. Large numbers of bulls, pigs, sheep and goats, and other animals were sacrificed every day; and casks of wine had been prepared and an immense quantity of barley groats mixed up in advance. Nor was it just the Celts, he says, who came there from their villages and cities who benefited; because the slaves in charge of the meal refused to let any foreigners who passed by get away until they had their share of the food being served (Athenaios 4.150d-f, trans. Olson).

Here Celtic banqueting is distinguished from Greek symposia on several counts: the integration of eating and drinking; the emphasis on a hierarchy within the banqueting group, rather than on equality; and the public display of wealth and provision for the community through massive feasts. Once again, we also see that wine was served alongside grain-based beverages. It is notable that a strict etiquette was supposedly observed regarding the consumption of food, as this description stands in contrast to the unruliness of Celtic banqueting more often described by classical authors, which will be shown presently.

Athenaios also quoted the philosopher Poseidonios, who lived in the second and first centuries BCE, on Celtic feasting. This passage is especially useful for the information it gives regarding cuisine in central and western Europe, and for the relationship it defines between social class and the kind of beverage consumed.

> Poseidonios the Stoic in his *Histories* (*FGrH* 87 F 15 = fr. 67 Edelstein-Kidd), which he compiles by recording numerous usages and customs

among many peoples that were germane to the philosophy he had adopted, says: The Celts (*Keltoi*) throw hay on the ground and serve their meals on wooden tables barely raised off of it. The food consists of a few loaves of bread and large quantities of meat that is either boiled or roasted on the coals or on spits. They consume the meat in a simple if lion-like way, taking whole joints in both hands and biting it off; if a piece proves difficult to tear away, they cut it off with a small knife that lies beside them in its own sheath. Those who live along the rivers or beside the interior or exterior sea (the Mediterranean Sea or Atlantic Ocean) also consume fish, which they eat roasted with salt, vinegar, and cumin. They also add cumin to their wine. They do not use oil, because it is scarce and because their lack of familiarity with it makes the taste seem unpleasant to them. Whenever a group of them has dinner together, they sit in a circle, and whoever is most important sits in the middle, like the leader of a dramatic chorus, whether he is distinguished from the others by his skill in warfare, the family he comes from, or his wealth. The host sits next to him; after that they sit in order on either side according to how prominent they are. Armed men bearing oblong shields stand behind the guests, and their bodyguards sit opposite them in a circle, just like their masters, and eat together. The servants bring the wine around in vessels that resemble spouted cups and are made of either earthenware or silver. The platters on which they serve the food are similar; but others use bronze platters or baskets made of wood or wickerwork. The rich drink wine imported from Italy or Massaliote territory; it is consumed unmixed, although occasionally they put a little water into it. Poorer people drink wheat-beer with honey added, or in most cases without it; they refer to this as *korma*. They sip it a bit at a time from the same vessel, which does not hold more than a fraction of a cup ("not a full kyathos"); but they do this repeatedly. The slave carries the cup around from right to left when they prostate themselves before their gods (Athenaios 4.151e-152d, trans. Olson).

The bias of Poseidonios against Celts and their dining practices is evident from his choice of certain phrases, like "simple if lion-like" (*kathareiōs men, leontōdōs de*), for the way meat was cut and held while eating, and describing tables as "barely raised off the ground" (*trapezōn xulinōn mikron apo tēs gēs epērmenōn*). In this passage, Celtic social hierarchies were described as being reified, not only by the order of drinking, but by the positioning of the drinkers, by the drink consumed, and probably also by the kinds of vessels used to hold drinks. Drinkers were seated in a circular fashion, similar to symposiasts, but they did not recline (indeed, it is possible from the description of the tables that they sat on the hay scattered on the floor). Poorer drinkers shared a cup; Arnold (1999, 73) has suggested the use of a common cup at banquets as one explanation for the low number of cups relative to other kinds of vessels in Hallstatt contexts. The potential for violence is clear, as armed men associated with individual drinkers were located in close proximity to the men they protected, and other men were employed by the host to prevent fights from breaking out. In another passage from Poseidonios, the violent behavior believed by Greeks to exist at Celtic banquets is described more fully:

> Poseidonios says in Book XXIII of his *Histories* (*FGrH* 87 F 16 = fr. 68 Edelstein-Kidd): The Celts (*Keltoi*) sometimes fight duels at dinner. For they have their weapons with them when they assemble, and they engage in imaginary battles or pretend to fight one another from a distance. But sometimes they go so far as to wound one another, and this makes them angry; if the bystanders do not restrain them, they do not stop until they are dead. In the old days, he says, whole joints of meat were served, and whoever was most powerful got the thigh; if someone else claimed it, they fought a duel to the death (Athenaios 4.154b, trans. Olson).

It is unclear whether such descriptions ought to be taken at face value or whether they should be identified as *Orientalism*-style stereotyping of the misunderstood Other. In any case, Poseidonios also recorded information about the entertainment available at banquets (if duels might not also be regarded as a kind of entertainment, as early gladiatorial combats were at Etruscan funerary banquets):

> Poseidonios of Apamea says in Book XXIII of his *History:* Even when they are at war, the Celts take companions they refer to as parasites around with them. These men eulogize them both to mass assemblies of people and to anyone who will listen to them in a private setting. Their musical entertainment is provided by the so-called *bardoi* (Bards); these are poets who literally sing their praises (6.246c, trans. Olson).

Although Poseidonios does not say so, the tradition of hiring poets to compose and sing poems in honor of a host (especially a tyrant) was well known to Greeks, and can be found in the works of Pindar and Bacchylides, among other authors of lyric poetry.

In all of these passages, the connection between feasting and representations of status was placed at the forefront by Greek authors: feasts were held by leaders, who supplied food and drink (sometimes in enormous quantities), perhaps even as a part of their role as leaders. Feasting seems to have been an exclusively male sphere of activity, since women were not mentioned at all. Certain behavior was expected at banquets, as at symposia, but in the Celtic world this behavior reinforced hierarchies among the participants, rather than equality. Leaders determined when feasting could begin, and presumably who would receive what kind of beverage in what kind of containers. At the same time, competition between individuals about portions of food was a fight by proxy over the relative status of those individuals. Determining the relationship between status and the use of Greek vessels in Hallstatt Europe will therefore be a primary interest in this investigation.

Iberian Banquets

Considerably less information is preserved from ancient texts regarding Iberian feasting practices. The few passages that are preserved, again primarily fragments found in the work of Athenaios, do emphasize the wealth of Iberian leaders and the presence of precious metals. In this respect, they are similar to the texts describing early colonization and interactions with Iberians, as described in Chapter 2. The historian Polybios, who lived in the second century BCE, was one author whose work discussed Iberia:

> Menelaos' house is the most luxurious; Homer conceives of it as being gloriously well-furnished as the home of a certain Iberian chieftain described by Polybios, who says that he had imitated the luxury of the Phaiakians except that the mixing-bowls (*kratēras*) standing in the middle of his house, although made of gold and silver, were full of barley [beer] (*oinou krithinou*) (Athenaios 1.16c, trans. Olson).

Despite archaeological evidence for the production of wine in Iberia from an early date, Polybios only mentions beer as a local beverage. The use of the word "krater" to describe the bowls used for consuming the beer is perhaps misleading here, since Greek authors (particularly Homer—*Iliad* 6.258, 8.232, *Odyssey* 2.431; also Aiskhylos in *Libation Bearers* 291) used it occasionally to describe drinking vessels or ritual vessels rather than ones meant for mixing. Phylarkhos, by contrast, seems to state that Iberians did not drink alcoholic beverages, even though the archaeological record clearly shows that this was not true:

> Phylarkhos asserts that Theodoros of Larissa, who was always at odds with King Antigonos, drank nothing but water. He also claims that the Iberians all drink only water, despite being the richest people on earth and he says that they always eat alone, because of their stinginess, but wear extremely expensive clothing (Athenaios 2.44b, trans. Olson).

Strabo is of little additional help with regard to feasting, though he did describe the use of metal vessels in Andalusia: "The wealth of Iberia is further evidenced by the following facts: the Carthaginians who, along with Barcas, made a campaign against Iberia found the people in Turdetania, as the historians tell us, using silver feeding-troughs and wine-jars" (*phatnais argurais kai pithois;* 3.2.14, trans. Jones).

SUMMARY

The history of scholarship on Greek pottery is a rich one, covering many different aspects of vases, including their distribution, decoration, shapes, and functions. At the same time, the concerns of scholars have developed since the 18th century from antiquarianism and connoisseurship to more anthropological issues related to the use and value of Greek vases in antiquity. One major question that remains to be fully resolved is the relationship, if any, between the distribution of metal and ceramic vessels. Despite the ubiquity of pot sherds in excavations, it is increasingly clear that extraordinary difficulties face archaeologists who want to use pottery to reconstruct ancient lifeways. Chief among these problems is the issue of quantifying the number of vessels or proportions of types of vessels that existed in the past on the basis of the sherds found in modern times. Although a method has been developed to transform measures and counts of diagnostic sherds into figures that can be treated like real counts in statistical tests, use of this method is hampered by the fact that the relevant measures (particularly the percentage of the diagnostic fragment that is preserved) are rarely published. The methodology adopted in this study therefore relies instead on the development of a consensus regarding pottery distribution that is derived from combining three different kinds of analysis: counts of sherds, the presence or absence of functional types, and the calculation of a statistic that measures the diversity (or evenness of distribution of types) of an assemblage.

The most common kind of study carried out by classical archaeologists using Greek pottery is related to the ritualized banquet known as the symposion. This is due to the fact that symposia appeared frequently in imagery and in literature from antiquity, and because the array of pottery produced by Greeks seems highly specialized for occasions on which wine would be consumed commensally. There were specific activities and architectural spaces where symposia were typically held. In addition, Greek commentary on drinking in a sympotic style shows that certain aspects of it, particularly the mixing of wine with water, were considered integral to Greek cultural identity, in opposition to the drinking practices of other groups. One of the primary questions facing this study of the relationship between imported pottery and the construction of local identity, then, is the extent to which Greek practices followed Greek vases into foreign contexts.

It is possible that ancient Greek literary descriptions of non-Greek feasting practices can shed some light on how Greek pottery was used, but these texts remain problematic for reasons of their late date, authorship, and bias. They appear to be consistent in describing Celtic feasting, for example, as deeply entangled with status competitions, but consideration of the actual distribution of vases may reveal different patterns. What is clear is that Greek authors saw non-Greek practices as having significant differences from their own.

NOTES

1. Only two examples of Greek major painting from the archaic and classical periods survive largely intact today (neither was known before the middle of the 20th century): a wooden plaque found near Sikyon showing a procession to a sacrifice, and the fresco paintings adorning the Tomb of the Diver from Paestum/Poseidonia, which show a symposion (see below).
2. In 1972, the Metropolitan Museum of Art's purchase of an Athenian red-figure krater painted by Euphronios and potted by Euxitheos (ca. 515 BCE, now on display in the Museo Nazionale Etrusco di Villa Giulia in Rome since its restoration to Italy in 2006) for $1 million firmly cemented ancient Greek pottery's status as "high" art (Hoving 1994), 319). The vase is now known to have been looted from an Etruscan tomb at Caere (modern Cerveteri; Watson and Todeschini 2006, 201–202). Only a few years earlier, the museum had paid $1.4 million at auction for the Impressionist master Claude Monet's "Garden at Sainte-Adresse" (Hoving 1994, 138).
3. The Beazley Archive pottery database (http://www.beazley.ox.ac.uk) was not used to carry out the analysis for this study for two reasons: its very heavy bias toward vases decorated with imagery, and the lack of a recorded provenance for so many of the vases listed in it (Hannestad 1996).
4. These arguments are made in much fuller form in Walsh and Antonaccio 2014.
5. For the same perspective, see Foxhall (1998, 299): "Surely what makes a 'luxury' must depend on who is consuming it and where it originated in relation to the consumer."
6. Similar ideas had already been formulated by Adolf Furtwängler and Georg Loeschke about Mycenaean and Geometric pottery found at Mycenae in the 1870s, but their work did not lead to the development of seriation techniques as in the United States.
7. For an example of a study that did subdivide weighed pottery by shape, see Walsh 2006.
8. Professor Orton kindly made Pie-slice available to me in 2010 for an unrelated project.
9. Nor, indeed, did any authors give the weight of published pieces in the publications consulted for this study.
10. I am grateful to Robert Fornango for his help in the preliminary analysis of the dataset. See also the introduction to Chapter 6 giving the basic characteristics of the dataset.
11. Jost (2006) has criticized the description of Simpson's D (or any other standard diversity formula) as a true diversity measure for ecological studies, where there can be dozens, if not hundreds of species represented in a sample, and many samples will not share any species at all. Since, however, the number of pottery types is constricted to the same range at every site, this does not seem to be a highly significant obstacle to the use of Simpson's D here.
12. Simpson's Index is also sometimes called the Gini-Simpson Index.

13. For the same reason, Villard's publication of pottery from Marseille (1960) was the sole source for vases found in that city, despite its age and the number of excavations carried out there in the meantime.

14. The regrettable absence of a significant and well-studied site from the database must be acknowledged here: Lattara (modern Lattes, in Hérault, Languedoc-Rousillon, southern France) is unfortunately not included. This site, which had a mostly indigenous Hallstatt population, probably supplemented by traders (especially from Etruria), has been excavated for several decades and publication has appeared in almost 20 volumes. Its absence is particularly painful to me because it has been the location of the fieldwork of Michael Dietler, whose work has so deeply informed the approach undertaken here—and because Professor Dietler very kindly welcomed me for a brief visit to the site during my ongoing research for this project in the summer of 2012. Apart from one publication, which catalogues the shapes and wares of Greek vases recovered, but not the contexts and findspots or the number of sherds (*Lattara 6* [Py 1993]), however, I was not able to use any of the final publications in the preparation of my database (especially the primary publication of Iron Age pottery, *Lattara* 14 [Py 2001]). They were not in the collection of any of the libraries that I was able to visit (including the Getty Research Institute, the University of California at Los Angeles, the American Academy in Rome, and the American School of Classical Studies at Athens; I was unable to visit the libraries of either the French School in Rome or the French School in Athens in my allotted time). Some of the Lattara volumes are available for download on the excavation team's website, but unfortunately not the sections related to the period covered in this study. Efforts to gain access to the relevant volumes through interlibrary loan were denied because the volumes could not be located in any participating library.

    It is unclear to me how the inclusion of data regarding Greek pottery at Lattara would change the results of this study. The site might have offered a counterweight to the very high number of vessels published from the similar town of Saint-Blaise, relative to other southern Hallstatt settlements in the database. If I have the opportunity to examine the Lattara volumes in the future, a statistical reanalysis could easily be performed to test this hypothesis.

15. See Boardman (2001, 260–261) for a discussion of the problems associated with the names used for this shape.

16. The extent to which families would dine together is debated; nonsympotic Greek dining was done seated on chairs rather than reclining on couches (Wilkins and Hill 2006, 64–73).

17. Corner (2012 n.27, following Murray 1995) has even described the symposion as "anti-domestic" in nature, since it put outsiders, rather than household slaves and the host's female relatives, in serving roles.

18. Travlos (1971, 482) proposed that the so-called Pinakotheke in the Mnesiklean Propylaia was a public dining space due to its off-center door, though not without problems for the size and arrangement of the couches (Hellström 1975, 87–89).

6 Analysis of the Dataset

CHARACTERISTICS OF THE DATASET

Having outlined the theoretical basis for understanding the significance of imported pottery in western Europe, it is now time to describe the distribution of that pottery. Certain basic characteristics of the dataset can be easily summarized:[1]

1. There were 23,928 artifacts (sherds or whole vessels) from 233 sites represented in the sample (Table 6.1).
2. Almost 99% of all artifacts were found in either France or Spain (Figures 6.1 and 6.2).
3. Four major sites were responsible for 58% of all artifacts: Emporion (N = 4,307), Massalia (N = 3,360), Nissan-lez-Ensérune (N = 1,463), and Saint-Blaise (N = 4,771). The nine largest sites had 76% of all artifacts. Sixty-three sites have only one artifact, 128 sites have five or fewer artifacts (59% of sites). Seventy-three sites have 10 or more artifacts (33% of sites).
4. Three fabrics dominated in the dataset: 66% of artifacts are Athenian black gloss (ABG), Athenian red-figure (ARF), or East Greek.
5. Fewer than half of the fabric types listed (44%) pertain to 10 or more artifacts. Only 28% of fabric types (N = 25) are represented by more than 50 artifacts.
6. Although there were 115 different vessel shapes, 69% of artifacts fall into eight shapes, and 49% in the top five shapes. All of the top seven shapes are related to drinking (Table 6.2).
7. Ninety-seven percent of artifacts for which contexts were given were found in cemeteries or settlements.
8. Two primary functions were represented by the pottery in the dataset: 88% were for eating or drinking; drinking alone accounts for 74% of artifacts.
9. Eighty-nine percent of artifacts were found in sites with three cultural identifications (South Hallstatt, Greek, Iberian [includes Ibero-Languedoc]; Figure 6.3)

Table 6.1   Count of artifacts by country and function

Provenance country	Drinking	Eating	Household	Storage	Transport	Unknown	Total
France	10775	1902	275	805	648	537	14942
Spain	6258	1151	588	200	243	191	8631
Portugal	86	28	3	5	1	44	167
Germany	27	0	2	1	57	3	90
Switzerland	36	0	0	2	47	13	98
Total	17182	3081	868	1013	996	788	23928

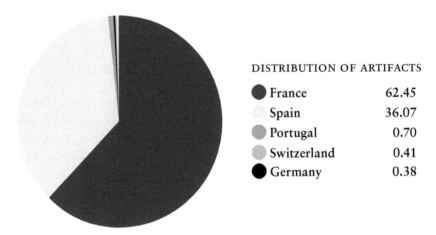

Figure 6.1   Chart showing percentage distribution of artifacts by country

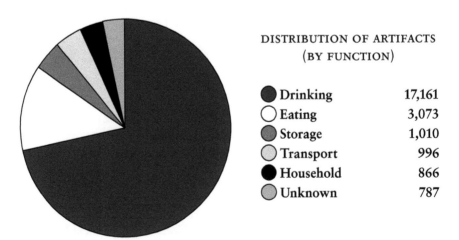

Figure 6.2   Chart showing distribution of artifact counts by functional type

Table 6.2 Major shapes

Shape	Count	Percentage of total artifacts
Stemmed cup	3012	13%
Ionian cup	2839	12
Cup	2035	9
Stemless cup	2007	8
Oinochoe	1842	8
Skyphos	1801	8
Krater	1640	7
Bowl	1347	6
Total	16523	69
		(does not equal sum of the above percentages due to rounding)

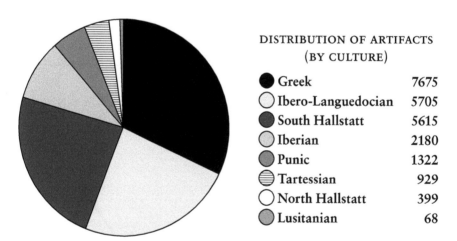

DISTRIBUTION OF ARTIFACTS
(BY CULTURE)

●	Greek	7675
○	Ibero-Languedocian	5705
●	South Hallstatt	5615
○	Iberian	2180
◓	Punic	1322
⊜	Tartessian	929
○	North Hallstatt	399
◓	Lusitanian	68

Figure 6.3 Chart showing distribution of artifact counts by cultural group

10. Two hundred eighty-eight combinations of artifact characteristics (0.1% of all possible combinations in the database) comprise three fabrics, eight shapes, two contexts, two functions, and three cultures. These 288 combinations account for 31.7% of all artifacts.
11. Broad examination of indigenous, Greek, mixed, and Punic settlements shows the following distribution: 46% indigenous (N = 10,888), 30% Greek (N = 7,038), 23% mixed (N = 5,449), 2% Punic (N = 490) (does not equal 100% due to rounding).
12. The chronological distribution of Greek pottery shows very limited presence in the eighth and seventh centuries (N = 16 and N = 229, respectively) followed by an explosive growth in the sixth century

(N = 4690) and relative stability in the fifth and fourth centuries (N = 5361 and N = 5122). Ninety-eight percent of all Greek pottery was made in the sixth through fourth centuries (Figures 6.4 and 6.5).

These facts show that the distribution of pottery as published was quite imbalanced both geographically and chronologically. Sites in

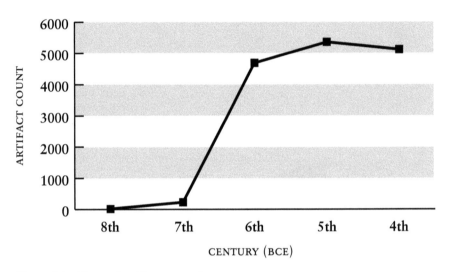

Figure 6.4   Chart of artifact counts by century

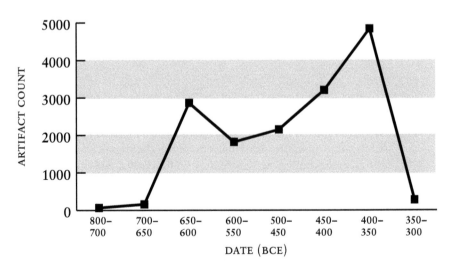

Figure 6.5   Chart of artifact counts by half-century

Portugal, Germany, and Switzerland together represent only 1% of the total. Indeed, sites in the deep interior of France and Spain add little more to this percentage. Almost all of the pottery was found within 100 kilometers of the coast.

MAPPING DISTRIBUTIONS

In this chapter, the analytical approaches described in Chapter 5—presence-absence, sherd counts, and Simpson's Index of Diversity—will be applied to the dataset of pottery. The analyses will be represented in a variety of ways. Lists, charts, and graphs present some of the data in a traditional fashion, and verbal discussion of the significance of the results will follow in the text. In some ways, however, the more important presentation will take the form of maps showing the results achieved. The method used to produce most of these maps, called kriging, deserves some description, since it may be unfamiliar to most classical archaeologists, and since it offers the ability to describe the probable distribution of Greek pottery in areas that were not or could not be sampled directly.[2]

Kriging is the application of an interpolative model to data that has a geographic component (Wheatley and Gillings 2002, 174–177). It requires the creation of a geographic information system (GIS), which is a file that consists of data that has some relationship to space defined by geographic coordinates. In this case, information about pottery and its location from the original Microsoft Access database was exported to a spreadsheet, where it underwent permutations to reflect the kind of analytical approach desired (see Chapter 5). It was then exported again in the comma-delimited text format (.CSV) so that it could be used for the GIS. The .CSV file, including the latitude and longitude coordinates for each site where a measurement was taken, was analyzed in ArcGIS Map, which includes a kriging feature in its Geostatistical Analyst set of tools. The sites and their values were mapped over two kinds of open-source georeferenced vector shapefiles: first, the boundaries of modern nations represented in the survey; and second, the region's river courses.

In a kriging interpolation, the software uses a defined set of values about a variable from different locations in order to make predictions for the values of the variable at points between or surrounding the known locations. In a relevant example, a krige of the pottery data's diversity will use the distribution of Simpson's Index of Diversity scores at various sites to predict what diversity index scores are likely to be found in areas that have not been sampled, between the sampled sites (Fig. 6.6). The prediction is based on the sampled values and on the predicted locations' distances from the known samples. As a result, in situations where the sampled sites are not evenly distributed (as is the case here, where most of the sites are arranged along the coasts of Spain and France, not inland), the quality of

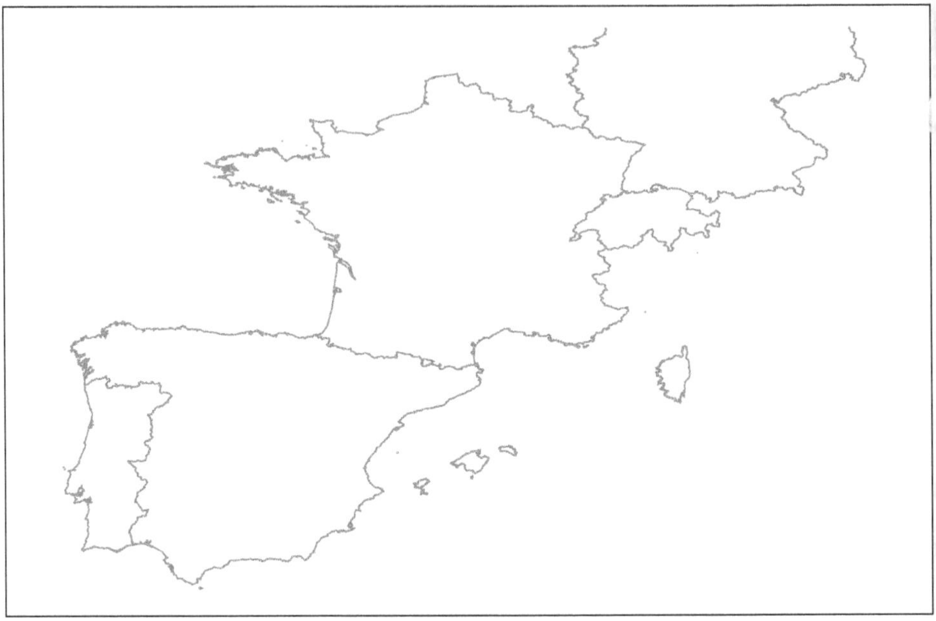

(a)

(b)

Figure 6.6 Sample maps showing the addition of different layers generated in kriging analysis. (a) National boundaries (b) River courses (c) Sites (d) Kriging prediction (e) Kriging error. For the sake of visual clarity, sites are not shown here with shading to represent local counts of artifacts.

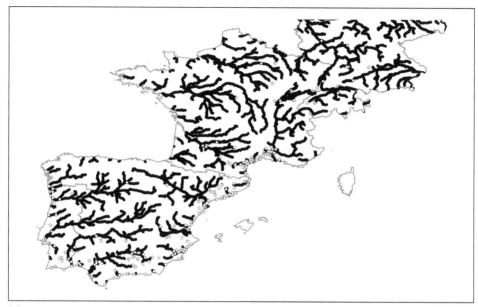

(c)

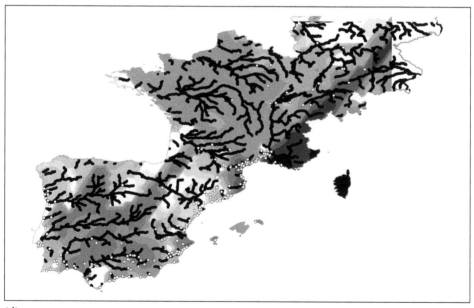

(d)

Figure 6.6   (Continued)

Figure 6.6 (Continued)

the prediction is not equal for all points on the map. Where sampled sites are clustered together, the prediction is likely to be of high quality, and where they are sparse, the prediction will accordingly be poor. The quality of the prediction can be assessed by mapping the standard error associated with the kriging. Regions with low standard error can be treated with greater confidence than regions with high standard error. The maps produced by kriging are highly informative, and often seem to offer a new perspective, not only on the consumption of Greek pottery generally, but also on the relationship (or lack of same) between topography and consumption. For example, in some regions there seems to be a strong correlation between the distribution of shapes at sites and the location of those sites along river courses, showing the importance of those rivers as transportation routes. In other cases, areas near the mouth of a river will show strongly different distributions from those at the headwaters (even when the river is relatively short), indicating the action of local preference on consumption.

The maps generated in ArcGIS are complex, presenting several types of information simultaneously. Each type of information is captured in a different layer: the location of sites in the sample and the number of artifacts (or a count of present types, or diversity index score) at each site; national boundaries to assist with orientation; the courses of rivers; the kriging interpolation results; and the amount of standard error associated with the kriging. Sites are represented by small dots whose shading corresponds to the amount of sherds, pottery types, or pottery diversity found at that site (lighter shading indicates lower values; darker shading indicates higher values). The colored areas on the maps are the kriging results, with blue representing low values, green and yellow representing medium values, and orange and red representing high values. The contour lines denote regions of similar standard error for the kriging, with regions enclosed by the black lines representing the areas with the lowest error, followed by the areas between the black and gray lines, the areas between the gray lines and the white lines, and finally the areas contained within the white lines. While all of this information is necessary for understanding the conclusions reached, such as regional patterns in pottery consumption, probable trade routes, or the amount of confidence that can be attributed to the kriging results in a given region, there is no effective way to translate these maps to a print format or to grayscale while retaining all aspects of their utility. For this reason, all of the maps are available for download from the publisher via the World Wide Web (http://www.routledge.com/books/details/9780415893794/). They are in two formats: high-resolution multilayer Portable Document Files (.PDF), so readers can view and manipulate them on any common computing platform using recent versions of the freely available Adobe Reader software, and the original ArcGIS map files (as map packages in .MPK format), which allow interested researchers to work directly with the original maps.[3] The names of the map files are given in the text **in boldface** when reference is made to their results. This digital presentation gives the reader an opportunity to turn layers on or off, and explore the different kinds of information available at varying scales. In addition, the Access database that was used to collect information is available for download in the standard Access 2010 format (.ACCDB). The two primary tables in the database, one containing information about pottery and the other about sites, are available separately in .CSV format for users who do not have the Access software and want to use the data in some other program. It is highly suggested that readers download the maps in order to follow the narrative below.

KRIGING ANALYSIS

Diachronic Overview

Some broad trends emerge when examining all of the pottery in the database simultaneously through a diachronic analysis of artifact counts (**Map: N**). The region that had the greatest amount of pottery is, perhaps unsurprisingly, the one encompassing Massalia and Saint-Blaise (the lack of data from sites to the east of Massalia reduces the amount of confidence the kriging has in predicting large quantities in that direction). In the South Hallstatt region, between the Rhône and the Hérault rivers, counts drop sharply, especially as one moves away from the coast. North of the Gard River, the low number of sites and relatively small quantities at Saint-Laurent-de-Carnols, Gaujac, and Mons-et-Monteils lead to the conclusion that few Greek pots were consumed more than about 60 kilometers inland in this area. If Arles was the site of a Greek settlement, as has been suggested (Dietler 2010, 117), it does not seem to have had much effect on consumption practices in its surrounding zone.

A clear contrast can be drawn between the quantity of Greek pottery found in the South Hallstatt region (eastern Languedoc) and the land on the west side of the Hérault (western Languedoc and Rousillon), where it appears that Iberians (or, as Dietler has called them in this region, "Ibero-Languedocians") were the primary cultural group. While the number of sites here is broadly similar to those recorded for the South Hallstatt region, many more examples of Greek pottery appeared in excavations, particularly near the coast and along rivers at Nissan-lez-Ensérune, Béziers, Pézenas, Bessan, Sigean (Pech Maho), and Castel-Rousillon (Ruscino).

The pattern of high Iberian consumption spreads south, as well, past Emporion to Ullastret. Beyond Ullastret, however, there is little evidence of Iberian interest in any Greek pottery at all until one arrives at the emporion of La Illeta dels Banyets. This site, seemingly alone in the coastal southeast, was a place where Greek pottery arrived in quantity. The reason for this pattern is not clear, though it may be related to the fact that this area was always the zone of greatest Phoenician presence in Iberia, from their emporia close to the Straits of Gibraltar to Cartagena and Ibiza. Inland, however, especially around the province of Jaén and the headwaters of the Guadalquivir River, was the area of the most intense Iberian consumption of Greek pottery. The town of Cástulo and its neighbors showed a strong interest in collecting Greek vases that was not present in other south Iberian settlements. In Tartessos, Greek vases were only found in significant numbers at a few special sites: the emporion of Huelva and the palace-sanctuary of Cancho Roano. Castro Marim, a fortified trading post on the west bank of the Guadiana River, if it can also be identified as a Tartessian site, could be added to that list. Although Greek pottery is distributed across Portugal, the pattern can only be described as sporadic. Likewise, in North Hallstatt areas, north and east of the Rhône and Saône valleys, few sites spread over large distances showed a relatively small number of vases. Châtillon-sur-Glâne, Heuneburg, and Vix had between 50 and 96 examples each, but as will be shown, these vases arrived only within a fairly constrained period of time.

A diachronic analysis of the distribution of Greek pottery according to the presence or absence of functional types presents a similar picture (**Map: Site_pres**). In this case, the analysis considers how many types of vases (drinking, eating, household, storage, and transport) were present at any time between 800 and 300 BCE. Quantities of sherds recovered are not considered. Ten sites had the full array of types; at 35 sites, no types could be identified with certainty. As noted above, the analysis does not tell which types were present at a given site, only the variety that were imported. The towns of the South Hallstatt cultural area showed the greatest number of types, in a broad band stretching from Massalia to the Hérault River. This band did not extend far from the coast, however; after about 25 kilometers, the number of types represented dropped, and north of the Gard River, the level declined again. In the Ibero-Languedocian zone, the number of types was slightly lower, except around Sigean and the lower Aude. In the foothills of the Pyrenees, the number dropped significantly. In addition, despite all five types being represented at both Emporion and Ullstret, other sites in Catalonia showed very little variety.

Most of the rest of the study area showed very little variety. The only exceptions to this rule in the Iberian Peninsula were the area near Cástulo, the coastal area controlled by Phoenicians on the Costa del Sol, and coastal Tartessos between Huelva and Seville. The variety of types present at Phoenician sites is striking, as it stands in contrast to the relatively low quantity of reported artifacts described above. In Portugal, only the coastal site of Alcácer do Sal showed almost a complete array of types (four out of five). Even less variety was seen in the North Hallstatt zone, where only Bourges (here an outlier in more than merely a geographical sense) had four types; Heuneburg and Breisach had three.

Analysis of total distribution by means of Simpson's Index of Diversity relied on the 106 sites in the sample where an index score could be calculated

(45% of all sites; **Map: Site_SDI**). Recall that this analysis differs from the presence-absence analysis because it also considers how many artifacts of each type are present. Since the set of sites is smaller, the region where confidence can be high that the kriging results are valid is correspondingly smaller—indeed, it only spans the area between Saint-Blaise and Olèrdola (just west of Barcelona). In this region, however, the results were clear and in accordance with the presence-absence analysis: in South Hallstatt eastern Languedoc, there was clearly greater diversity (index scores of between 0.5 and 0.6) than in the northern Iberian area, especially western Languedoc (0.29–0.39). In the South Hallstatt area, diversity again dipped in correlation with distance from the shore, but the opposite was true in western Languedoc and Rousillon—sites that generally had lower quantities of pottery showed greater diversity. The great exception to Rousillon's low overall consumption of Greek pottery, Castel-Rousillon, also had the lowest diversity index (0.15).

In areas where there is somewhat less confidence in the kriging due to the sparsity of reported samples, there are still some potentially important trends to notice. Diversity was low around Cástulo (the site itself had an index score of only 0.18), and much higher in southern Portugal due to high index scores at Almôdovar, Alcácer do Sal, and Castro Marim. The extreme sparsity of sites in the North Hallstatt region only permits us to say that diversity was in a low to medium range, particularly in the area around the upper Rhine where Germany, Switzerland, and France meet (the location of Breisach, Illfurth, and Châtillon-sur-Glâne).

In summary, there appear to be several important points that will be examined in further detail below: the areas of greatest importation seem to be those closest to Greek settlement, especially between the Greek colonies of Massalia and Emporion (although this point is suggested by the least reliable kind of evidence, artifact counts); the areas with large quantities of Greek pottery do not show a single pattern of consumption with regard to functional types, but rather several different patterns; areas where fewer Greek vessels were found could still display a variety of types (or, to put it more precisely, a high level of diversity in their assemblages); and finally, the different patterns of distribution do not necessarily correspond to broad cultural groupings, since some regions thought to be inhabited by a single group (particularly Iberia) seem to exhibit more than one pattern.

Change over Time

In the introduction to this chapter, an examination of vessel counts that did not take geographic location into account showed the general trend of pottery consumption in the western Mediterranean and trans-Alpine Europe: very low in the eighth and seventh centuries, followed by a boom in the sixth century (likely attributable to the foundation of Massalia and Emporion and the corresponding availability of desirable products), and a plateau in the fifth century. The number of artifacts declined slightly in the fourth century. What local or regional patterns emerge when those trends are plotted on a map? For this section of the analysis, the material will be divided both by century and by half-century for the artifact count and presence-absence analysis. For the analysis of diversity index scores, the material will only be divided by century (and is only available for the sixth, fifth, and fourth centuries) because the number of sites available with enough imported pottery is too small to make a more fine-grained approach possible. The dates used for this analysis are median production dates, since statistical software cannot handle date ranges directly.

Eighth Century

In the eighth century, only two small regions showed the presence of Greek vases: the area around the Phoenician emporion at Vélez-Málaga, and the Tartessian coast between El Puerto de Santa Maria and Huelva (**Map: Site_N_8th**). But even here, the most that might be expected to be found are one or two vessels. From the presence-absence analysis, Phoenician consumption of Greek pottery seems slightly more widespread, extending east to Sexi and west to Guadalhorce, but it was no more diverse than indicated by the artifact counts: only one type was present at each site (drinking at Sexi and Vélez-Málaga; transport at Guadalhorce; **Map: Site_Pres_8th**).

Seventh Century

The seventh century brought a rise in the number of vessels—minuscule compared to what would come in the sixth century, but substantial relative to the eighth (a tenfold increase). No site shows more than 59 artifacts (Vélez-Málaga) during the seventh century; Guadalhorce had 47 and Saint-Blaise 53. Growth was particularly strong in the Phoenician emporia of the Costa del Sol and coastal Tartessos (including Castro Marim), but for the first time, Greek vessels also began to appear in smaller quantities at inland sites in both regions, such as Medellín and Pinos Puente, too (**Map: Site_N_7th**). Both of these sites lie on routes along rivers—the Guadiana and a tributary of the Guadalquivir, respectively. During the seventh century, trade also began to open up along the coast of France, with Saint-Blaise and Massalia showing some of the highest counts of artifacts in this period. Massalia's foundation at or around 600 is confirmed by the fact that all of the vessels there dating to the seventh century (N = 10) belong to the last few decades at the earliest. Some scholars have argued that these vessels may represent heirlooms, evidence of an advance party of Greek colonists or of Etruscan merchants (Dietler 1997, 278, with references), but I would suggest that they may simply be examples of imprecision in the attribution of manufacture dates to the imported types. A pattern similar to Massalia also appears at Saint-Blaise. To the west, five sites—all of them on the west side of the Hérault, apart from the indigenous predecessor to Agathe, which overlooks the river—began to consume Greek pottery. Eleven vessels at Emporion mark the only presence of Greek pottery from the seventh century in Catalonia.

There were no Greek vessels recorded in the North Hallstatt zone in this period. The yellow colors, which represent a prediction of moderate presence of Greek vessels in some parts of this region by the kriging model, are the result of the clustered arrangement of all the sites in this survey along a northeast-southwest axis, and are not due to any actual Greek pottery in that specific area. This phenomenon shows why it is necessary to note the placement of the standard error contour lines on the map. These lines show that confidence can only be held in the small areas around sites, which are, of course, blue because there were no Greek vessels there in the seventh century. Similarly erroneous kriging patterns will appear from time to time in sparsely populated sections of other maps, which is why it is always important to be aware of both the prediction for a given location and its associated standard error (from this point forward, problems with the kriging prediction will be noted in footnotes rather than the main text).

Looking more closely at the transition from the first half of the seventh century to the second half, it becomes clear that early on, there is only one place where Greek pottery is being consumed in any quantity: Vélez-Málaga, where 53 of the artifacts (including 31 transport amphorai and 18 drinking vessels) dated to 700–650 (**Map: Site_N_1sthalf_7th**). This pattern shows clearly how sporadic trade in Greek goods was in the western Mediterranean prior to the middle of the seventh century—apart from Vélez-Málaga, no site received more than four artifacts. It is correspondingly unlikely that many Greek traders ventured west beyond Sicily or Italy in this period. Only in the second half (and especially in the fourth quarter) of the seventh century did more Greek vases arrive (**Map: Site_N_2ndhalf_7th**). A view of the second half of the sixth century by itself reveals that not only were the Phoenician emporia, Saint-Blaise, and eastern Languedoc growing in their interest for Greek wares, there was also some limited desire present at, and perhaps around, the area where Emporion would be founded.

There is little variety to be seen in the presence or absence of types in seventh-century assemblages, except at the sites where greater numbers of vessels were found, in a few Phoenician emporia, and at Saint-Blaise and Massalia (**Map: Site_Pres_7th**). In fact, the pattern matches what was seen in the artifact counts: the Phoenician sites showed more variety in the first half of the seventh century, and those in France showed a great deal of variety only in the second half (**Maps: Site_Pres_1sthalf_7th** and **Site_Pres_2ndthalf_7th**).

Sixth Century

The picture becomes much more detailed in the sixth century. Massalia and Emporion are solidly established in this period, and Greek pottery is found from the northernmost coast of Portugal around the entire Iberian Peninsula and the coast of southern France. For the first time, Greek vases also penetrated deep into the interior, traveling hundreds of kilometers into central Spain, and north into central France, Switzerland, and southwestern Germany (**Map: Site_N_6th**). The greatest number of artifacts from this point forward would be found consistently at Massalia and Saint-Blaise, followed by Emporion (there may not be much point in making a distinction between these three sites given that they have been published to varying degrees). But the divergence of distribution between eastern Languedoc on one hand, and western Languedoc and Rousillon on the other, also firmly took root in the sixth century. Far fewer artifacts were found between the Rhône and Hérault rivers than west and south of the Hérault. Saint-Gilles-du-Gard and Calvisson were the only South Hallstatt sites with more than a dozen artifacts represented. Several sites inland, in Midi-Pyrénées, also received a few pieces of pottery. In Iberia, people at the recently founded center of Ullastret became significant consumers of Greek pottery, acquiring 196 artifacts. This point may be taken in concert with Cabrera Bonet's contention (1996, 53–54) that initially there was not a high demand for Greek products in Catalonia, and it took a long time for local people to want them. Indeed, it is clear that even a short distance away from Emporion and the coast, there was not a great amount of interest in Greek pottery. Cabrera Bonet argued that the growth of native culture allowed Emporion to flourish, not the other way around.

Greek vessels also began to make inroads in southeastern Spain (albeit to a lesser extent than farther north), between Guardamar del Segura and Cuevas de Almanzora, for the first time. They continued to be somewhat popular in the Phoenician emporia and especially at Huelva, which accounts for the bright coloration of Tartessos on the map. Over 300 artifacts were found at Huelva, but hardly any were found elsewhere in the region. Perhaps the most striking development, however, was the transport of dozens of Greek vases, if not a few hundred of them, north from the Mediterranean coast. These vessels traveled 400 kilometers or more (the closest North Hallstatt site to the sea in this survey is Bragny-sur-Saône) and 69 of them went at least 800 kilometers (to Heuneburg, likely via the Saône, Aar, Rhine, and Danube river valleys).

Generally speaking, the pattern of distribution for the presence of pottery types again aligned with what was seen from artifact counts (**Map: Site_Pres_6th**). There was growth inland in southern France and Catalonia; the Phoenician emporia and Huelva were foci for trade in Greek vessels, and some variety could be detected in the North Hallstatt region. In western Languedoc and Rousillon, especially along the Aude River, the range of types was still broader, often approaching what was found in Greek settlements. Despite the lower counts of artifacts in eastern Languedoc, there were many sites with high variation in their assemblages. This was also true in the southernmost part of Spain, particularly the lower Guadalquivir valley around Seville. The very different range of colors in the presence map shows that in general, only a few types tended to be emphasized—clearly, drinking vessels above all else, trailed by those for eating or transport.

The nuances revealed by study of presence and absence are emphasized when diversity index scores are examined (**Map: SDI_6th**). It was possible to calculate scores for 54 sites in the sixth century (23% of sites). Hot spots for the relatively even distribution of vases across types (index scores of 0.55–0.72) appeared in the South Hallstatt region. Coastal Ibero-Languedoc showed lower diversity (0.44–0.55), and Emporion and coastal Catalonia were less diverse still. Guardamar de Segura and Cuevas de Almanzora had relatively few artifacts (10 and six, respectively) in the sixth century, but they were evenly distributed across types, showing the presence of an interesting pattern in the southeast of the Iberian Peninsula.

The growth in consumption of Greek vases was relatively sudden: 2864 artifacts date to the first half of the sixth century alone (**Map: Site_N_1sthalf_6th**). The second half of the century actually showed a significant decline from the first half (N = 1826). Such a decline has already been noted by several authors for Andalusia alone (Cabrera Bonet 1994, 370–371, Domínguez 2002). In fact, while total numbers may have decreased, the geographic spread grew slightly. The variety of types present remained low. In the second half of the sixth century, southern France is the only area where sites regularly show a variety of functions represented in the assemblages (**Map: Site_N_2ndhalf_6th**). In the previous half-century, similar patterns appeared around Tartessos and the Phoenician emporia, but these areas lost their interest in a wide range of types later on. Around the lower Rhône and Gard Rivers, and in western Languedoc and Rousillon (even—or perhaps especially—inland), indigenous groups showed desire for many different kinds of Greek pottery throughout the sixth century.

The complex and occasionally violent history of the sixth century, encompassing as it did the foundation of at least two major Greek settlements, the abandonment of Cerro de Villar and foundation of Malaka, and the Phokaian diaspora and the Battle of Alalia, among other incidents, has led scholars to wonder if trade might have been deeply affected by the tumultuous events. As noted, in some regions such as Andalusia, there seems to have been a break in trade around 560, lasting until about 530. Did the Greek cession of Alalia lead to Carthaginian and Etruscan dominance of the western Mediterranean?

Fifth Century

The consumption of Greek pottery seems to have begun to increase again in the fifth century, but at a much slower rate than before (**Map: Site_N_5th**). In the first half of the century, there were 2105 artifacts, while in the second half that number climbed to 3206. The growth occurred particularly in the south of Spain, where the Tartessian inland "palace-sanctuary" at Cancho Roano (Zalamea de la Serena) received 443 artifacts (almost entirely Cástulo-type stemless cups), and the headwaters of the Guadalquivir River in Jaén province began to show significant interest in Greek pottery for the first time. The zone around the mouth of the Segura River and particularly the emporion at La Illeta dels Banyets also showed consumption of Greek wares at an increased rate. Importation decreased at the Phoenician emporia and at Huelva, even as sites in the southern Portuguese interior began to receive some small amounts of Greek pottery.[4]

As in the seventh and sixth centuries, the south coast of France continued to be the zone of greatest consumption. Marseille and Saint-Blaise were again important centers for Greek pottery, but they were joined along the lower Rhône valley by Beaucaire (89 examples), located just where that river and the Gard meet. Other sites in this area showed elevated consumption relative to previous periods, but were still fairly limited when compared to western Languedoc and Rousillon. Across the Hérault River, there were three sites (Nissan-lez-Ensérune, Béziers, and Bessan) that reported more than 350 artifacts each in the fifth century; two more sites (Montlaurès and Castel-Rousillon) had over 190 artifacts. These sites did not all decide to consume large quantities of Greek pottery simultaneously; two-thirds of the artifacts at Bessan arrived in the first half of the fifth century, compared to half of those at Béziers, and less than 10% (49 out of 533) at Nissan-lez-Ensérune (**Map: Site_N_1sthalf_5th, Map: Site_N_2ndhalf_5th**). Another hot spot for consumption was farther south, from Elne in France to Emporion and Ullastret. Most notable in this area was the confinement of very high quantities of Greek pottery to just those centers, while other sites nearby seem not to have participated in such trade at a high level. The area with the lowest interest in Greek pottery along the Mediterranean coast continued to be the zone between Barcelona and Valencia. In this region, only the Phoenician colony of Ibiza (located 100 kilometers from the mainland), was a significant purchaser of Greek wares—particularly household vessels used for deposit in tombs.

In the fifth century, the North Hallstatt region showed a sharp overall decline in the quantity of Greek vessels imported. Even as Greek pottery spread to far-off sites where none had been present before, such as Somme-Bionne in northeastern France, and Asperg, northwest of Stuttgart, it appeared only in highly isolated cases. Apart from Bourges, where 75 artifacts were found, none of the North Hallstatt sites had more than two pieces dating to the fifth century. In a surprising development, 80% of the Greek vessels at Bourges (61 out of 75) arrived in the second half of the century.

With respect to the presence and variety of functional types dating to the fifth century, it is again clear that there were few areas where consumers were interested in buying the full range that was available (**Map: Site_ Pres_5th**). Instead, the maps make clear that people at certain scattered centers such as Cástulo did buy a wide range of types, but that their close neighbors tended to be less interested. The sites where many types were found were also, broadly speaking, the ones where large numbers of artifacts appeared, marking them out as regional centers. Saint-Gilles-du-Gard is an exception to this rule, showing all five types distributed among only 44 artifacts. The number of types found in eastern Languedoc dropped slightly as the fifth century went on; the same small decrease could also be found in western Languedoc and Rousillon, except for the five major sites of Bessan, Béziers, Nissan-lez-Ensérune, Montlaurès, and Sigean (Pech Maho).

A striking contrast is presented, then, by the diversity index scores for sites in the fifth century (**Map: Site_5th_SDI**). Scores could be calculated for 41 sites (18% of the total, but representing the vast majority of all the Greek pottery reported from this period). The area with the highest diversity, or even spread of artifacts across types, was the zone from Barcelona south to La Illeta dels Banyets, where artifact counts were low, and confidence is also lower. Ibero-Languedoc, where the cluster with the most high-count sites appeared, showed much lower diversity (0.19–0.29), compared to South Hallstatt sites east of the Hérault River (0.41–0.49). Three of 10 sites sampled in eastern Languedoc had diversity scores between 0.56 and 0.83, and another five had scores between 0.35 and 0.56. The diversity index scores combined with the quantity of artifacts present allows for an interpretation to be advanced. It must be assumed, from the presence of Massalia and Emporion at either end of the coast, that the full range of Greek vessels was available to all who lived between those towns. The diversity index scores and counts suggest that people in western Languedoc and Rousillon were avid consumers of Greek vases, but despite the fact that all of the major types were present, Ibero-Languedocians had strong desires particularly for specific types. The South Hallstatt population living in eastern Languedoc did not feel so strongly about acquiring large quantities of Greek pottery, or all of the functional types, but they spread their consumption evenly across the types they did buy. Perhaps these two patterns reflect different uses of Greek pottery to define elite status through display. In one model, the procurement of a large number of vessels belonging to a limited range of specific shapes that were locally determined to be of interest could show refined taste, while in another model a broad range of types could be purchased by a limited number of people who could thus display a "set" of equipment to their neighbors.

In other areas, such as Andalusia, artifact counts were lower, and few types were represented on a per-site basis; it was difficult to determine trends with regard to diversity, due to the low number of sites for which scores could be calculated.

Fourth Century

Even more than the sixth century, the fourth century shows a dramatic difference between the first and second halves of the century. Although almost as many artifacts were dated to the fourth century overall as the fifth, there was growth in the first half, followed by a steep and sudden decline in the second half, from 4844 to only 278. Some trends that have already been recognized continued to strengthen in the fourth century (**Map: Site_N_4th**). For example, there was hardly any sign of Greek vessels in the North Hallstatt region—in fact, just two vases were found, one at Chassey-le-Camp, on the upper Saône, and the other at Châtillon-sur-Glâne. In addition, consumption at South Hallstatt sites decreased, while Ibero-Languedocian sites maintained their strong interest in Greek pottery (although fewer vessels seem to have traveled into the interior here). The inland part of southeast Spain, especially around Cástulo and up into the hills where the Guadalquivir's tributaries begin, became a significant area of focus for Greek wares (even as lower Guadalquivir sites seemingly lost all interest). On the coast, La Illeta dels Banyets, with over 600 artifacts, was the single site where high consumption was evident. Although the counts were small in Portugal, a pattern clearly emerged to show the gradual spread of Greek vases, from the lower Guadiana and especially Castro Marim well into central Portugal—not only on the coast, but in the interior as well. A few vases—generally only one or two per site—were even found in northern Portugal, as at Facha and Murça. In the latter half of the fourth century, however, only one region continued to buy Greek vessels in any numbers: coastal western Languedoc and Rousillon. Apart from Nissan-lez-Ensérune (N = 132), only two sites in the survey, Béziers and Montlaurès, had more than 25 artifacts between 350 and 300.[5] Even Saint-Blaise, previously a prolific consumer of Greek vases, had only 11 examples in this period, and 12 in the preceding half-century.

In the fourth century there is no site with more than four functional types present, and in the second half of the century, there are none with more than three types (**Map: Site_Pres_4th**). Cástulo and its neighbors are confirmed by presence-absence analysis to have collected the richest assemblages in the entire survey area—only two of the 10 sites in the region had fewer than two different types of Greek vases. This region remained the only one with a local pattern of multiple types represented in the second half of the fourth century (**Map: Site_Pres_2ndhalf_4th**). In western Languedoc and Rousillon, a subtle distinction seems to appear between the areas to the north and south of the Aude River. Despite the presence on the north side of the Aude of the five major centers where a wide range of types was collected, the presence of many smaller sites offsets the richer sites and reduced the overall variety of the area. South of the Aude there was no major center (except for Castel-Rousillon, well inland), but almost all the sites had one or more types accounted for.

Multiple types were also broadly represented in the South Hallstatt region, and it was here that the highest diversity scores were recorded (**Map: Site_SDI_4th**). Western Provence and eastern Languedoc were characterized by a broad region where scores ranged from 0.52 to 0.74, decreasing from east to west, so that for the western part of the Gard *département* the scores dipped as low as 0.49. Rousillon and most of western Languedoc, by contrast, show extremely low diversity scores (0.08–0.24, with narrow bands of up to 0.46 close to the Hérault River). Around Cástulo, diversity indexes were essentially the same as for Rousillon and western Languedoc, in the low-to-medium range of 0.34 to 0.45.

Chronological Summary by Region

The focus of the previous discussion on chronology may have obscured some regional patterns, so a brief summary grouped by geographic regions is presented below.

- South Hallstatt: The earliest Greek imports to the South Hallstatt region, between Massalia and the Hérault River, date to the late seventh century. It seems likely that their appearance is connected to the foundation of Massalia, perhaps with Saint-Blaise created to function as an intermediary point of exchange. This region never imported as much pottery as its neighbors on the other side of the Hérault, but it did follow a similar pattern of high growth in the sixth and fifth centuries followed by decline in the second half of the fourth. South Hallstatt sites showed the consumption of a limited number of types of pottery (generally not more than two in most areas in any given period). There was, however, a remarkable and stable balance shown in the evenness of distribution of artifacts across types over time— more than in any other region. In earlier periods, the coastal zone consumed more Greek pottery than did sites just to the north, but in the fifth and fourth centuries, this distinction faded. The Gard River valley seemed to form the northern limit of significant consumption of Greek pottery.
- Ibero-Languedoc: This region, essentially comprising western Languedoc from the Hérault River west and Rousillon south to the border of Spain, was the area of the greatest indigenous consumption of Greek products between 600 and 300. The high level of interest in Greek pottery was sustained especially at five major centers, four between the Hérault and the Aude rivers (Bessan, Béziers, Montlaurès, Nissan-lez-Ensérune), and one south of the Aude (Castel-Rousillon). Together, these sites accounted for 4526 artifacts (roughly 20% of all examples in the corpus).

- Iberia: The Iberian region showed multiple patterns in several different zones: northeastern Catalonia, the east coast between Barcelona and Múrcia, the southeast, the Costa del Sol, and the central interior (Tartessos is treated separately below). The earliest centers for consumption of Greek pottery were the Phoenician emporia scattered along the south coast, especially Vélez-Málaga. After the sixth century, however, the emporia ceased to import many Greek vases. The region that imported the most Greek pottery in the fifth and fourth centuries was instead northeastern Catalonia, though this pattern was almost entirely due to the very high number of vases at the Greek colony of Emporion, with the Iberian regional fortified center of Ullastret following well behind, and other Iberian sites practically absent. Both Emporion and Ullastret consumed all five types of vases. The Iberian emporion of La Illeta dels Banyets emerged as a major locus of exchange in the fifth and especially the fourth centuries, getting almost 600 vases between 400 and 350. Although the interior sites in the province of Jaén are relatively close to La Illeta dels Banyets and show a similar jump in consumption during the late fifth and fourth centuries, the two areas were probably not directly connected, since travel over the Sierra de Segura would have been problematic (likewise, there was probably little connection between Cástulo and the Phoenician emporia of the southern coast due to the Sierra Nevada range).
- Tartessos: Consumption of Greek pottery focused primarily on one site, the emporion of Huelva. From the earliest period of trade in Greek vases, the late eighth century, Huelva received some vessels (as did El Puerto de Santa Maria, located across the bay from the Phoenician emporion of Cádiz). In the seventh and sixth centuries, Huelva was one of the biggest recipients of Greek vases in the West, but its interest in consuming them dwindled after this period. If the site of Cancho Roano had not been discovered and excavated since the 1970s, it would be easy to think that Tartessos ceased consuming Greek pottery at the end of the archaic period, when its mines were no longer exploited to the same degree. The enormous number of vases found at Cancho Roano forces us to reconsider what form local interest took in the fifth and fourth centuries, particularly since at least one imitation Greek vessel was found there. Cancho Roano also is one of the few sites in the corpus with a recognizably strong religious component, which may have had some effect on the somewhat limited range of types found there (see drinking function).
- Lusitanian: Perhaps unsurprisingly, given their distance from Greek colonies, sites in Portugal generally had very low numbers of Greek vases, and the ones that did arrive were of fairly late date—the second half of the fifth century or first half of the fourth. A different way of regarding the situation might be to note the number of sites where any Greek pottery was found: 24. These sites were located in all parts of the country, from the coast to the hilly interior, from south to north. The greatest number of vases was found in the south at Castro Marim, which may have been

a Tartessian emporion, since it was located at the mouth of the Guadiana River, which led into Tartessos's heartland, but an almost equal number were found in central near-coastal Portugal at Alcácer do Sal.

- North Hallstatt: The earliest Greek vases to appear in the North Hallstatt region had a median production date of 550; the latest dated to the early fourth century. This region therefore had a much more circumscribed period of consumption than other areas. Most of the major consumers of Greek pottery were at the large hilltop settlements known as Fürstensitzen, particularly Heuneburg, Châtillon-sur-Glâne, and Vix, in the sixth century, though no site in the region received even 100 vases. The true outlier in this region was Bourges, which began receiving Greek vases relatively late, and which consumed far more vases over the course of the fifth century than any other North Hallstatt site. Bourges also was the only site to receive all five functional types; most others received only one or two types.

INTEREST IN TYPES OF GREEK POTTERY

The foregoing discussion frequently mentioned that "many types" or "only a few types" of pottery were found at some sites or in some regions, or that some sites were more or less diverse than others. Very little mention has yet been made about precisely which types were prevalent or rare, because the presence-absence and Simpson's Index of Diversity tests for entire assemblages cannot reveal that information directly. It is instead necessary to look at each functional type individually. This section will proceed through the functional types, discussing the distribution of drinking, eating, household, storage, and transport vessels each in turn. Because the overwhelming majority of the Greek pottery found in western Europe was (at least in its home context) associated with drinking at banquets like the symposion, additional attention will be devoted to the distribution of cups and kraters. Finally, the distribution of a specific kind of Athenian stemless cup known as the Cástulo type will also be considered, since it has frequently been suggested to have been designed specifically for export to western markets.

Drinking

For the purposes of this analysis, the following shapes were defined as having a function related to drinking: askos, bolsal, calyx-cup, chalice, cup (usually for cups that could not be identified with greater specificity because diagnostic features were missing), cup-kantharos, cup-kotyle, cup-skyphos, dinos, goblet, Ionian cup, jug, juglet, kantharos, kotyle, krater, mastoid cup, oinochoe, olpe, rhyton, skyphos, stemless cup, and stemmed cup. Drinking vessels were the most popular type of Greek pottery at almost every site and certainly in every region surveyed (Fig. 6.7).

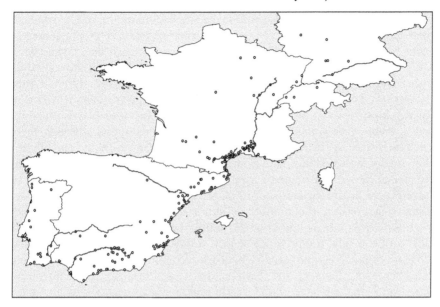

Figure 6.7   Sites where drinking vessels were found

By count of artifacts, however, the distribution of drinking vessels was far from even (**Map: Site_N_Drinking**). The area of highest counts was around Massalia and Saint-Blaise. The next highest set of counts, generally over 400 vessels per site, occurred at Emporion and the Iberian/Ibero-Languedocian sites of northeastern Catalonia, Rousillon, and western Languedoc. These numbers drop off dramatically as one's attention moves away from the coast, and east across the Hérault River. South Hallstatt sites continued to show a clearly different pattern from those that surrounded them, in this case a predicted value only one-tenth as great (or even less) as that for Ibero-Languedocian sites, Saint-Blaise, or Massalia.

In the southern Iberian Peninsula, the most drinking vessels appeared in the province of Jaén, along with La Illeta dels Banyets and Cancho Roano. Very low numbers of drinking vessels were found at sites up the Segura River from the coast, perhaps a sign that there was little direct connection between the southeast coast and the Jaén area. Huelva and the Phoenician emporia on the south coast also received drinking vessels, albeit at lower levels. At the sites in southern and northern Portugal where there was enough data to make high-confidence predictions, the number of drinking vessels (like the overall number of vessels imported) was quite low, ranging only as high as five to 14 vessels, and frequently lower than that. The smallest number of vessels according to artifact counts was in the North Hallstatt sites, where confidence about predictions was also fairly low or even very low.[6]

Of the 23 types of drinking vessels, no site (including the Greek colonies) had more than 14 present (**Map: Site_Drinking_Pres**). This phenomenon may be the result of the fact that certain shapes (such as kotylai) were only made early in history, when some sites were big consumers, while other shapes (like calyx-cups) were made only later, when different sites had eclipsed those early big consumers. In comparing regional distribution of drinking types, it appears that the sharp breaks seen between certain areas seem to be smoothed over somewhat. For example, although there was certainly a difference between Massalia/Saint-Blaise and Ibero-Languedoc on one hand, and South Halstatt sites on the other, the difference was between a range of three to four types at the latter and five to seven types at the former—not at all the tenfold difference seen in artifact counts. Moreover, the number of types found at sites in northeastern Catalonia was just as low as at the South Hallstatt towns. In the southern Iberian Peninsula, the province of Jaén stands out, with between three and four types per site, compared to between zero and two for the area around La Illeta dels Banyets and between two and three for the Phoenician emporia. Cancho Roano, with Cástulo-type stemless cups making up almost all of its drinking vessels, had a very narrow range and thus did not stand out among the towns of Tartessos in the same way that Huelva, and, to a lesser extent, Castro Marim did. Portugal showed the least variety of drinking shapes, while North Hallstatt sites were only slightly richer.

The map of diversity index scores opens up another useful perspective on the distribution of drinking vessels (**Map: Site_Drinking_SimpsonDI**). This analysis calculated scores for 97 sites (41% of the total). It should be noted that the range of diversity scores is biased toward the high end of the spectrum, with the top eight intervals (in this case, spaced geometrically) covering the range between 0.52 and 0.93. This range means that at 82% of sites for which index scores were calculated (80 out of 97), the likelihood that one could randomly choose two different types on successive tries was better than even. At 41 of the 97 sites, the chance rose from 50% to 75%. In other words, people throughout western Europe seemed to want drinking vessels, but with only a few exceptions, they did not express a strong preference for only one or two types to the exclusion of others.

As in the chronological analysis, South Hallstatt sites, especially those bordering the Hérault River, showed slightly higher diversity scores than Ibero-Langudocian sites, Massalia and Saint-Blaise, despite their lower overall counts and narrower range of types. Diversity was not high (0.52–0.62) in the eastern part of Andalusia and Múrcia and it could even be described as low (0.35–0.51) in the western part of the Iberian Peninsula (including Portugal). Cancho Roano had the lowest score of any site (0.11), again due to the high number of Cástulo cups and the low number of any other types.

Although the North Hallstatt zone was characterized by extreme spatial sparsity, leading to reduced confidence in the kriging results, a broad trend does seem to appear. Index scores rise as one moves from west to east, and at the far eastern end of the survey, Heuneburg (0.80) and Bopfingen (0.83) have two of the highest scores.[7] The lowest-scoring North Hallstatt site was the one farthest west, Bourges, but even its score was not terribly low (0.49).

The inclusion of presence-absence analysis and diversity index scores allows us to see that for most locations, a narrow range of types of vessels was preferred to a wider array, but that equal numbers of each of the types present could also often be found. In the South Hallstatt region, the total number of vessels was low compared to that of their neighbors, but more types were represented, and the count was evenly distributed across types. In western Languedoc, Rousillon, and northeastern Catalonia, there were many, many more vessels, and a few more types per site, but the counts were slightly less evenly distributed. Another way of stating this is that sets of Greek drinking vessels in Ibero-Languedoc were likely more widely held as well as more specialized than in South Hallstatt towns. In North Hallstatt towns, by contrast, there were far fewer vessels, and, apart from two sites, relatively few types were represented, but the diversity scores were universally high. The pattern seems to show that at least some consumers in this area were able to collect rich assemblages of the kinds of vessels they wanted, regardless of their distance from the pottery's point of manufacture or from a Greek colony. In the area of Cástulo, there was a fairly high number of drinking vessels, but few types and relatively low diversity, showing a great interest in Greek pottery, but only in two or three kinds from the available range. Although Cancho Roano is several hundred kilometers from Jaén province, it presents the most extreme version of this pattern: of 443 total vessels, 417 were for drinking; of these, 393 were stemless cups (94% of drinking vessels, 89% of all vessels). Apart from Cancho Roano, the number of drinking vessels in Tartessos, the number of types, and the diversity of assemblages were all low compared to the regions already mentioned, perhaps signaling a general lack of interest in Greek pottery for drinking. In Portugal, the level of interest was, if anything, lower still.

Eating

Vessels used for eating were the second most common group in western Europe, but they only appeared at 74 sites. These shapes included bowls, dishes, fish plates, large bowls, lekanai, lekanides, one-handlers, pateras, plates, saltcellars, small bowls, stemmed dishes, and stemmed plates. Although the earliest examples appeared around 650 or sometime thereafter, most of the eating vessels belong to the fifth and fourth centuries. The sites where the most examples were found were Massalia (904), La Illeta dels Banyets (653), Saint-Blaise (422), and Emporion (209) (Fig. 6.8).

In the South Hallstatt region, counts were again lower than in surrounding areas (**Map: Site_N_Eating**). Only Saint-Gilles-du-Gard (46) had more than 14 examples. To the west of the Hérault, there were more eating

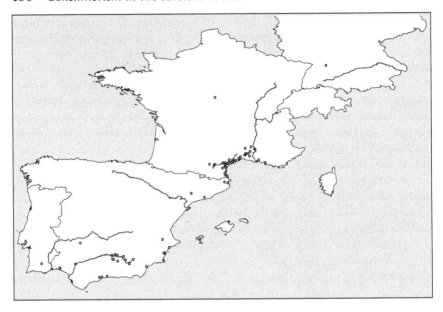

Figure 6.8   Sites where eating vessels were found

vessels, but they seemed to be associated only with the sites that were otherwise major consumers of Greek pottery—Nissan-lez-Ensérune, Béziers, Montlaurès, and Bessan. The distribution of eating vessels dropped off sharply as one moved away from the coast. South of the Pyrenees in Catalonia, Emporion and Ullastret were not the only recipients of eating vessels; Olèrdola, in the hills west of Barcelona, had 30 examples, but it appears to be an outlier in the region. Likewise an outlier is La Illeta dels Banyets in southeastern Spain, where the appearance of more than 650 eating vessels contrasts sharply to their total absence from the six closest sites. Even near the Phoenician emporion at Guardamar del Segura, there are no more than two examples at any given site. These patterns may be related to the dates of the sites' active periods. Guardamar del Segura was a point of exchange in the eighth, seventh, and sixth centuries, when western Europeans showed little interest in Greek eating vessels, while La Illeta dels Banyets flourished particularly in the fourth century (63% of the eating vessels had median production dates between 363 and 350), when demand for these kinds of vases was much greater. Two areas in southern Spain where there were slightly higher counts of eating vessels are the provinces of Jaén (including Cástulo) and especially Granada. In the latter area, two sites in the highland of the Sierra Nevada, Baza and Galera, where the farthest tributaries of the Guadalquivir begin, had 40 and 20 examples, respectively.[8] Farther west, on the coast, Huelva and

Castro Marim each received some eating vessels, but these did not generally penetrate into the interior (Cancho Roano being the only site of significant consumption in the hinterland). All of the eating vessels that came to Huelva dated to the sixth century. In the North Hallstatt region, eating vessels were essentially absent; only Bourges (four examples) received any at all.[9]

Presence-absence analysis of eating vessels shows quite different results in some areas from the analyses already conducted for drinking and for chronological change over time. In broad terms, and perhaps unsurprisingly, given that only one-third of sites had any eating vessels at all, the kriging predicts that no eating vessel types will be found in the vast majority of the survey area (**Map: Site_Eating_Pres**). In this way, the presence-absence analysis is robust (that is to say, resistant to the effects of isolated cases such as La Illeta dels Banyets, Olèrdola, Cancho Roano, or Huelva).There are three primary areas where any variety is found: Ibero-Languedoc, extending south to Emporion; Massalia and Saint-Blaise; and the provinces of Jaén and Granada. Particularly in western Languedoc and Rousillon, a group of sites can be seen just a few kilometers inland, circling the coast-line. These sites include the four with the highest number of types repre-sented, all with between eight and 10 of the 13 eating types. Eight sites in this region rank within the top 13 in the survey. For once, in other words, South Hallstatt sites do not show greater variety than Ibero-Languedocian ones. The area around the Aude River specifically shows both high counts and a large number of types. In Catalonia, only Emporion shows a variety of eating vessels. Massalia and Saint-Blaise form a high-value cluster on their own, as usual. Despite the quantity of eating vessels in the Jaén-Granada region, sites there showed hardly any variety, with a predicted value of one or two types.

There were only 39 sites for which Simpson's Index of Diversity scores could be calculated. These showed a uniform area where eating vessels were somewhat evenly distributed (0.61–0.67) stretching from Massalia along the Mediterranean coast to Emporion (**Map: Site_Eating_SimpsonDI**). Diversity was lower in Jaén and Granada (0.47–0.54), although those results are associated with lower confidence. Only at Peal de Becerro was there more even distribution: five types from a population of 14 artifacts (SDI = 0.71). By comparison, Cástulo had six types from a population of 30 arti-facts, but 24 of the artifacts belonged to one type, bowls (SDI = 0.36).

It is clear from this discussion that interest in consuming eating vessels was highly variable—much more so than for drinking vessels. This there-fore implies that the decision to buy and display eating vessels was made on the basis of local concerns, rather than regional ones. Most consumers who were interested in buying Greek pottery (and able to do so) did not choose pottery that was designed for eating. Obviously, many of the shapes that have been designated for drinking or for eating could be used for the other function instead (even in Greek contexts)—serving soup, stew, or porridge in a cup, for example, or drinking out of a bowl or one-handler.

Even so, apart from the sites of Massalia, Emporion, and, perhaps strangely, La Illeta dels Banyets, there is only one region where people were definitely interested in buying the vases Greeks used for dining and food preparation: western Languedoc and Rousillon. In this region, there were high counts at many sites, many types present at those sites, and a moderate diversity to the assemblages. There is very little evidence to suggest that Greek eating vessels were popular elsewhere. Their wide geographic availability is made clear, however, by their presence in high numbers on the coast of southeastern Spain and in low numbers at sites across the interior of Andalusia, Portugal (specifically Alcácer do Sal), and in South Hallstatt towns.

Household

Greek vessels for general household use were found at just 55 sites (24% of the total). The category of household vases includes personal containers for oil and perfumes, cosmetics, jewelry, vessels used for washing, and vases intended for ritual use (including miniature vases). The shapes are alabastra, amphoriskoi, aryballoi, kotha, krateriskoi, lamps, lebetes gamikoi, lekythoi, loutrophoroi, lydia, miniature skyphos-kraters, perfume vases, phialai, plemo-choai, pyxides, pyxis-tripods, and stamnoi. Only three sites revealed more than 100 household artifacts: Emporion (336), Ibiza (125), and Massalia (119); just 12 sites had 10 or more examples (Fig. 6.9). Twenty-three sites had only a single example. Fifteen household vases arrived in the survey area during the eighth and seventh centuries, followed by 173 in the sixth, 323 in the fifth, and 193 in the fourth century (**Map: Site_N_Household**).

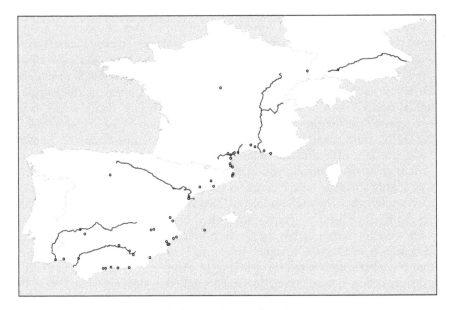

Figure 6.9   Sites where household vessels were found

With regard to the counts of household vessels per site, Ibiza's presence toward the top of the list may be most striking. This fact may be linked to the function for which these vases were put. The excavations of Puig de Molins brought to light dozens of Phoenician tombs in a necropolis where household vases were deposited, mostly lekythoi and lamps—a practice remarkably similar to Greeks' use of vases in burials. A regional interest in household vases may be seen in coastal Rousillon, and to a lesser extent, western Languedoc. This interest was not very strong, though. Only two sites in the area had more than 20 examples, and none had more than 36. Similarly weak interest was evident among the Phoenician emporia on the Costa del Sol. The kriging prediction of low numbers of household vessels in Tartessos is entirely based on 36 examples found at Huelva. Only five household vessel artifacts were found in Portugal; another five were found at North Hallstatt sites.

As might be expected from the analysis of artifact counts, the number of sites where many of the 17 household types appeared was very low (**Map: Site_Household_Pres**). No site had more than 11 types; no non-Greek site had more than six. Almost half of all sites where any types of household vessels were identified only showed one type (26 out of 53 sites; 49%). The island of Ibiza showed the highest range of types, between about three and five, after Massalia. The regions of coastal Rousillon and northeastern Catalonia, the Costa del Sol, the area around the mouth of the Almanzora River in south-eastern Andalusia, coastal Tartessos, the zone around Cancho Roano, and the zone surrounding Heuneburg all only showed at most the likelihood of finding a single type of household vessel. No other areas showed any probability of different kinds of household vases being purchased and used.

Only 21 sites had enough household vessels for Simpson's Index of Diversity scores to be calculated. Half of these sites were located in western Languedoc, Rousillon, and northeastern Catalonia, but the rest were widely scattered, making it impossible to compare regions or to attribute any confidence to the kriging predictions. What can be said is that the cluster of sites in the south of France confirms the consumption of a *relatively* broad range of household vessels in this area, and, at least, a moderate range of evenness in those assemblages (at three of the 10 sites, diversity index scores were 0.70 or higher). None of the Ibero-Languedocian sites were as interested in household vases as the Greek colonies or Ibiza, but no other region besides Ibero-Languedoc showed interest in household vases as a characteristic feature.

Storage

Of the Greek storage vases that could be dated, the earliest appeared in limited numbers in the second half of the seventh century (N = 16; **Map: Site_N_Storage**).These were followed by 490 artifacts in the sixth century, 50 in the fifth, and 96 in the fourth century This category includes vessels used for holding liquid or grain: amphorai, hydriai, jars, pelikai, pithoi,

Figure 6.10   Sites where storage vessels were found

and situlae. Although storage vessels were found at 55 sites, 75% of them appeared at either Massalia (N = 638) or Emporion (N = 117) (Fig. 6.10).

The largest non-Greek importers of storage vases were Pézenas (56), Huelva (25), Bessan (14), Sigean (14), and Saint-Blaise (13). These numbers are significantly lower than in the Greek colonies. In the South Hallstatt region, only Saint-Gilles-du-Gard (8) had more than five artifacts. Slightly more appeared around the coast of western Languedoc and Rousillon. The high kriging prediction for northeastern Catalonia is due to Emporion's large quantity of storage vases; even Ullastret, otherwise a large consumer of Greek pottery, only had four instances. A similar pattern appeared in Jaén and Granada provinces in Spain, around Málaga on the Costa del Sol, at Huelva, and at Vix. In none of these cases does the prediction show that a large number of storage vases could be expected in these regions, however. The prediction instead ranges from as low as two to as many as nine—hardly a sign of great interest in these vases on the part of consumers, even though some of the shapes, like amphorai, might have played an important role in the full-scale performance of a symposion.

Massalia was the only site with five of the seven types present, while Emporion and three Ibero-Languedocian sites followed with three each (**Map: Site_Storage_ Pres**). Two of the three non-Greek sites—Pézenas and Nissan-lez-Ensérune—and five more with two types were all located between the Hérault and the Aude rivers, leading to the conclusion that as a region, western Languedoc was (again, relatively speaking) more interested in multiple types of storage vessels than other regions. Any other places where more than one type appeared, such as Cuevas de Almanzora, Vix, or Châtillon-sur-Glâne, were so isolated that they cannot be taken as symptomatic of any regional trends. There were so few sites where multiple storage vases appeared that it was not possible to calculate enough diversity index scores for a comparison.

Fundamentally, then, there seems to have been little to no interest among non-Greeks in owning storage vessels. It could certainly be argued that the size of these vessels might have made them more cumbersome for trade, and that this reason might be more significant for determining distribution than local taste (or lack thereof). This reasoning could explain why Massalia, closest to Greek production centers (and a production center itself), received the most storage vessels, and why even Emporion received fewer. Further comment on this point will wait until the description of the distribution of other large shapes, namely transport amphorai and kraters, is complete.

A related issue is the extent to which storage shapes served as vectors for the transmission of Greek imagery to non-Greeks. These vases (together with kraters) were the largest to bear figured images, and images on them would be larger and easier to see than on cups or other small vessels. Of the 1013 storage vessels in the database, 214 had painted images (all Athenian black-figure or red-figure). By the same token, of the 8431 figured vases, only 214 had storage as their intended function. It seems from these numbers that there was no great desire in western Europe for large painted vases, perhaps because the images they bore were meaningless or incomprehensible to audiences.

Transport

The presence of transport amphorai has, understandably, often been seen as signifying the presence of wine, too. It has been generally accepted that wine was introduced to this part of Europe in the archaic period. Phoenicians brought wine to the Iberian Peninsula in the eighth century, and Iberians had begun producing wine by 700 BCE (Dietler 2006, 232). In France and trans-Alpine Europe, Greeks have usually been seen as responsible for this introduction. The foundation of Massalia may have led to some of the earliest plantings of vines (Bertucchi 1992), and wine from Massalia became a major export product. Recent work, however, has identified the earliest direct evidence of wine in France from residue found in Etruscan amphorai dating to 500–475 at Lattes (McGovern et al. 2013). The number of datable amphorai grew over time, from three in the eighth century to 44 in the seventh, 235 in the sixth, 210 in the fifth, and then dropped again to 28 in the fourth century. The absence of locally produced wine, especially in the interior of France and trans-Alpine Europe, was noted by ancient authors, who attributed the need for imported wine to what they perceived to be a climate that was not conducive to growing grapevines (or olives, for that matter; Diod. Sic. 5.26). The same authors identified alcoholic beverages other than wine as being consumed by local populations. These beverages seem to have been grain-based, like beer, or honey-based, like mead.

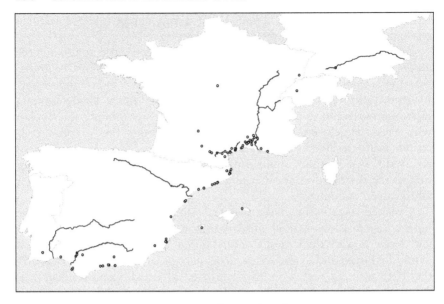

Figure 6.11   Sites where transport vessels were found

Almost 1000 transport amphorai were catalogued in the database (N = 996). Of these, at least 41% originated in Massalia. Transport amphorai were found at 77 sites (33% of the total). Saint-Blaise led all sites with 188 amphorai, followed by Massalia (Fig. 6.11, **Map: Site_N_Transport**). The next two sites, Beaucaire and Saint-Gilles-du-Gard, with 84 examples each, therefore direct attention to a larger pattern that is identified in the kriging: the prominence of the South Hallstatt region as the largest consumer of transport amphorai (and thus, apparently, of imported wine). A number of sites with relatively high counts are clustered in this area. The Rhône and Gard valleys seem to form the particular focus of consumption, with the trend dropping off somewhat with distance from Massalia. The amphorai in this area tend to date later than 550 BCE. The next two sites after the ones in eastern Languedoc are Heuneburg (N = 57) and Bourges (N = 53), while Châtillon-sur-Glâne had 47 examples, showing that certain parts of the North Hallstatt region not only had access to amphorai but were also highly interested in acquiring them relative to towns in other regions. Other North Hallstatt sites, including Vix, however, had few or, more frequently, no amphorai represented among their assemblages.

On the west side of the Hérault, where we have already noted the very high consumption of Greek pottery generally, and vessels for drinking in particular, the counts for transport amphorai are, however, much lower. Pézenas had the most amphorai of any Ibero-Languedocian site, with eight examples, and hardly any amphorai were found between the Aude River and the Pyrenees. Once again, in northeastern Catalonia, consumption of

Greek pottery seems to have been restricted to Emporion and Ullastret, but even at these sites, the number of transport amphorai is fairly low (N = 32 and 22, respectively). Scattered sites here and there along the east coast of Spain—Calafell and Benicarlo, Guardamar del Segura and San Fulgencio—have a few amphorai, but otherwise, there is little evidence for them in this area, just as there is little evidence for the presence of Greek pottery generally here. No examples were reported from the site that consumed the most Greek pottery in this area, La Illeta dels Banyets.

Consumers in the Phoenician emporia of Málaga and Vélez-Málaga, on the other hand, purchased some amphorai, particularly in the seventh and early sixth centuries, and a few examples appeared slightly inland at Guadalhorce in this period as well. Huelva and, to a lesser extent, El Puerto de Santa María, both on the Atlantic coast, similarly bought amphorai early on but not later. Just one transport amphora appeared in Portugal, at Monte Beirao in Almôdovar.

The presence-absence kriging offers a similar perspective, since this functional category only includes a single shape, but it removes the effects of very high vessel counts (**Map: Site_Transport_Pres**). The initial pattern identifying South Hallstatt sites as the most frequent consumers of transport amphorai is confirmed by the cluster of sites with amphorai in that area. At the same time, the picture of western Languedoc and Rousillon as low-level consumers given by artifact counts needs some revision. Specifically, while sites between the Hérault and Aude rivers show fewer presences, there is also a clear route of sites with amphorai along the Aude itself. That route leads into the interior, likely being used to supply Albas (N = 3) and Toulouse (N = 1) with at least some wine. The presence-absence map also helps to show how the south of Spain was also a common destination for amphorai, particularly along the lower Guadalquivir (but not farther upstream in Jaén or Granada provinces).

Summary of Functional Analysis

Consumers of Greek pottery did not want the same things in every part of western Europe. Regional and local trends are visible for each of the five functional types. In some cases, regions show the same trends across all or most of the types, particularly where consumption was low: the east coast of Spain between Barcelona and Valencia, for example, did not display evidence of interest on the part of consumers for any type of Greek pottery. The same pattern appeared in central and northern Spain, and western France. By contrast, western Languedoc and Rousillon showed evidence for greater interest in three of the different types of Greek vessels (drinking, eating, and storage) than any other non-Greek area. The South Hallstatt region had consistently lower numbers of imports (except transport amphorai), but also broader, and often more evenly distributed, ranges of drinking and eating vessels. A subregion of Iberia, equivalent to the provinces of

Jaén and Granada in Andalusia, which has attracted much scrutiny for the presence of a kind of Athenian cup, showed elevated (though not high) numbers of drinking and eating vessels, but little or no variety within those types, indicating the existence of strong preferences for specific shapes. There was also no evidence for the consumption of wine from Greek sources in this area, though local wine could certainly have been drunk. Consumers at North Hallstatt and Lusitanian sites seemed exclusively interested in vases for drinking. Hardly any sites or regions had much household pottery.

SHAPE STUDIES

The extraordinary emphasis on vessels used for drinking in the consumption of Greek pottery in western Europe deserves closer attention. The very large numbers allow for the treatment of several shapes and a group of shapes by themselves. In this section, the distribution of cups of all kinds and Cástulo cups specifically will be examined, as well as kraters, by the same means used previously for functional types.

Cups

It was already shown in the introduction to this chapter that the most common shapes in the survey were various kinds of cups. There were 12,511 cups in the database, for 52% of the total, and 73% of drinking vessels. Focusing scrutiny on cups will help distinguish between vases intended for individuals to use in drinking and those associated with other parts of the Greek symposion banquet, like pouring or mixing. At the same time, the smaller size of cups must be noted, since they were likely less expensive than larger vessels, and more of them could be transported at the same time than larger vessels. Both of these facts might help explain their wider distribution.

The distribution of cups according to artifact count is essentially the same as those for drinking as a whole, a fact that is unsurprising given the dominance of cups in that category (**Map: Site_N_Cups**) (Fig. 6.12). But other analyses provide some useful counterpoints. Two different presence-absence studies were conducted. One grouped all cups together, and the other treated the various shapes separately. In the first case, a map of binary states (the presence or absence of any kind of cup) reveals that sites along the Iberian coast were not totally excluded from trade in Greek vessels; they only received very few of them (**Map: Site_Pres_ Cups_Simple**). Moreover, the type of vessels they did receive at least included cups in almost every instance. In contrast, there were several subregions that did not receive cups, including inland Tartessos (apart from Cancho Roano) and the lower Guadalquivir; southern Catalonia; Lusitanian sites along the Douro River; the confluence of the Tarn, Lot,

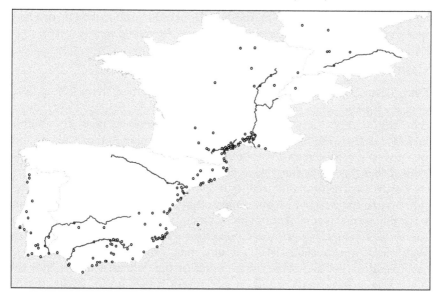

Figure 6.12   Sites where cups appeared

and Garonne rivers in eastern Aquitaine; the upper Rhine around Breisach and Uetliberg (even though cups did travel farther along similar routes to sites like Heuneburg and Asperg). Consideration of the presence of types of cups reinforces the impression that Ibero-Languedoc had the most intense interest in Greek pottery of any non-Greek region (**Map: Site_Pres_Cups_Complex**). Of the eight sites with at least eight types of cups present, six were in Ibero-Languedoc (including the only site with nine types, Montlaurès). Coastal South Hallstatt sites also seem to have a slightly higher level of consumption of cups in this analysis. The sites along Spain's east coast once again show how limited interest in a wide variety of Greek vases was there, with only two sites having two or more types. Greater variety is apparent around Cástulo and the upper Guadalquivir, where 10 sites have at least two types, and two sites have five or more. North Hallstatt sites generally show lower variety, with only two sites (Heuneburg and Bourges)having four or five types, and the rest having two, one, or zero.

It was possible to calculate Simpson's Index of Diversity scores for cups at 81 sites (35% of the total, accounting for 98% of all cups; **Map: Site_ SDI_Cups**). A remarkable degree of evenness was found for sites from the Rhône to Emporion (0.70–0.82). This pattern was not only along the coast but inland as far as the Gard River and the headwaters of the Aude. Around Cástulo, the level of evenness was lower (0.49–0.61), showing that preferences were more pronounced for certain kinds of cups, like the Athenian stemless shape now named for the site. There was too little data to draw broad regional conclusions about Portugal or the North Hallstat region, though diversity index scores were low at the few sites where they could be calculated.

Cástulo Cups

Since Brian Shefton named the Athenian heavy-walled stemless cup with concave lip and offset inside after the site of Cástulo (Pellicer 1982), much scholarly attention has been directed to understanding their distribution and role in the west. Shefton gave the designation due to the large number of cups with these features found in tombs around Cástulo.[10] He also argued that this shape must have been intended for trade, both because of its sturdy construction and because it seemed to have been shipped in large numbers to the western Mediterranean (Shefton 1996, 88). Other scholars have followed this line of thought, while introducing new ideas to explain the shape's popularity to non-Greeks (see Chapter 5; Antonaccio 2003, Walsh and Antonaccio 2014). One intriguing example of a cup similar to the Cástulo type, and which was found in the Athenian agora, had the word *xenon* (foreigner) incised on its underside, perhaps indicating that in Greece, too, this shape was especially interesting to (or associated with) non-Greeks (Camp 1999, 274; Walsh and Antonaccio 2014).

The survey presented here is, to my knowledge, the most comprehensive to consider the distribution of Cástulo cups as a type, and the evidence continues to support Shefton's assertion concerning the shape as one primarily intended for export to non-Greeks. Of the 37 sites where Cástulo cups were found, none were Greek (**Map: Site_N_Castulo**) (Fig. 6.13).

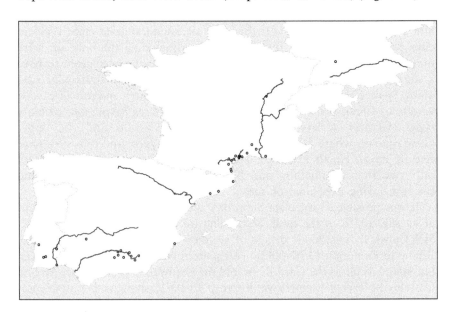

Figure 6.13   Sites where Cástulo cups appeared

At some of the sites, particularly Cancho Roano and Cástulo itself, hundreds of examples appeared. The areas with the greatest regional distribution of Cástulo cups coincided with those for cups generally (**Map: Site_N_Castulo_0**). Hot spots included inland Tartessos around Cancho Roano, although this was due to the very high number found at that site alone (N = 370); Jaén and Granada provinces, where six more sites joined Cástulo; and Ibero-Languedoc, with seven sites totaling more than 160 examples. The contrast between Greek and non-Greek sites is clearest in northeastern Catalonia, where Ullastret, just 20 kilometers from Emporion, had 22 examples. Hallstatt sites, on the coast or in trans-Alpine Europe, consumed almost no Cástulo cups (the production dates for the Cástulo type (ca. 480–375, with most examples dating ca. 450–400; Gracia Alonso 2003) are later than the period of greatest consumption for Greek pottery in the North Hallstatt region). Two unusual exceptions to that trend were the red-figure and black-gloss examples found at Kleinaspergle, near Asperg (see the description of that site in Chapter 3).

The effect of sites with enormous quantities of Cástulo cups (like Cancho Roano) on the kriging prediction is eliminated by a presence-absence analysis (**Map: Site_Pres_Castulo**). Ibero-Languedoc and Jaén and Granada still appear as important clusters of consumption, but to these is now added southern Portugal. The South Hallstatt region also shows a slightly higher presence of Cástulo cups than in the artifact count analysis. The pattern of low consumption in northeastern Catalonia seen in artifact counts is confirmed in the presence-absence kriging.

These maps thus confirm indigenous interest in purchasing Cástulo cups, and lack of interest on the part of Greeks. The desire among non-Greeks, as we have seen before, was not universal but instead focused in certain areas: the southern part of the Iberian Peninsula, and, to a lesser extent, Ibero-Languedoc. The fact that the sites where large numbers of Cástulo cups were found in Andalusia and Extremadura were a 200-kilometer journey inland (or more) emphasizes the distinction between regions where consumers did and did not want these cups—the products must have passed through or by many markets where potential buyers simply did not want them.

Kraters

As described amply in Chapter 5, the krater has long been considered the vessel most representative of the Greek-style commensal banquet known as the symposion. Greeks constructed their identity in opposition to foreigners—"barbaroi"—partly by emphasizing the fact that they mixed their wine with water. The krater, as the primary locus of the action of mixing, thus became a material expression of Greek identity. In trying to understand the ways in which people far from Greece consumed Greek vessels, therefore, examination of the distribution of kraters seems to be a particularly important endeavor. In addition, the spectacular finds of bronze kraters and other vessels made for mixing at Vix and elsewhere has attracted attention and raised questions about how such shapes might have been used in non-Greek contexts (if they were not used in the same fashion that they were in Greece; see discussion of the Vix krater in Chapter 3).

Kraters were found at 55 sites in the survey area (24% of sites; N = 1648, 7% of the total), but only 18 sites had 10 or more examples (Fig. 6.14). The top five sites were Emporion (N = 549), Nissan-lez-Ensérune (246), Saint-Blaise (115), and Galera-Cerro del Real (107). The regions where these sites were located stand out for their high concentrations of kraters: Ibero-Languedoc, northeastern Catalonia, and the provinces of Jaén and Granada (**Map: Site_N_Krater**). Low levels of consumption appear in the South Hallstatt region, while some limited distribution occurred in the north, particularly at Châtillon-sur-Glâne (N = 14). In Ibero-Languedoc and northeastern Catalonia, kraters seem to be confined mostly to just a few towns: Nissan-lez-Ensérune and Montlaurès in the first case, and Emporion and Ullastret in the second case. Elsewhere, there are only a few or no examples. Kraters were more widely distributed in Jaén and Granada, as Peal de Becerro, Huelma, Hinojares, and Baeza joined Galera and Cástulo in each having more than 10 examples. There was inter- and intraregional variation in the contexts where kraters were found at various sites. At Nissan-lez-Ensérune, almost 100 kraters appeared in tombs, but none of the kraters at Montlaurès did. Likewise, at Cástulo, 80 examples (out of 81) came from tombs, while at Galera, only seven were found in tombs. Further discussion of this kind of contextual information will follow below.

Figure 6.14   Sites where kraters appeared

The significant interest in kraters in Jaén and Granada provinces is confirmed by presence-absence analysis, as this is the region where the most sites with kraters are clustered (**Map: Site_Pres_Krater**). Indeed, the maps showing the distribution of kraters are the only ones that suggest a possible connection between the eastern Andalusian interior and the southeastern coast. The interpretation of trade routes or a similar relationship between these zones still seems unlikely, however, given the intervening mountainous territory. The spread of kraters, though obviously in small numbers, as far as northern Portugal is revealed in the presence-absence map.

The distribution of kraters shows that they were rare in non-Greek contexts. A third of all examples were found at Emporion; the rest appeared almost exclusively in only three regions. Where they have been found in non-Greek areas, they are frequently not found in settlement contexts, but rather in tombs (280 examples out of 1013; 28% of the total)—a practice not carried out by Greeks. Quite often, then, we can see that native people did not want kraters, even though these vases were available throughout the full extent of the survey area. When they did buy them, they sometimes put them to new uses (and this statement assumes that they were used in the Greek fashion when they were found in settlements).

Distribution of Large Vases

In the earlier discussion of the distribution of storage vessels, the size of these vases was suggested as a possible reason for their limited spread, not only to indigenous sites, but also to Emporion. Their size would have made them, from this perspective, bulky and difficult to transport, particularly to distant areas far from waterways. It is now possible to evaluate this argument on the basis of comparison with the spread of other large vases, particularly transport amphorai and kraters. The spread of transport amphorai to North Hallstatt Europe, and the range of kraters throughout the entire survey area—although admittedly neither of these groups was present in very large numbers—would seem to suggest that size did not prevent vases from being part of long-distance trade. If we combine the numbers for all three groups (storage, transport, and kraters), there were 3657 artifacts, or 16% of all vases. While not very great, this proportion is clearly not indicative of an absence of large vases. Instead, I believe that consumer preference still remains as the best explanation for the patterns of distribution for these types.

CONTEXTUAL ANALYSIS

Only limited contextual information was recorded in the database. Few publications indicated the specific context (locus, trench, house or tomb, etc.), and the compendia of vases that were the primary sources for the database sometimes did not even identify whether the vases came from a cemetery, settlement, or sanctuary. As a result, examination of the different contexts where Greek vases were found in western Europe ought to be considered provisional.

Funerary Contexts

Greek vases were found in association with graves at 51 sites (22% of sites; N = 1974, 8% of all examples, 13% of vases for which a context is known) (Fig. 6.15, Table 6.3). A small proportion of these vases were

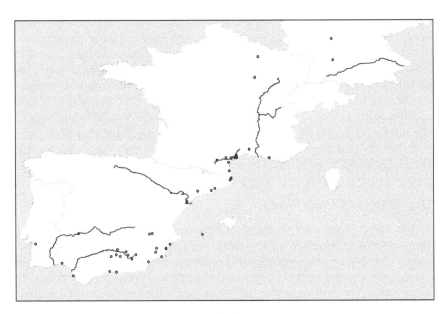

Figure 6.15   Sites where vases appeared in funerary contexts

Table 6.3   Artifact counts from 10 largest funerary contexts

Provenance site	Artifact count
Nissan-lez-Ensérune	515
Cástulo	414
Pézenas	339
Ibiza	132
Peal de Becerro	97
Emporion	85
Baza	75
Hinojares	61
Mailhac	35
Cuevas de Almanzora	28

found at Greek colonies (**Map: Sites_Cemetery_N**). At Massalia, the vases were almost exclusively lekythoi, but at Emporion, a wider range was found, including vases for drinking and eating. Strabo's report of the mixed nature of Emporion's foundation may serve to explain how vases not normally associated with funerary behavior found their way into tombs (see Chapter 3).

Only one region shows a relatively consistent spread of sites where Greek vases had a funerary function: Jaén and Granada provinces. Ibero-Languedoc seems from the kriging prediction to have a relatively high concentration of vases in graves, but in fact, the prediction is skewed by very large numbers at just two sites, Pézenas (N = 339; 100% of all vases from the site) and Nissan-lez-Ensérune (N = 515; 35% of all vases; **Map: Sites_Cemetery_Percentage**). Five other sites from this area had between one and nine vases in tombs, and one had 35 vases. The difference between these two regions is somewhat clarified by presence-absence analysis (**Map: Sites_Cemetery_Pres**). In the South Hallstatt region, only three sites had any vases in graves, and two of these were along the Hérault River. Only one of them, Agde, had more than one vase (N = 4, all dating to the seventh century, before Greeks settled the city).

Drinking vessels were by far the most prominent in tombs, forming 72% of the examples. Household vessels formed 13% of grave goods, followed by eating (8%), and storage (4%). Transport amphorai did appear in a small number of tombs, forming 1% of the total. This ranking of types was confirmed by presence-absence analysis, as drinking vessels appeared in tombs at 40 sites, household vessels at 24 sites, eating vessels at 13 sites, storage vessels at 11 sites, and transport amphorai at seven sites. These proportions may indicate that drinking formed part of the burial ritual, or that drinking as part of commensal leisured activity was connected symbolically with the afterlife (or even was considered to form a part of the deceased's activities following death). The spectacular examples of the Vix krater and the Hochdorf dinos, which do not appear in the database because they are not ceramic, may be recalled here. The outfitting of some tombs with wine in transport amphorai—or mead, as confirmed by residue analysis conducted on the dinos—also reinforces this theory.

Settlement Contexts

It would have been helpful to know which vases were found intact or broken in use levels of houses, as opposed to use levels of public contexts like monumental buildings or central open spaces, or discarded in streets, foundation trenches, fill for construction, or in refuse pits like the *koprones* found in houses on the Greek mainland (Ault 1999, Cahill 2002, Walsh 2006). Knowing which spaces held the most Greek pottery might allow connections to be made between the consumption of imports and social categories such as class or gender. Although a high level of contextual detail was reported for certain sites, such as Ullastret, Heuneburg, and Châtillon-sur-Glâne, as well as for Athenian red-figured pottery at Emporion (Miró i Alaix 2011), it was unfortunately not available for the vast majority of sites. It was, however, often possible to determine that vases were at least found within the inhabited boundaries of a town, as opposed to a cemetery. While most vases from settlement contexts were probably used in private, domestic situations, scholars have interpreted some deposits of pottery found in settlements in very different ways (e.g., as evidence for public dining or as merchandise from pottery workshops; Rotroff and Oakley 1992, Roberts and Glock 1986, 4).

Greek vases were confirmed to have been found in settlement contexts at 93 sites (40% of sites; N = 12,446, 52% of all vases, 84% of vases for which a context is known) (Fig. 6.16, Table 6.4). The imports found at many other sites may also have been found within settlements, but this could not be confirmed.[11] One large area, comprising Ibero-Languedoc and northeastern Catalonia, showed high concentrations of vases in multiple settlements (**Map: Sites_Settlement_N**). Emporion and Ullastret again were the primary consumers of imported pottery found in Catalonian settlements. In Ibero-Languedoc, Nissan-lez-Ensérune, Sigean, and Mailhac were the four sites where the most pottery was clearly found in settlements. Two isolated sites, Saint-Blaise and La Illeta dels Banyets (both of which were emporia set up by natives or with their cooperation), also showed high counts for settlement contexts. A middling amount of pottery was attributed to settlement contexts across Andalusia and southern Portugal; the important centers were the Phoenician

Table 6.4   Artifact count of vases from 10 largest settlement contexts

Provenance site	Artifact count
Saint-Blaise	4771
Emporion	3446
El Campello–La Illeta dels Banyets	954
Nissan-lez-Ensérune	948
Ullastret	739
Sigean–Pech Maho	227
Mailhac	145
Bourges	128
Châtillon-sur-Glâne	96
Málaga	87

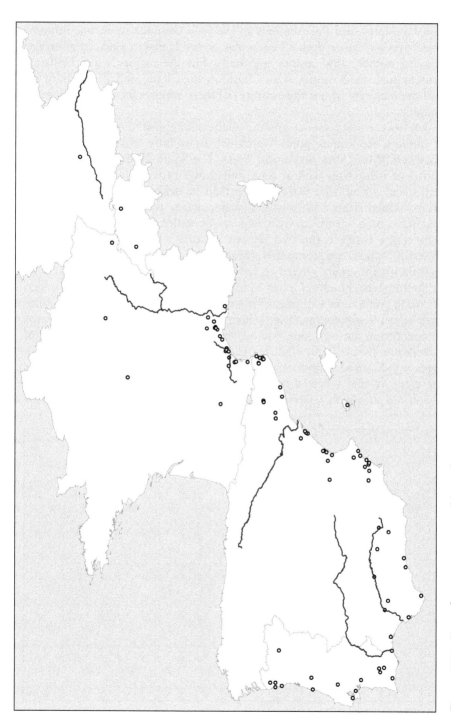

Figure 6.16   Sites where vases appeared in settlement contexts

emporia on the Costa del Sol, Huelva and Castro Marim in Tartessos, and Hinojares and Puentetablas in the Jaén/Granada area, but none of these sites had more than 87 examples. South Hallstatt sites, by contrast, showed notably low counts regionally, but the major North Hallstatt centers such as Bourges, Vix, Châtillon-sur-Glâne, and Heuneburg all had the majority (if not the entirety) of their imports found in settlement contexts.

For once, when presence-absence analysis is applied to remove the effects of outliers, the kriging predictive model shows little significant patterning anywhere (**Map: Sites_Settlement_Pres**). The South Hallstatt region had a cluster of many sites with at least some range of types (even though their settlement assemblages were smaller than in neighboring regions). There are no similar clusters in Ibero-Languedoc, where there are only a few sites that have been identified with imports in settlement contexts. A similar comparison between the two regions appears when Simpson's Index of Diversity scores are computed (**Map: Sites_Settlement_SDI**). Sites that showed high diversity tended to have relatively small artifact counts, such as Pontos, Elne, Huelva, Castro Marim, and Almôdovar. There is little sign of strong preferences with regard to vessel functions at these locations. Sites with higher vessel counts in settlement contexts, on the other hand, tended to concentrate on only one type of vessel. Examples of this phenomenon include Hinojares (0.13), Mailhac (0.20), Ullastret (0.24), Saint-Blaise (0.26), Sigean (0.27), and Emporion (0.31). In each of these cases, drinking was the category that received special emphasis. Only in the North Hallstatt region did sites with relatively large counts of vases in settlement contexts

Figure 6.17   Sites where vases appeared in sanctuary contexts

also have somewhat higher index scores, such as Châtillon-sur-Glâne (0.52) and Bourges (0.59).

Sanctuary Context

Sanctuaries were specifically identified at only six sites in the corpus: Cancho Roano, Huelva, La Illeta dels Banyets, Ourique, Santuario de la Luz, and Gaujac (Fig. 6.17). Cancho Roano's function seems to have been primarily religious (although it may also have been a center of regional administration), and it preserved an enormous quantity of Greek pottery. The other sites, though, only had between one and eight vessels preserved. No regional patterns can be distinguished from this small sample, but drinking vessels were the most frequent at most sites besides Ourique (where two vessels had unknown functions) and La Illeta dels Banyets (where there were four eating vessels and three for drinking).

NOTES

1. This basic analysis was carried out partly by the author and partly by statistician Robert Fornango as part of a preliminary consultation. All other analyses, including the kriging, were carried out entirely by the author.
2. Pronounced "KREEG-ing," the method is named for its inventor, the geostatistician Danie Krige.
3. To turn individual layers on or off in Adobe Reader XI, click the Layer button in the Navigation Pane (on the left side of the application window) and select the desired layer(s) by clicking the "eye" symbol next to each one. The Layer function can also be selected from the menu at the top of screen by selecting the following options in order: View > Show/Hide > Navigation Panes > Layers. Mobile versions of Adobe Reader such as those for tablets and phones do not yet support multiple layers. In these environments, the entire map may be viewed because all the layers are shown, but they cannot be turned on or off.
4. The bright orange colors predicted by the kriging model for central Spain must be disregarded as a function of the very high quantity of artifacts at Cancho Roano combined with the low values and sparse arrangement of other sites in the area (note particularly the standard error contour lines, which demonstrate lower levels of confidence).
5. These sites had 533, 165, and 380 artifacts, respectively, for the fourth century as a whole.
6. These results are notwithstanding the very unlikely prediction of hundreds or thousands of drinking vessels for the area around Uetliberg in Switzerland and Heuneburg in Germany, where the actual counts were one and 14, respectively.
7. To this pair could be added Vix, with a score of 0.73.
8. Although both Baza and Galera are located on a high plateau between the steepest parts of the Sierra Nevada and the Sierra de Segura, and thus are relatively open to transit from the southeast coast, the similarity in the pattern of consumption to sites like Cástulo that are closer to the Guadalquivir seems to argue for trade coming upstream from the west instead (even on foot, since the rivers were apparently not easily navigable beyond Córdoba (see Chapter 2).

9. These examples, uncertainly identified as West Greek bowls, were not given a date by the excavators (Augier et al. 2007).

10. Villard (1959) first drew attention to the shape in his publication of a necropolis at Cherchel in Algeria.

11. These numbers do not include any vases from Massalia, for example, because even where the excavation site was named in the relevant publication (Villard 1959), the type of context was not explicitly indicated (apart from a few objects stated to have been found in tombs). Most of the 3360 vases recorded by Villard were probably from settlement contexts.

7 Interpreting the Evidence
Consumerism, Signaling, and Identity

At this point, it is worth reiterating how the distributions of Greek pottery described above can lead us to an understanding of consumer preference and identity construction in the ancient world. Beginning from what statisticians call a null hypothesis, we might expect to find that the distribution of vases was random, without organization, and unaffected by any external factor such as location, cost, vessel shape or size, or desire. This randomness would persist at all levels of the distribution, from the quantity of vases, to their types, to their places of origin, and so on. Testing of the null hypothesis shows it is not correct; there are many nonrandom patterns that can be identified, and there are significant differences between the distributions of various kinds of vases in different places across western Europe.

What features of the pottery or the people who bought it can explain the patterns? We might choose to suggest that the availability of different types in different locations was a primary factor causing the appearance of trends. Yet it is difficult to say that the Ibero-Languedocians had access to a significantly different range of goods than their South Hallstatt neighbors to the east, particularly since the two regions were bounded by Greek colonies that were founded within 50 years of one another. It is particularly telling that Emporion apparently failed to be a conduit of Greek vases to its own close neighbors, apart from Ullastret (Cabrera Bonet 2000, 313–314). In areas farther south, far from Greek settlements (at least, those that can be identified archaeologically), one could point to the lower levels of consumption in the Iberian Peninsula south of Barcelona, continuing along the coast to Portugal as an example of lower availability of Greek pottery. Perhaps, in our new hypothesis, Phoenicians blocked Greek merchants from traveling beyond their emporia on the Costa del Sol, especially after the Battle of Alalia. Yet this theory also cannot be completely true; many Greek vases arrived at Huelva early on, at Cancho Roano in the fifth century, and at Cástulo and its neighbors in the fifth and fourth centuries. Likewise, the presence of Greek vases at North Hallstatt sites in the second half of the sixth century and first half of the fifth, occasionally in significant numbers, shows that it was theoretically possible for them to arrive there at any time—but instead, they were not consumed there in any other time period but that one.

The only explanation that remains is that people made purposeful selections from an array of available choices. This is not to say that all types were available everywhere in every period, but rather that variations that can be spotted between consumption in different regions (especially neighboring regions) at the same time are indeed significant signs of consumers making choices, selecting some types and rejecting others. Absence can be as important to track as presence, since we can be certain from the preserved evidence that ancient merchants would travel to serve a demand if it existed, regardless of distance (Blomqvist 1979, Lacroix 1998). A low number of Greek vases in areas that did receive them therefore probably indicates a general lack of interest in them on the part of local consumers.

SIMILARITIES AND DIFFERENCES

It is now possible to draw some more solid conclusions about regional variation in the consumption of Greek pottery across the western Mediterranean and trans-Alpine Europe between 800 and 300 BCE. The ability to compare sites and regions visually while also taking relevant geographic features into consideration that is provided by the kriging tool has been particularly useful, since it is likely that the process of making distinctions between distributions in Ibero-Languedoc and the South Hallstatt region (for example) would have been quite difficult had the data only been available as a spreadsheet. The inclusion of even relatively coarse contextual information also allows some understandings to be formed about how Greek vases were used in foreign environments.

It is clear that no site in the survey (apart from the Greek colonies and Saint-Blaise) revealed enough examples of every type of Greek vase for an argument to be made that natives gave up their own foodways and became fully or even mostly Hellenized. Similarly, there is no sign of symposia or even pseudosympotic behavior in any non-Greek region.[1]

In the South Hallstatt region, closest to Massalia, and with plentiful access to the entire range of Greek pottery, consumers bought relatively few vases compared to their neighbors and showed no particular preferences for any shape beyond the drinking vessels that were also consumed everywhere else in the survey and transport amphorai. They tended to buy more types of Greek pottery than any other group in this survey, but they spread their purchases evenly across those types. This pattern of distribution was visible, not only at a few major centers, but was also seen at many sites across that region. Ibero-Languedocians, Iberians around Jaén and Granada, and Greeks themselves all bought much more Greek pottery, if the numbers derived from artifact counts can be believed. Despite the unimpressive consumption of Greek pottery, however, Greek wine seems to have been of significant interest for Hallstatt people along the Mediterranean coast. Yet it is difficult to say that consumption practices in this region mirrored the Greek model of the symposion, particularly since importation of kraters was so meager. Although it is perhaps surprising given the presence of Massalia (and later Agathe), Greek influence on behavior has to be marked as "mixed" at most in this region. Presumably the features of Greek pottery that interested these consumers were not related to specific shapes, but maybe to their unusual decoration.

Ibero-Languedocian contrasts with South Hallstatt sites were clear in almost every examination of the data. This region was also completely within the orbit of Greek traders from Emporion and Massalia, and presumably Greek pottery was equally available here as it was in the colonies or to the east of the Hérault River. Much more pottery was found in Ibero-Languedoc, but it represented a smaller range of shapes and a less even distribution of individual vases across functional types. Moreover, not all Ibero-Languedocian sites participated in the consumption of Greek pottery to the same intensive extent. Instead, distribution was centered on five or six towns, mostly north of the Aude River, while other towns were only involved in the consumption of Greek vases at a marginal level, if at all. In addition, at some of the larger sites, Greek vases were used—either exclusively or occasionally—as grave goods, especially drinking and eating vessels. Finally, the relative absence of transport amphorai potentially signals very different uses for the very high number of drinking vessels (especially cups) besides the drinking of wine.

The distribution of Greek pottery in the Iberian Peninsula was highly variable. In Catalonia, there were essentially only two settlements where Greek vessels were consumed in any significant quantities: Emporion and Ullastret. The very large amount of pottery found in all categories at Emporion confirms that Greeks continued to practice their own foodways, even when at a remove from other Greeks. The presence of almost 550 kraters, more than at any other site, also indicates strong local interest in mixing wine, and probably in sympotic activity (a point reinforced by the "hēdukoitos" mosaic inscription described in Chapter 3). There does not seem to have been a significant fine ware pottery industry at Emporion (although certainly Ionian cups may have been made here, as elsewhere in the western Mediterranean), so the majority of items intended for public display and use must have been imported. It is clear from Ullastret's size and development that it was an important Iberian regional center, but its domination of local indigenous consumption of imported pottery is over-whelming. Hardly any Greek vases have been reported from other sites close to these two, and the numbers are even lower in the interior and to the south (including along the coast). Ullastret consumed large numbers of drinking vases, including many kraters, as well as some transport amphorai, but not many eating or household vessels.

The fact, noted several times in the analysis, that Iberians along the east coast showed almost no interest in Greek products, combined with a paucity of evidence for Greek settlements, or even influence, beyond Emporion, raises questions about what the colony's *raison d'être* was, and whether it achieved the goals that were the cause of its foundation. Emporion was a success in the sense that it survived, and even thrived for many centuries, but its success also seems to have been constrained, particularly in the extent to which the town was able to create new markets for Greek goods. Cabrera Bonet (2000, 313–314) has already drawn attention to some of these problems. The difficulties faced by Greek traders who wanted to compete with Etruscans and especially Phoenicians were described in Chapter 2. Although there is some literary evidence for other Greek settlements in Iberia, perhaps even in the south, such evidence is not strongly confirmed by archaeology. Even if we accept that Mainake was a Greek emporion situated alongside a Phoenician one at Cerro del Villar (Aubet 2005), that town was temporary and ultimately even less successful than Emporion, since it was clearly abandoned, as Strabo reported. The view of demand presented in this study for Greek products in Iberia shows that interest was so much lower there—especially in non-Phoenician contexts early on—than it was north of the Pyrenees that there was, in fact, no need for more Greek settlements, especially emporia. Only the province of Jaén and the interior of Granada showed a higher level of demand, although they did not begin consuming Greek pottery until around the middle of the fifth century, after Greeks had stopped their colonial expansion in Iberia. In any case, these settlements were so far from Emporion along the coast and then up the Guadalquivir valley that it is difficult to attribute their interest in Greek products to the effect of Emporion. So what was Emporion's function? Cabrera Bonet has suggested that the colony was primarily a center for redistribution, but it is not clear what products it offered that natives wanted. This problem remains unanswered.

There was one significant exception to the limited quantities of Greek pottery found on the southeastern and southern coasts of Iberia: the emporion at La Illeta dels Banyets. At this site alone were Greek vases acquired in large numbers and across all types, with particular interest given not only to drinking but also to eating. When Greek vases appeared at other coastal sites, whether Iberian, Phoenician, or Tartessian, they were almost as rare as along the east coast. The same pattern holds true for Portugal. In these areas, imports truly take on the appearance of unusual or special luxuries, limited editions or one-of-a-kind pieces whose value was much more for display than for their utilitarian design. It is difficult to know the extent to which wine was consumed in these regions, although the lack of transport amphorai is not necessarily significant—as already noted, wine was introduced by Phoenicians at an early date, and Iberians did produce their own wine from the seventh century onward. There is no direct evidence, however, that practices involving Greek pottery in these regions had any relationship with Greek cultural traditions. It is clear that Greek vases were sometimes given funerary significance, as happened around

Cástulo, in addition to whatever uses they were put prior to burial. Sites where Greek pottery was found in graves tended to have it in abundance, and it was used in many, rather than only a few tombs. The only reason to believe that vases might have also maintained their basic functions—that is, that vessels intended for drinking in Greece were also used for drinking in the southern and western Iberian Peninsula, even if the beverage consumed or the style of drinking might have been different—is the fact that the proportions of functional types that were found here in the south and west of the Iberian Peninsula were broadly similar to those found at sites in other regions of the survey area, including the Greek colonies. Even this suggestion is admittedly circumstantial and relies heavily on assumptions about broad similarities between western European cultures.

In the North Hallstatt region, there are signs that commensal banqueting was the primary arena for the use of Greek vases, and the proportions of functional types—almost exclusively for drinking, with some consumption of transport amphorai—underlines that usage. They were found associated with monumental architecture in settlement contexts at Vix and Heuneburg. Secondarily, Greek vases were appropriate grave goods in tombs belonging to members of the very highest levels of society, but not in other kinds of graves. These patterns suggest the very limited scope of consumption in this region, and the significance specifically attributed to Greek pottery and wine as a marker of elite status.[2]

CONSUMPTION AND FEASTING

As is perhaps painfully clear by now, people use pottery for eating and drinking, among other activities; the range of shapes identified in Greek pottery shows that these were the most common functions to which it was put in their home context. Analysis of evidence from shipwrecks from the western Mediterranean has led to the argument that indigenous people, especially around the south of France, really only wanted wine and Greek drinking vessels, and were indifferent to other types of pottery (Dietler 2010, 133–135). In many respects this analysis supports that claim, and even broadens it to the other regions included in the dataset. What remains to be determined is why drinking vessels and wine were important, how they fit into indigenous societies, and whether any other conclusions can be drawn about the consumption of Greek pottery.

In addition to Dietler's work on the consumption of foreign goods in southern France, he has also made efforts to understand the social and cultural significance of feasting, which he has connected directly to community-wide status competitions. He defined three categories of commensalism: empowering feasts, in which hosts attempt to demonstrate their ability to hold higher-status roles by holding elaborate feasts for the community; patron-role feasts, which are provided by high-status hosts to lower-status guests, often to acknowledge labor provided by the guests in fulfillment of their social obligations; and diacritical feasts, which are not open for participation by all members of the community, but only to high-status individuals (Dietler 2001, 75–88). In the first two kinds of feasting, reciprocity is the focus of activity, either as a way to take part in a status competition or to reinforce existing hierarchies. The political function of diacritical feasts, on the other hand, has nothing to do with reciprocity, but instead is to mark out elites as separate from other members of the community.[3] This is accomplished not only through their participation in an exclusive event, but is also emphasized by the use of specialized equipment and by the consumption of special foods and drink.

In the South Hallstatt region, around the mouth of the Rhône, Dietler argued that wine was introduced to the local indigenous population along with sympotic equipment by Greeks, which "initiated an escalation of social competition centered around . . . feasting" (1996, 112). Additionally, the coastal location of the region meant that contact with shipborne merchants could not be controlled as effectively by local elites. Wine and equipment became available to a wider cross-section of society than just the elites because contact between the general population and traders was more frequent. Dietler especially saw the introduction of local imitations of Greek pottery as a sign that elites were not the only participants in competitive feasting.[4] Members of other classes were thus involved in the same kinds of commensal hospitality as elites, hoping to achieve gains in status in the process. In other words, people living at the mouth of the Rhône participated in empowering feasts, according to Dietler's schema.[5]

In northern and central Europe, only certain members of the Hallstatt culture received Greek objects and a small amount of wine through trade—not enough for it to be redistributed widely. Competition between elites in Hallstatt settlements was based on the display of imports at feasts. Notably, both men and women were buried with large assemblages of drinking equipment, as at Vix. Elites had monopolistic access to Greek imports that allowed them to use those objects as an identification and confirmation of their high status. North Hallstatt consumption and use of Greek pottery was thus suggested by Dietler to fit the category of diacritical feasting (1996, 112).

It should be noted that ancient literary sources for feasting in Celtic regions, for whatever they are worth—the lack of geographic or chronological specificity in the texts makes it particularly difficult to know how to apply them to this region and period—are mixed at best with respect to supporting Dietler's identification of diacritical feasting practices at North Hallstatt sites. On the one hand, elites and common people are described as drinking separately, in different ways (a common cup versus individual cups), using different kinds of equipment, and imbibing different beverages (Athenaios 4.151e–152d). On the other hand, regional leaders sometimes set up massive feasts in multiple locations to serve all comers (Athenaios

4.150d–f), which seems to fit the mold of patron-role feasts better. It was also apparently common for fights to break out within groups of elites over status (in the previously cited passage and Athenaios 4.154d), behavior that does not correlate neatly with any of Dietler's three modes of feasting.

WASTEFUL ADVERTISING

As useful as Dietler's framework is—and it can certainly be seen as an important effort to categorize feasts so that they might be better understood—there are certain aspects of pottery consumption and status that are not fully elucidated by it. Some kinds of feasts are, of course, not included in the list of types, while others might incorporate aspects of several types at once.[6] It also remains unclear precisely how the use of specialized equipment might have been related to status in antiquity. More importantly, we have seen from the presence of Greek vases in non-Greek contexts that are not directly related to feasting—burials and sanctuaries— that they were not only used for commensal functions. These other functions also need to be incorporated into our understanding.

During the description of this study's theoretical approach in Chapter 4, I suggested that a Darwinian understanding of wasteful advertising (also known as costly signaling) as a strategy that improves or reinforces individuals' evolutionary fitness might be a useful way of interpreting the consumption of luxury goods. I have already posited the identification of Greek pottery as a luxury due to the efforts and costs associated with its transport, and the interest of non-Greeks in obtaining authentic versions. An assumption underpinning my use of wasteful advertising theory here is that Greek pottery was bought and used in arenas of public display. Only in that way could members of the community see it and recognize it as a luxury representing greater fitness on the part of the owner/user, and attribute status to him or her as a result. This assumption relies in part on the distinctive visual features of Greek pottery in western Europe, including its decoration and the range of shapes, which were different from locally produced wares. These features would have allowed ancient consumers to attribute codified meanings to Greek pottery easily. Such meanings were locally determined and so varied from place to place, but they almost certainly were related to higher status, given the cost and relative rarity of Greek pottery in non-Greek contexts. Even though imitations of Greek pottery existed in some (but not all) of the regions studied here, these varied in their slavishness to the originals and in any case can be differentiated visually from authentic Greek products fairly easily today. It can be assumed that ancient consumers were equally well attuned to these distinctions, too.

To summarize the explanation of wasteful advertising offered earlier, according to biologists' formulation of the theory, there are three primary factors at play in determining the extent to which members of a community engaged in the practice. First, there is the competitive ability of the worst advertiser; second, the amount of variance in competitive ability; and third, the value to be gained from advertising (Neiman 1997, 270, Boone 2000, 84–89). When the worst advertiser can hardly participate in the contest, or there is little variance among competitors, or there is little or no value to be gained from competing, there will be little evidence of wasteful advertising. Conversely, if even the lowest-status competitor is able to make some effort, or if there is a wide range of participants, or much at stake for competitors, wasteful advertising can be an extraordinarily useful strategy for defining status. Moreover, honesty in advertising is enforced by the competition, because higher-status (i.e., fitter, evolutionarily speaking, within the community) individuals can always advertise at a level beyond those with lower status, and if lower status individuals advertise at too high a cost, they will not be able to support themselves or their dependents. At the same time, community members must be able to accurately assess the meaning of the advertising signal for wasteful advertising to be a useful strategy.

How, then, can regional or local patterns of consumption of Greek pottery reflect status competitions carried out through wasteful advertising? Comparison of the two Hallstatt regions can be illuminating. Consumption of Greek pottery in the north was extremely limited. In this area, only a small number of people received any, and what they received consisted almost entirely of drinking vessels and transport amphorai. These facts indicate the importance of these vases to feasting, but the funerary context in which many examples were found is also worth noting. The fact that so great a proportion of the few drinking vessels that were imported were deposited in elite tombs (some of the burials quite spectacular) hints at how special these vases were perceived to be. Further, including Greek vases among grave goods seems to bind those vases tightly to the deceased as their owners, and reinforce the connection between an individual person, their identity, and these special vase(s). In this case, Dietler's diacritical feasting category does seem particularly apt, with regard both to equipment and to food.

In the south, Greek table wares were widely consumed, as we have seen, but at a low level relative to its availability, while no strong preferences for particular shapes were manifest, apart from the function of drinking. Such a pattern indicates that Greek pottery was not an important vector for signaling status in this area, perhaps because there was a more equal distribution of power across the region, as suggested by Dietler in his labeling of feasts in this area as "empowering." The homogeneous but relatively low distribution probably shows that South Hallstatt elites participated in region-wide status competitions that were carried out partly through the display of varied and somewhat small sets of luxurious imported Greek pottery. Such displays could have included the consumption of wine, perhaps unmixed, and probably not served from a communal storage vase, since kraters were not common. The high consumption of Massaliote wine, however, might show that access to the beverage was a more important marker of status than the display of pottery.[7] A third possibility—if we follow Boone's definition of social status as an attributed identity—is that in South Hallstatt communities, consumers bought Greek pottery for what it meant to them personally, making an individuated, rather than a codified, identification with it instead.

Continuing in this vein, we can examine Ibero-Languedoc, where very large quantities of Greek pottery were concentrated in a small number of places, and there were stronger preferences for certain types and shapes. Between the Hérault and Aude rivers especially, individuals wanted Greek vases, and they wanted certain types more than others; wine received less interest in this region. The vases were mostly used in domestic settings, but occasionally also as grave goods. In the five major centers of consumption, Greek pottery was highly desirable, and its value as an object of display (perhaps especially for particular shapes that had been locally identified as interesting or useful) within those communities must accordingly have been high. This pattern seems to show that status competitions may have been local rather than regional, with Greek vases being put to different purposes in different towns. Those uses seem to have involved much stronger preferences for specific types or shapes than at South Hallstatt sites. Furthermore, the fact that many smaller Ibero-Languedocian towns were not big consumers of Greek pottery could be seen as an indication of great stratification between settlements, with luxuries monopolized by inhabitants of politically important communities where status competitions were fiercer. Similar patterns might also be visible at Ullastret and around Cástulo. In the latter area, once the mining of metal brought wealth to the area in the fifth century, consumption of Greek pottery took off. In this case (pending the excavation of more settlement contexts), it appears that public display might have been particularly effective during burial rituals as vases were deposited by the decedents' survivors in tombs.

The presence of only a small number of vases or a limited range of shapes is not enough on its own to suggest the importance of Greek vases in diacritical feasting. At Portuguese sites, overall consumption was even more limited than in northern France and central Europe, and there were hardly any transport amphorai reported, so there is little clear connection to feasting. The contexts in which the vases were found are likewise equivocal regarding their importance for commensal banqueting, as opposed to private dining. The fact that Greek vases were consumed at all does suggest that they were seen to have some value for display, but there might have been little variability within the community, or a particularly low level of competitive ability associated with the lowest-status members. For these reasons, Greek pottery was little more than a novelty in the western Iberian Peninsula.

In Tartessos, the period of greatest local wealth did not coincide with high availability of Greek pottery. In the seventh and early sixth centuries, when the mines of the area flourished, Phoenician imports were more readily available than Greek ones in this area, since the closest Greek cities were in Italy and Sicily. The example of Cancho Roano is intriguing, though, not only for its later date, but because it shows very high demand for just one subtype of Greek pottery, the Cástulo cup, to the exclusion of others. The overwhelming predominance of this shape in a ritual sphere (where feasting may also have occurred) suggests that it almost became a rule associated with worship here to offer one or several Cástulo cups. In this case, access to a source for Cástulo cups, and not to just any Greek pottery, enabled a community member to have access to the palace-sanctuary and participate in activities here according to established etiquette. This, too, is wasteful advertising, although of a different kind than we have seen before.

CONCLUSION

This study has shown how the use of an admittedly complex but nonetheless robust system of theory can clarify the appearance of imported goods in different ancient societies. Ancient people may not have been wholly conscious of themselves as consumers, but they acted in ways that suggest similarities with certain aspects of consumerism. These actions are visible to us in the presence of the objects found through excavation, especially imported goods, which do not qualify as necessities for sustaining life. Regional variations in distribution patterns of imports demonstrate the agency of consumers to make choices. These goods, which were luxury items in foreign contexts, were acquired and used by local consumers because they could signal positive information about their owners to the surrounding community. As spectators saw the imports on display in domestic, religious, or funerary environments, they understood that the person who displayed them had expendable resources, access to (relatively) unusual or rare items, the taste to select the ones that were locally meaningful, and the knowledge of how to use them in locally appropriate ways. As a result, they attributed an identity of high status to the owners of imports. Likewise, consumers who bought imports were attempting to create a self-identity that included membership in an elite group of people. The display of imports in public arenas depended entirely on the limitations constraining wasteful advertising in the local community—the ability of low-level individuals to participate, the range of ability across all competitors, and the potential value (status) that could be gained by signaling. In areas where even low-status individuals could participate (likely when availability of luxury goods was high), wealth was broadly distributed, and status rewards for display of luxury goods were high, more luxury goods were purchased. Such a system is perhaps similar to the pattern seen for Greek colonies. In these contexts, as at Massalia and Emporion, Greek vases from other centers were different, and therefore special. Their high availability might appear to have limited their ability to signal something important about consumers, but the extremely high consumption of Athenian vases in the fifth and fourth centuries at Emporion (N = 3630 for red-figured vases alone) shows that this was not the case (but compare with discussion of South Hallstatt sites below). Greek pottery seems to have served a similar, if less intense, role in Ibero-Languedoc and, in the fifth and fourth centuries, in eastern Andalusia near Cástulo.

In areas where only high-status individuals were able to procure luxury goods, there was little variability in status among individuals, and there was little reward for display of luxuries, few were purchased. There are few examples of unstratified societies in the Western world today, though one might point to 20th-century communist societies as possible illustrations of this pattern. In ancient western Europe, eastern Iberia and Portugal seem to be good examples of persistent low consumption and low value for wasteful advertising using Greek pottery. The two Hallstatt regions, Phoenician emporia, and Tartessos show mixed patterns. North Hallstatt sites had low consumption, apparently because there was a wide gulf between elites and other members of the community. Greek pottery still had display value, but only within a limited group. It is highly interesting that Greek vases seem to have lost their ability to send positive signals about their owners around the time of the transition from the Hallstatt culture to the La Téne culture, circa 450. Tartessos and the Phoenician emporia may be examples of similar phenomena in an earlier period. The South Hallstatt region showed low consumption compared to its neighbors, but medium consumption relative to all the groups in the survey. In this case, the value that could be gained from display of Greek pottery must have been somewhat limited, perhaps as a result of its easy availability from Massalia via Saint-Blaise, or, as mentioned earlier, because the drinking of wine had a higher display value than the vessels used for drinking in this region.[8]

Much future work remains to be done in this area—mapping the consumption of other kinds of luxury goods in these regions during the same period, or in the preceding or succeeding periods, or of Greek pottery in other parts of the Mediterranean and beyond, would present the possibility for comparison with these results and confirmation or rejection of them. Such evaluations would be of enormous help in advancing archaeologists' understanding of costly signaling, consumption, and identity in the ancient world.

NOTES

1. This point was already made by Dietler (1996, 112) with regard to the south of France, criticizing Bouloumié (1988).
2. Arnold (1995, 50) has argued that only spectacular imports like the Vix krater seem linked to very high status in both Late Hallstatt and Early La Téne burial contexts; imported metal vases (especially Etruscan or local imitations of Etruscan bronze situlae) appeared in a broader range of burials.

3. Miller (2011) has used Dietler's categorization of diacritical feasting to understand Persian drinking practices.
4. Unlike the imitations of Greek pottery that were made in Sicily and the south of Italy, which copied decorations and shapes simultaneously (and thus can be considered true counterfeits), potters who made imitations in France only incorporated certain elements (i.e., either decoration or shapes, but generally not both) into otherwise local vases.
5. Dietler called this type of feast "entrepreneurial" in his initial work on the subject (1996, 114–115), which is described here, but he later altered it to "empowering" in order to avoid modern economic overtones (2001, 76).
6. Dietler does acknowledge the possibility or even likelihood of a single society using more than one kind of feast, but he is not so clear about the mixing of types (2001, 93–94).
7. Contrast this observation with Bettina Arnold's very similar statement for North Hallstatt consumption of pottery and wine (1999).
8. Note that it is possible to say that high availability could be a reason for Greek pottery having a low display value in South Hallstatt sites but not in Greek colonies, not only because their levels of consumption differed, but also because the meanings of objects are always locally determined.

Appendix

Sites and counts of artifacts by function

"Site total" counts include artifacts whose function could not be identified

Site	Drinking	Eating	Household	Storage	Transport	Function subtotal	Site total
Adra	1	0	1	0	0	2	3
Agde	4	0	0	0	0	4	4
Agen	1	0	0	0	0	1	1
Alarcos	2	0	0	0	0	2	3
Albas	1	0	0	0	3	4	5
Alcácer do Sal	20	8	1	3	0	32	33
Alcáçova de Santarém	2	0	0	0	0	2	2
Alcala de Chivert	1	0	0	0	0	1	1
Alcantarilla	1	0	0	0	0	1	1
Alcoutim	0	0	0	0	0	0	2
Alcoy	2	0	0	0	0	2	3
Algarrobo	4	0	0	0	1	5	5
Algeciras	1	0	0	0	0	1	1
Alicante	2	0	0	0	0	2	2
Aljaraque	0	0	0	2		2	2
Almada	2	0	0	0	0	2	2
Almassora	0	0	0	0	0	0	1
Almodôvar	2	1	0	0	1	4	4
Almodovar del Campo	1	0	0	0	0	1	1
Amposta	1	0	0	0	0	1	1

(*Continued*)

Site	Drinking	Eating	Household	Storage	Transport	Function subtotal	Site total
Ampurias	3532	209	336	117	32	4226	4307
Arbeca	1	1	0	0	0	2	2
Archena	3	0	0	0	0	3	3
Argeles-sur-Mer	2	0	0	0	0	2	2
Asperg	2	0	0	0	0	2	2
Aumes	20	2	0	0	1	23	29
Baeza	4	1	0	0	0	5	5
Banyeres	3	0	0	0	0	3	3
Barcelona	0	0	0	0	0	0	1
Barcelos	1	0	0	0	0	1	1
Baza	32	40	3	0	0	75	75
Beaucaire	11	0	0	1	84	96	98
Beaujeu-Saint-Vallier-Pierrejux-et-Quitteur	1	0	0	0	0	1	1
Beja	0	0	0	0	0	0	1
Bellcaire d'Emporda	0	0	1	0	0	1	1
Benahadux	4	0	0	0	0	4	4
Benicarlo	4	0	0	0	5	9	12
Bessan	637	60	12	14	6	729	736
Béziers	464	77	36	4	0	581	703
Bopfingen	4	0	0	0	0	4	4
Borriol	1	0	0	0	0	1	1
Bourges	49	4	3	3	53	112	128
Bragny-sur-Saône	2	0	0	0	0	2	3
Breisach	4	0	1	1	0	6	7
Cabanes	2	0	0	0	0	2	2
Cabrera de Mar	3	0	0	0	1	4	4
Cadiz	3	0	0	0	3	6	6
Calaceite	4	0	0	0	0	4	4
Calafell	12	0	0	0	6	18	18
Calvisson	26	8	2	1	6	43	43
Carcassonne	7	4	0	1	1	13	15
Carmona	1	0	0	0	3	4	5
Cartagena	5	0	0	0	0	5	5

Site	Drinking	Eating	Household	Storage	Transport	Function subtotal	Site total
Casillas de Martos	2	0	0	0	0	2	2
Castelnau-le-Lez - Sextantio/ Substantion	32	6	0	2	1	41	44
Castelo de Serpa	0	0	0	0	0	0	1
Castel-Rousillon	589	36	10	4	0	639	639
Castro Marim	22	19	2		0	43	48
Castro Verde	1	0	0	0	0	1	1
Castulo	373	30	4	7	0	414	414
Caudete de las Fuentes	3	0	0	0	0	3	3
Cerdanyola del Valles	4	0	0	0	0	4	4
Cerro Furado	1	0	0	0	0	1	1
Chassey-le-Camp	3	0	0	0	0	3	4
Châtillon-sur-Glâne	34	0	0	2	47	83	96
Chinchilla	1	0	2	0	0	3	3
Ciutadilla	1	0	0	0	0	1	1
Clermont-Dessous	2	0	0	0	0	2	2
Collias	3	1	0	0	2	6	9
Collioure	19	8	1	1	0	29	30
Conimbriga	1	0	0	0	0	1	1
Córdoba	1	0	0	0	0	1	1
Coria del Rio	0	0	1	1	1	3	3
Couffoulens	8	1	0	0	0	9	9
Cox	2	0	0	0	0	2	2
Crevillente	0	0	2	0	0	2	2
Cuevas de Almanzora	13	4	10	2	0	29	29
Damerey	1	0	0	0	0	1	1
Durban-Corbières	25	3	0	1	2	31	43
El Brull	0	0	0	0	0	0	1
El Campello	277	653	9	1	0	940	962

(*Continued*)

Site	Drinking	Eating	Household	Storage	Transport	Function subtotal	Site total
El Carambolo	2	0	0	0	0	2	2
El Castell – Almenara	1	0	0	0	0	1	1
El Puerto de Santa Maria	3	0	0	0	7	10	10
Elche	2	0	0	0	2	4	4
Elne	144	32	5	3		184	186
Ermedas	0	0	0		3	3	3
Escacena del Campo	0	0	0	1	0	1	1
Esposende	1	0	0	0	0	1	1
Fabregues	17	3	0	1	0	21	21
Facha	5	0	0	2	0	7	30
Faro	1	0	0	0	0	1	1
Figueira da Foz	1	0	0	0	0	1	2
Florensac	13	2	0	0	1	16	16
Fortuna	1	0	0	0	0	1	1
Fuengirola	2	0	0	0	0	2	2
Gailhan	6	0	0	0	1	7	7
Galera	134	20	0	10	0	164	164
Gandesa	1	0	0	0	0	1	1
Gaujac	21	0	0	0	1	22	22
Granada	2	0	0	0	0	2	2
Guadalhorce	47	1	1	10	9	68	74
Guardamar del Segura	9	1	1	0	5	16	17
Heuneburg	14		1	0	57	72	74
Hinojares	92	9	2	1	0	104	105
Hochdorf	1	0	0	0	0	1	1
Hoya Gonzalo	0	0	3	0	0	3	3
Huelma	46	3		1	0	50	50
Huelva	205	32	39	25	49	350	395
Ibiza	6	8	125	0	1	140	140
Illfurth	6	0	0	0	1	7	7
Ivorra	1	0	0	0	0	1	1
La Guardia	2	1	0	0	0	3	4
La Palma	0	0	1	0	0	1	1

Site	Drinking	Eating	Household	Storage	Transport	Function subtotal	Site total
La Rinconada	0	1	0	0	4	5	5
Lagos	2	0	0	0	0	2	2
L'Escala	0	0	1	0	0	1	1
Librilla	0	0	0	0	1	1	1
Lisbon	1	0	0	0	0	1	1
Lliria	2	0	1	0	0	3	3
Magalas	23	2	0	0	4	29	30
Mailhac	145	14	4	7	4	174	180
Málaga	44	5	5	4	27	85	87
Manresa	0	0	1	0	0	1	1
Marbella	1	0	0	0	0	1	1
Marguerittes	4	0	0	0	6	10	10
Maria	0	0	0	0	0	0	1
Marseille – Massalia	1518	904	119	638	115	3294	3360
Medellín	2	0	1	0	0	3	3
Mengibar	12	3	0	0	0	15	15
Menorca	0	0	0	0	1	1	1
Mertola	6	0	0	0	0	6	6
Mèze	40	7	0	0	0	47	47
Milmanda	0		1	0	0	1	1
Mirador de Rolando	1	0	0	0	0	1	1
Mogente	1	1	0	1	0	3	3
Moncada	1	0	0	0	1	2	2
Mons-et-Monteils	9	3	0	0	1	13	13
Mont Lassois	27	0	0	9	0	36	57
Monteagudo	1	0	0	0	0	1	1
Montfaucon	2	1	0	1	1	5	7
Montlaurès	892	61	22	5	2	982	985
Moura	10	0	0	0	0	10	10
Mourèze	1	0	0	1	0	2	3
Moux	0	0	0	0	2	2	2
Murça	1	0	0	0	0	1	1
Nîmes	11	1	0	2	10	24	27
Nissan-lez-Ensérune	1320	121	9	5	1	1456	1463
Olèrdola	28	30	0	2	0	60	60

(*Continued*)

Site	Drinking	Eating	Household	Storage	Transport	Function subtotal	Site total
Olius	2	0	0	0	0	2	2
Orihuela	3	0	0	0	0	3	3
Ourique	1	0	0	0	0	1	4
Ouveillan	6	7	0	2	0	15	15
Palenzuela	0	0	1	0	0	1	1
Palmela	1	0	0	0	0	1	1
Peal de Becerro	83	7	1	6	0	97	97
Penarrubia	1	0	0	0	0	1	1
Peniscola	1	0	0	0	0	1	1
Peyriac-de-Mer	30	3	0	0	0	33	36
Pézenas	259	15	1	56	8	339	355
Picanya	0	0	1	0	0	1	1
Pinos Puente	1	0	0	0	1	2	2
Pontos	1	2	0	0	1	4	5
Portiragnes	11	2	0	0	0	13	13
Porto	0	0	0	0	0	0	4
Pretin	0	0	0	0	0	0	1
Puentetablas	25	6	0	0	0	31	31
Puissalicon	0	0	0	0	0	0	2
Puisserguier	2	0	0	0	0	2	2
Rodenbach	1	0	0	0	0	1	1
Rojales	22	1	3	0	0	26	28
Roquemaure	13	3	0	0	2	18	19
Rosas	6	0	0	0	1	7	8
Rosell	1	0	0	0	0	1	1
Saguntum	5	0	0	1	0	6	6
Saint-Blaise	3931	422	39	13	188	4593	4771
Saint-Bonnet (d'Aramon)	2	0	0	0	0	2	2
Saint-Côme-et-Maruéjols	60	14	0	1	2	77	78
Saint-Dionisy	12	3	0	0	31	46	46
Sainte-Anastasie	5	0	0	0	2	7	7
Saint-Gilles-du-Gard	60	46	1	8	84	199	200
Saint-Laurent-de-Carnols	14	4	0	0	1	19	20

Site	Drinking	Eating	Household	Storage	Transport	Function subtotal	Site total
Saint-Thibéry	22	6	0	4	0	32	35
Salins-les-Bains	6	0	0	0	0	6	8
Salles d'Aude	8	1	0	0	1	10	11
San Fulgencio	15	2	2	1	5	25	26
Sanilhac-Sagriès	4	0	0	0	0	4	6
Sant Just Desvern	13	0	0	0	1	14	15
Sant Pere de Premia	0	0	0	0	1	1	1
Sant Vincenc de Castellet	2	0	0	0	0	2	2
Santa Barbara	0	0	1	0	0	1	1
Santa Coloma de Gramenet	2	0	0	0	1	3	4
Santa Perpetua de Mogoda	1	0	0	0	0	1	1
Santa Pola	1	0	0	0	0	1	1
Santomera	1	0	0	0	0	1	1
Santuario de la Luz	0	0	0	0	0	0	1
Sernhac	2	0	0	0	0	2	2
Serra d'Almors	1	0	0	0	0	1	1
Serra de Daro	2	0	0	1	0	3	3
Sevilla	1	0	0	0	1	2	2
Sexi	3	0	1	0	1	5	5
Sigean – Pech Maho	172	9	11	14	0	206	235
Silves	3	0	0	0	0	3	4
Solsona	1	0	0	0	0	1	1
Somme-Bionne	1	0	0	0	0	1	1
Sommières	14	2	0	0	11	27	29
Tarragona	0	0	0	0	1	1	1
Torroella de Montgri	0	0	0	0	1	1	1
Tortosa	1	0	2	0	0	3	3
Toulouse	7	0	0	0	1	8	10

(*Continued*)

Site	Drinking	Eating	Household	Storage	Transport	Function subtotal	Site total
Ubeda	5	0	0	0	0	5	5
Uetliberg	1	0	0	0	0	1	1
Ullastret	634	52	16	4	22	728	739
Valencia	0	0	0	1	0	1	1
Vall de Uxo	6	0	0	1	0	7	7
Vallfogona de Balaguer-Termens	0	0	0	0	0	0	1
Valros	14	0	0	2	0	16	19
Vélez-Málaga	43	4	5	0	42	94	94
Vic-la-Gardiole	4	1	0	0	1	6	6
Vila Chã	1	0	0	0	0	1	1
Vila da Feira	0	0	0	0	0	0	1
Vilaharelho	0	0	0	0	0	0	1
Vilanova i la Geltru	0	0	0	0	0	0	1
Villajoyosa	0	0	1	0	0	1	1
Villasavary	3	1	0	0	1	5	5
Villeneuve-la-Comptal	2	0	0	0	1	3	3
Villeneuve-les-Beziers	1	0	0	0		1	1
Villeneuve-lès-Maguelonne	0	1	0	0	4	5	5
Villetelle – Ambrussum	4	1	0	1	1	7	7
Vinaroz	2	0	0	0	2	4	4
Weißenthurm-Urmitz	1	0	0	0	0	1	1
Yverdon-les-Bains	1	0	0	0	0	1	1
Zalamea de la Serena	417	24	2	0	0	443	443

Bibliography

Adroher, A. M. 1987. "Digresiones sobre la Forma de Barniz Negro 21–25 B y Sus Imitaciones: El Caso de Baza (Granada)." *Cuadernos de Prehistoria de la Universidad de Granada* 12: 195–203.

Aldhouse-Green, M. 1995. *The Celtic World.* London; New York: Routledge.

Almagro Basch, M. 1952. *Las Inscripciones Ampuritanas: Griegas, Ibéricas y Latinas.* Monografías Ampuritanas 2. Barcelona: Departamento de Barcelona del Instituto Rodrigo Caro de Arquelogía del C.S.I.C.

Almagro-Gorbea, M. 1988a. "El Palacio de Cancho Roano y Sus Paralelos Arquitectónicos y Funcionales." *Zephyrus* 41: 339–382.

———. 1988b. "Société et Commerce Méditerranéen dans la Peninsula Ibérique aux VIIᵉ-Vᵉ Siècles." In *Les Princes Celtes et la Méditerranée*, 71–80. Paris: La Documentation Francaise.

———. 1997. "Die Kelten auf der Iberischen Halbinsel." In *Die Welt Der Kelten: Dia-Vortragsreihe in Hochdorf/Enz 1991—1997: 30 Vorträge—Zusammenfassung*, edited by T. Bader. Hochdorf an der Enz: Keltenmuseum. 73–83.

Amyx, D. A. 1956. "The Attic Stelai." *Hesperia* 25: 178–328.

———. 1988. *Corinthian Vase-Painting of the Archaic Period.* Berkeley: University of California Press.

Amyx, D. A., and P. Lawrence. 1996. *Studies in Archaic Corinthian Vase Painting.* Princeton, NJ: American School of Classical Studies at Athens.

Antonaccio, C. M. 1997. "Urbanism at Archaic Morgantina." *Acta Hyperborea* 7: 167–194.

———. 2000. "Architecture and Behavior: Building Gender into Greek Houses." *Classical World* 93 (5): 517–533.

———. 2001. "Ethnicity and Colonization." In *Ancient Perceptions of Greek Ethnicity*, 113–157. Washington, DC: Center for Hellenic Studies; Boston: Harvard University Press.

———. 2003. "Hybridity and the Cultures within Greek Culture." In *The Cultures within Ancient Greek Culture*, edited by C. Dougherty and L. Kurke, 57–74. Cambridge: Cambridge University Press.

———. 2004. "Siculo-Geometric and the Sikels: Ceramics and Identity in Eastern Sicily." In *Greek Identity in the Western Mediterranean: Papers in Honour of Brian Shefton*, 54–81. Leiden: Brill.

———. 2005. "Excavating Colonization." In *Ancient Colonizations: Analogy, Similarity, and Difference*, 97–114. London: Duckworth.

———. 2009. "(Re)defining Ethnicity: Culture, Material Culture, and Identity." In *Material Culture and Social Identities in the Ancient World*, 32–53. Cambridge: Cambridge University Press.

Appadurai, A. 2009. *The Social Life of Things: Commodities in Cultural Perspective*. Cambridge: Cambridge University Press.

Arafat, K., and C. Morgan. 1994. "Athens, Etruria, and the Heuneburg: Mutual Misconceptions in the Study of Greek-Barbarian Relations." In *Classical Greece: Ancient Histories and Modern Archaeologies*, edited by I. Morris, 108–134. New Directions in Archaeology. Cambridge: Cambridge University Press.

Arcelin, P. 1986. "Le Territoire de Marseille Grecque dans Son Contexte Indigene." In *Le Territoire de Marseille Grecque: Actes de La Table-ronde d'Aix-en-Provence, 16 Mars 1985*, 43–104. Etudes Massaliètes, 1, Travaux du Centre Camille Jullian, 1. Aix-en-Provence: Université de Provence.

———. 1990. "Les Habitats Indigenes des Environs de Marseille Grecque." In *Voyage en Massalie: 100 Ans D'archéologie en Gaule du Sud*, 26–31. Marseille/Aix-en-Provence: Musées de Marseille/Edisud.

Arnold, B. 1995. "The Material Culture of Social Structure: Rank and Status in Early Iron Age Europe." In *Celtic Chiefdom, Celtic State*, edited by B. Arnold and D. B. Gibson, 43–52. Cambridge: Cambridge University Press.

———. 1999. " 'Drinking the Feast': Alcohol and the Legitimation of Power in Celtic Europe." *Cambridge Archaeological Journal* 9 (1): 71–93.

———. 2012a. "Gender, Temporalities, and Periodization in Early Iron Age West-Central Europe." *Social Science History* 36 (1): 85–112.

———. 2012b. "The Vix Princess Redux: A Retrospective on European Iron Age Gender and Mortuary Studies." In *La Arqueología Funeraria desde una Perspectiva de Género. II Jornadas Internacionales de Arqueología y Género en la UAM*, edited by L. Prados Torreira, 215–232. Madrid: Ediciones Universidad Autónoma de Madrid.

Arruda, A. M. 1997. *As cerâmicas áticas do castelo de Castro Marim: No quadro das exportações gregas para a Península Ibérica*. Colecção Arqueologia & História Antiga 2. Lisboa: Edições Colibri.

———. 1998. "Cerâmicas Áticas de Mértola." *Conimbriga* 37: 121–149.

———. 2000. "Tartessos y El Territorio Actual de Portugal." In *Argantonio, Rey de Tartessos*, 165–178. Seville: Fundacio El Monte.

———. 2007. "Ceramicas Gregas Encontradas Em Portugal." In *Vasos Gregos Em Portugal—Aquém das Colunas de Hércules*, edited by M. H. da Rocha Pereira, 135–140. Lisbon: Museu Nacional de Arqueologia.

———. 2009a. "Castro Marim: Un Santuario en la Desembocadura del Guadiana." In *Santuarios, "Oppida" y Ciudades: Arquitectura Sacra en el Origen y Desarrollo Urbano del Mediterráneo Occidental*, 79–88. Anejos de Archivio Español de Arqueología 45. Mérida: Consejo Superior de Investigaciones Científica, Instituto de Arqueología de Mérida.

———. 2009b. "Phoenician Colonization on the Atlantic Coast of the Iberian Peninsula." In *Colonial Encounters in Ancient Iberia: Phoenician, Greek, and Indigenous Relations*, edited by M. Dietler and C. López-Ruiz, 113–130. Chicago: University Of Chicago Press.

Athenaios. 2007–2011. *The Learned Banqueters*. Translated by S. D. Olson. 8 vols. Loeb Classical Library. Cambridge, MA: Harvard University Press.

Aubet, M. E. 1993. "El Comerç Fenici i les Comunitats del Ferro a Catalunya." *Laietania* 8: 23–40.

———. 2005. "Mainake: The Legend and the New Archaeological Evidence." In *Mediterranean Urbanization, 800–600 BCE*, 187–202. Proceedings of the British Academy 126. Oxford: Oxford University.

Aubet Semmler, M. E., ed. 1989. *Tartessos: Arqueología Protohistorica Del Bajo Guadalquivir*. Sabadell: Editorial AUSA.

———. 2002a. "Notes on the Economy of the Phoenician Settlements in Southern Spain." In *The Phoenicians in Spain*, edited by M. R. Bierling, 79–96. Winona Lake, IN: Eisenbrauns.

———. 2002b. "Phoenician Trade in the West: Balance and Perspectives." In *The Phoenicians in Spain*, edited by M.R. Bierling, 97–112. Winona Lake, IN: Eisenbrauns.

———. 2002c. "Some Questions on the Tartessian Orientalizing Period." In *The Phoenicians in Spain*, edited by M.R. Bierling, 199–224. Winona Lake, IN: Eisenbrauns.

———. 2002d. "The Phoenician Impact on Tartessos: Spheres of Interaction." In *The Phoenicians in Spain*, edited by M.R. Bierling, 225–240. Winona Lake, IN: Eisenbrauns.

Augier, L., O. Buchsenschutz, and I.B.M. Ralston. 2007. *Un complexe princier de l'âge du fer l'habitat du promontoire de Bourges (Cher), VIe-IVe s. av. J.-C.* Bourges: Bourges plus, Service d'archéologie préventive.

Ault, B.A. 1999. "Koprones and Oil Presses at Halieis: Interactions of Town and Country and the Integration of Domestic and Regional Economies." *Hesperia* 68 (4): 549–573.

Avramidou, A. 2006. "Attic Vases in Etruria: Another View on the Divine Banquet Cup by the Codrus Painter." *American Journal of Archaeology* 110: 565–579.

Azuar, R., P. Rouillard, E. Gailledrat, P. Moret, F. Sala, and A. Badie. 2001. "L'établissement Orientalisant et Ibérique Ancien de La Rábita, Guardamar Del Segura (prov. d'Alicante)." In *Échanges Transdisciplinaires sur les Constructions en Terre Crue: Actes de la Table-ronde de Montpellier, 17–18 Novembre 2001*, 283–297. Montpellier: Éditions de l'Espérou.

Bader, T. 1997. *Die Welt der Kelten: Dia-Vortragsreihe in Hochdorf/Enz 1991–1997: 30 Vorträge—Zusammenfassung.* Eberdingen: Keltenmuseum Hochdorf/Enz.

Balzer, I. 2010. "Neue Forschungen Zu Alten Fragen: Der Früheisenzeitliche 'Fürstensitz' Hohenasperg (Kr. Ludwigsburg) und Sein Umland." In *'Fürstensitze' und Zentralorte der frühen Kelten: Abschlusskolloquium des DFG-Schwerpunktprogramms 1171 in Stuttgart, 12. –15. Oktober 2009*, 209–238. Stuttgart: Theiss.

Bats, M. 1986. "Le Territoire de Marseille Grecque: Réflexions et Problèmes." In *Le Territoire de Marseille Grecque: Actes de la Table-ronde d'Aix-en-Provence, 16 Mars 1985*, edited by M. Bats and H. Tréziny, 17–42. Aix-en-Provence: Université de Provence.

———. 1992. *Marseille grecque et la Gaule: Actes du Colloque international d'histoire et d'archéologie et du Ve Congrès archéologique de Gaule méridionale (Marseille, 18–23 novembre 1990).* Etudes massaliètes 3. Travaux du Centre Camille Jullian 11. Lattes/Aix-en-Provence: A.D.A.M. éd.; Université de Provence.

Beazley, J.D. 1928. *Greek Vases in Poland.* Oxford: Clarendon.

———. 1944. *Potter and Painter in Ancient Athens.* London: G. Cumberledge.

———. 1956. *Attic Black-Figure Vase-Painters.* Oxford: Clarendon Press.

———. 1963. *Attic Red-Figure Vase-Painters.* Oxford: Clarendon Press.

———. 1971. *Paralipomena: Additions to Attic Black-Figure Vase-Painters and to Attic Red-Figure Vase-Painters (Second Edition).* Oxford: Clarendon Press.

Bell, M. 1984–1985. "Recenti Scavi nell'Agora di Morgantina." *Kokalos* 30–31: 501–520.

———. 2000. "Camarina e Morgantina al Congresso Di Gela." In *Un Ponte fra l'Italia e La Grecia: Atti del Simposio in Onore di Antonino Di Vita*, 291–297. Padua: Bottega d'Erasmo.

———. 2006. "Rapporti Urbanistici Fra Camarina e Morgantina." In *Camarina 2600 Anni Dopo: Nuovi Studi sulla Città e Sul Territorio. Atti Del Convegno Internazionale, Ragusa, 7 dicembre 2002/7–9 aprile 2003*, 253–258. Rome: Centro studi Feliciano Rossitto.

———. 2008. "Continuità e Rotture a Morgantina nel V Sec. a.C." In *Morgantina a Cinquant'anni dall'Inizio delle Ricerche Sistematiche. Atti dell'Incontro di Studio, Aidone, 10 Dicembre 2005*, 9–21. Caltanissetta: Salvatore Sciascia Editore.

Benoit, F. 1965. *Recherches sur L'Hellenisation du Midi de la Gaule.* Aix-en-Provence: Faculté des lettres et sciences humaines d'Aix-en-Provence.

Bergquist, B. 1990. "Sympotic Space: A Functional Aspect of Greek Dining-Rooms." In *Sympotica: A Symposium on the Symposion,* 39–65. Oxford: Oxford University Press.

Bertucchi, G. 1992. *Les amphores et le vin de Marseille, VIe s. avant J.-C. – IIe s. après J.-C. Revue Archéologique Narbonnaise* Supp. 25. Paris: CNRS.

Bhabha, H.K. 1994. *The Location of Culture.* London; New York: Routledge.

Bieg, G. 2002. *Hochdorf V: Der Bronzekessel aus dem Späthallstattzeitliche Fürstengrab von Eberdingen-Hochdorf (Kr. Ludwisburg). Griechische Stabdreifüsse und Bronzekessel der archaischen Zeit mit figurlichem Schmuck.* Forschungen und Berichte zur Vor- und Frühgeschichte in Baden-Württemberg 83. Stuttgart: Theiss.

Biel, J. 1981. "The Late Hallstatt Chieftain's Grave at Hochdorf." *Antiquity* 55: 16–18.

Bittel, K., and A. Rieth. 1951. *Die Heuneburg an der oberen Donau: Ein Frühkeltischer Fürstensitz z. Vorläufiger Bericht Über die Ausgrabungen 1950.* Stuttgart: Kohlhammer.

Blázquez, J.M. 1984. *Cástulo IV.* Excavaciones Arqueológicas en España 131. Madrid: Ministerio de Cultura, Dirección General de Bellas Artes y Archivos, Subdirección General de Arqueología y Etnografia.

———. 1985. *Castulo V.* Excavaciones Arqueológicas en España 140. Madrid: Ministerio de Cultura, Dirección General del Patrimo nio Artístico, Archivos y Museos, Subdirección General de Arqueología.

Blázquez, J.M., M.P. García-Gelabert Pérez, and F. López Pardo. 1984. "Evolución del Patrón de Asentamiento en Castulo: Fases Iniciales." *Arqueología Espacial* 4: 241–252.

Bliege Bird, R., and E.A. Smith. 2005. "Signaling Theory, Strategic Interaction, and Symbolic Capital." *Current Anthropology* 46 (2): 221–248.

Blomqvist, J. 1979. *The Date and Origin of the Greek Version of Hanno's Periplus: With an Edition of the Text and a Translation.* Lund: Liber Läromedel/Gleerup.

Boardman, J. 1987. "Silver Is White." *Revue Archéologique* 2: 279–285.

———.1990. "Symposion Furniture." In *Sympotica: A Symposium on the Symposion,* 122–131. Oxford: Oxford University Press.

———. 1999. *The Greeks Overseas: The Early Colonies and Trade.* 4th ed. Thames & Hudson.

———. 2001. *The History of Greek Vases: Potters, Painters and Pictures.* London: Thames & Hudson.

Böhr, E. 1988. "Die griechische Schalen." In *Das Kleinaspergle: Studien zu einem Fürstengrabhügel der frühen Latenezeit bei Stuttgart,* edited by W. Kimmig, 176–190. Forschungen und Berichte zur Vor- und Frühgeschichte in Baden-Württemberg 30. Stuttgart: Theiss.

Böhr, E., and B.B. Shefton. 2000. "Die griechische Keramik der Heuneburg." In *Importe Und mediterrane Einflusse auf der Heuneburg,* 1–42. Mainz am Rhein: v. Zabern.

Bolay, G., A. Krüger, F. Müller, and H. Paul. 2010. *Kelten am Hohenasperg.* Asperg: Keltenfürst-Verl.

Bookidis, N. 1993. "Ritual Dining at Corinth." In *Greek Sanctuaries: New Approaches,* edited by N. Marinatos and R. Hägg, 45–61. London; New York: Routledge.

Bookidis, N., and R. Stroud. 1997. *Corinth XVIII, Part 3: The Sanctuary of Demeter and Persephone:Topography and Architecture.* Princeton: American School of Classical Studies at Athens.

Boone, J. 2000. "Status Signaling, Social Power, and Lineage Survival." In *Hierarchies in Action: Cui Bono?*, 84–110. Southern Illinois University Center for Archaeological Studies Occasional Papers 27. Carbondale: Southern Illinois University Press.

Bouiron, M., and H. Tréziny. 2001. *Marseille, trames et paysages urbains de Gyptis au roi René: actes du colloque international d'archéologie, Marseille, 3–5 novembre 1999.* Edisud: Centre Camille Jullian.

Bouloumié, B. 1982. "Saint-Blaise et Marseille au VIe Siècle avant J.-C: L'hypothèse Étrusque." *Latomus* 41: 74–91.

———. 1984. "Saint-Blaise, Oppidum du Sel." *Dossiers D'archéologie* 84: 5–96.

———. 1988. "Le Symposion Gréco-étrusque et L'aristocratie Celtique." In *Les Princes Celtes et la Méditerranée*, 343–383. Paris: La Documentation Francaise.

———. 1992. *Saint-Blaise, Fouilles H. Rolland. L'habitat Protohistorique. Les Céramiques Grecques.* Travaux du Centre Camille Jullian 13. Aix-en-Provence: Publications de l'Université de Provence.

Bourdieu, P. 1984. *Distinction: A Social Critique of the Judgment of Taste.* Cambridge, MA: Harvard University Press.

Bowser, B. 2000. "From Pottery to Politics: An Ethnoarchaeological Study of Political Factionalism, Ethnicity, and Domestic Pottery Style in the Ecuadorian Amazon." *Journal of Archaeological Method and Theory* 7 (3): 219–248.

Braun, D. 1983. "Pots as Tools." In *Archaeological Hammers and Theories,* edited by A. Keene and J. Moore, 107–134. New York: Academic Press.

Bräuning, A., W. Lohlein, and S. Plouin. 2012. *Die frühe Eisenzeit zwischen Schwarzwald und Vogesen = Le Premier Âge du Fer entre la Forêt-Noire et les Vosges.* Stuttgart: Landesamt für Denkmalpflege im Regierungspräsidium Stuttgart.

Bresson, A. 1992. "Les Cités Grecques et Leurs Emporia." In *L'emporion,* edited by A. Bresson and P. Rouillard, 163–231. Paris: Publications du Center Pierre.

Brijder, H. A. G., and G. Strietman. 1983. *Siana Cups I and Komast Cups.* Amsterdam: Allard Pierson Museum.

Brughmans, T., S. Keay, and G. Earl. 2012. "Complex Networks in Archaeology: Urban Connectivity in Iron Age and Roman Southern Spain." *Leonardo* 45 (3), 280.

Brun, P. 1987. *Princes et Princesses de La Celtique: Le Premier Age du Fer en Europe, 850–450 Av. J.-C.* Paris: Editions Errance.

———. 1988. "Les <<Résidences Princières>> commes Centres Territoriaux: Éléments de Vérification." In *Les Princes Celtes et la Méditerranée,* 129–144. Paris: La Documentation Francaise.

———. 1992. "L'influence Grecque sur le Société Celtique Non-méditerranéene." In *Marseille Grecque et La Gaule: Actes du Colloque Internationale D'histoire et de Archéologie et du Ve Congrès Archéologique de Gaule Meridionale,* edited by M. Bats, G. Bertucchi, G. Congès, and H. Tréziny, 389–399. A.D.A.M. éd.; Université de Provence.

———. 1995. "From Chiefdom to State Organization in Celtic Europe." In *Celtic Chiefdom, Celtic State,* edited by B. Arnold and D. B. Gibson, 13–25. New Directions in Archaeology. Cambridge: Cambridge University Press.

———. 1997. *Vix et les éphémères principautés celtiques: Les VI et Ve siècles avant J.-C. en Europe centre-occidentale: Actes du colloque de Châtillon-sur-Seine (27–29 octobre 1993).* Paris: Editions Errance.

Burton, J. 1998. "Women's Commensality in the Ancient Greek World." *Greece and Rome* Second Series 45 (2): 143–165.

Buxó, R., and E. Pons i Brun, ed. 2000. *L'hàbitat protohistòric a Catalunya, Rosselló i Llenguadoc occidental. Actualitat de l'arqueologia de l'edat del ferro: Actes del XXII col·loqui internacional per a l'estudi de l'Edat del Ferro.* Museu d'Arqueologia de Catalunya-Girona: Generalitat de Catalunya.

Cabrera Bonet, P. 1994. "La Presencia Griega en Andalucía (siglos VI al IV a. C.)." *Huelva Arqueológica* 14: 367–390.

———. 1996. "Emporion y el Comercio Griego Arcaico en el Nordeste de la Península Ibérica." In *Formes Archaïques et Arts Ibériques,* 43–54. Collection de La Casa de Velázquez 59. Paris: Boccard.

———. 1998. "Greek Trade in Iberia: The Extent of Interaction." *Oxford Journal of Archaeology* 17 (2): 191–205.

———. 2000. "Cádiz y Ampurias. Relaciones Económicas y de Intercambio. Siglos V y IV a.C." In *Actas del IV Congreso Internacional de Estudios Fenicios y Púnicos: Cádiz, 2 al 6 de Octubre de 1995,* 313–317. Cádiz: Servicio de Publicaciones, Universidad de Cádiz.

Cabrera Bonet, P., and P. Rouillard. 2003. "La Céramique Attique dans les Necropoles Ibériques." In *Le Vase Grec et Ses Destins,* 179–186. Munich: Biering and Brinkmann.

Cahill, N. 2002. *Household and City Organization at Olynthus.* New Haven, CT: Yale University Press.

Camp, J. 1999. "Excavations in the Athenian Agora, 1996 and 1997." *Hesperia* 68 (3): 255–283.

Camporeale, G. 2004. *The Etruscans Outside of Etruria.* Los Angeles: Getty Publications.

Carme Belarte, M. 2009. "Colonial Contacts and Protohistoric Indigenous Urbanism on the Mediterranean Coast of the Iberian Peninsula." In *Colonial Encounters in Ancient Iberia: Phoenician, Greek, and Indigenous Relations,* edited by M. Dietler and C. López-Ruiz, 91–112. Chicago: University of Chicago Press.

Carpenter, T.H. 1986. *Dionysian Imagery in Archaic Greek Art: Its Development in Black-Figure Vase Painting.* Oxford Monographs on Classical Archaeology. Oxford: Clarendon Press.

———. 1997. *Dionysian Imagery in Fifth-Century Athens.* Oxford Monographs on Classical Archaeology. Oxford: Clarendon Press.

Carrier, J.G. 2006. *A Handbook of Economic Anthropology.* Northampton, MA: Edward Elgar Publishing.

Casson, L. 1959. *The Ancient Mariners: Seafarers and Sea Fighters of the Mediterranean in Ancient Times.* New York: Macmillan.

———. 1971. *Ships and Seamanship in the Ancient World.* Princeton, NJ: Princeton University Press.

———. 1984. *Ancient Trade and Society.* Detroit, MI: Wayne State University Press.

Celestino Pérez, S. 1993. *El Palacio-santuario de Cancho Roano.* Badajoz: Gil Santacruz.

———. 1996. *El Palacio Santuario de Cancho Roano V, VI, VII: Los Sectores Oeste, Sur y Este.* Madrid: Bartolomé Gil.

———. 2009. "Precolonization and Colonization in the Interior of Tartessos." In *Colonial Encounters in Ancient Iberia: Phoenician, Greek, and Indigenous Relations,* 229–253. Chicago: University of Chicago Press.

Celestino Pérez, S., and F. Gracia Alonso. 2003. *Cancho Roano VIII: Los materiales arqueológicos.* Merida, Spain: Instituto de Arqueología de Mérida, CSIC: Junta de Extremadura, Consejería de Cultura, Dirección General de Patrimonio Cultural.

Celestino Pérez, S., and C. López-Ruiz. 2003. "Sacred Precincts: A Tartessian Sanctuary in Ancient Spain." *Archaeology Odyssey* 6(6): 20–29.

Chaume, B., and P. Brun, ed. 1997. *Vix et les Éphèmères Principautés Celtiques. Les 6ᵉ et 5ᵉ Siècles avant J.-C. en Europe Centre-occidentale. Actes du Colloque de Châtillon-sur-Seine, 27–29 Octobre 1993.* Archéologie Aujourd'hui. Paris: Éditions Errance.

Chaume, B., C. Mordant, and C. Allag. 2011. *Le complexe aristocratique de Vix: nouvelles recherches sur l'habitat et le système de fortification et l'environnement du Mont Lassois.* Dijon: Editions universitaires de Dijon.

Chaume, B., N. Nieszery, and W. Reinhard. 2012. "Ein Frühkeltischer Fürstensitz im Burgund: Der Mont Lassois." In *Die Welt der Kelten—Zentren der Macht, Kostbarkeiten der Kunst,* 132–138. Stuttgart: Thorbecke.

Chaume, B., L. Olivier, and W. Reinhard. 2000. "L'enclos Cultuel Hallstattien de Vix, Les Herbues." *Ocnus: Quaderni della Scuola di Specializzazione in Archeologia* 8: 229–249.

Chaume, B., and W. Reinhard. 2009. "Le Cas des Statues de Vix-Les Herbues et Le Phénomène des Stèles Anthropomorphes Hallstattiennes." In *Stèles et Statues des Celtes du Midi de la France (8ᵉ–4ᵉ s. av. J.-C.),* edited by P. Gruat, 67–69. Rodez: Conseil Général de l'Aveyron.

Chaume, B., W. Reinhard, and N. Nieszery. 2007. "Le Palais de La Dame de Vix." *Bulletin Archéologique et Historique du Châtillonnais* 6: 23–27.

Cook, L.J., R. Yamin, and J.P. McCarthy. 1996. "Shopping as Meaningful Action: Toward a Redefinition of Consumption in Historical Archaeology." *Historical Archaeology* 30 (4): 50–65.

Cook, R.M. 1987. " 'Artful Crafts': A Commentary." *Journal of Hellenic Studies* 107: 169–171.

———. 1997. *Greek Painted Pottery.* London; New York: Routledge.

Cook, R.M., and P. Dupont. 1997. *East Greek Pottery.* London: Routledge.

Cooper, F., and S. Morris. 1990. "Dining in Round Buildings." In *Sympotica: A Symposium on the Symposion,* edited by O. Murray, 66–85. Oxford: Oxford University Press.

Corner, S. 2012. "Did 'Respectable' Women Attend Symposia?" *Greece & Rome* 59 (1): 34–45.

Cuadrado Díaz, E. "Las Fíbulas Anulares de la Ría de Huelva." *Archivio Español de Arqueología* 42: 40–45.

Cunliffe, B. 1979. *The Celtic World.* Maidenhead, UK: McGraw-Hill.

———. 1988. *Greeks, Romans and Barbarians: Spheres of Interaction.* London: Batsford.

Curtis, R.I. 2001. *Ancient Food Technology.* Leiden: Brill.

Dalby, A. 1993. "Food and Sexuality in Classical Athens: The Written Sources." *Food, Culture & History* 1: 165–190.

Deamos, M.B. 2009. "Phoenicians in Tartessos." In *Colonial Encounters in Ancient Iberia: Phoenician, Greek, and Indigenous Relations,* edited by M. Dietler and C. López-Ruiz, 193–228. Chicago: University of Chicago Press.

De Angelis, F. 1998. "Ancient Past, Imperial Present: The British Empire in T.J. Dunbabin's *The Western Greeks*." *Antiquity* 72: 539–549.

De Angelis, F., and G. Tsetskhladze, eds. 2004. *The Archaeology of Greek Colonisation.* 2nd ed. Oxford School of Archaeology.

Dechelette, J. 1913. "Le Tumulus de Motte Saint-Valentin (Commune de Courcelles-en-Montagne, Haute-Marne)." *La Collection Millon: Antiquités Préhistoriques et Gallo-Romaines,* 101–151. Paris: Librarie Paul Geuthner.

de Hoz, J. 1993. "La Lengua y Escritura Ibéricas y las Lenguas de los Iberos." In *Lengua y Cultura en la Hispania Prerromana: Actas del V Coloquio sobre Lenguas y Culturas Prerromanas de la Península Ibérica,* 635–666. Salamanca: Universidad de Salamanca.

Demetriou, D. 2012. *Negotiating Identity in the Ancient Mediterranean: The Archaic and Classical Greek Multiethnic Emporia.* Cambridge: Cambridge University Press.

Diels, H.A. 1962. *Die Fragmente der Vorsokratiker,* 6th ed., rev. by W. Kranz. Berlin: Weidmann.

Dietler, M. 1990. "Exchange, Consumption, and Colonial Interaction in the Rhône Basin of France: A Study of Early Iron Age Political Economy." Dissertation, Berkeley: University of California.

———. 1996. "Feasts and Commensal Politics in the Political Economy: Food, Power, and Status in Prehistoric Europe." In *Food and the Status Quest,* edited by P. Wiesner and W. Schiefenhövel, 87–125. Providence and London: Berghahn Books.

———. 1997. "The Iron Age in Mediterranean France: Colonial Encounters, Entanglements, and Transformations." *Journal of World Prehistory* 11 (3): 269–358.

———. 1998. "Consumption, Agency, and Cultural Entanglement: Theoretical Implications of a Mediterranean Colonial Encounter." In *Studies in Culture Contact: Interaction, Culture Change and Archaeology,* 288–315. Carbondale: Southern Illinois University Press.

———. 1999. "Consumption, Cultural Frontiers, and Identity: Anthropological Approaches to Greek Colonial Encounters." In *Confini e Frontiere nella Grecità d'Occidente,* 1:475–501. Naples: Arte tipographica.

———. 2001. "Theorizing the Feast: Rituals of Consumption, Commensal Politics, and Power in African Contexts." In *Feasts: Archaeological and Ethnographic Perspectives on Food, Politics, and Power,* edited by M. Dietler and B. Hayden, 65–114. Smithsonian Series in Archaeological Inquiry. Washington, DC: Smithsonian Institution Press.

———. 2004. "Review of Claude Rolley (ed.), *La Tombe Princière de Vix,* 2003." *Mélanges de la Casa de Velázquez* 34 (1): 362–366.

———. 2005. *Consumption and Colonial Encounters in the Rhône Basin of France: A Study of Early Iron Age Political Economy.* Monographies d'Archéologie Méditerranéenne 21. Lattes: CNRS.

———. 2006. "Alcohol: Anthropological/Archaeological Perspectives." *Annual Review of Anthropology* 35: 229–249.

———. 2009. "Colonial Encounters in Iberia and the Western Mediterranean: An Exploratory Framework." In *Colonial Encounters in Ancient Iberia: Phoenician, Greek, and Indigenous Relations,* edited by M. Dietler and C. López-Ruiz, 3–48. Chicago; London: University of Chicago Press.

———. 2010. *Archaeologies of Colonialism: Consumption, Entanglement, and Violence in Ancient Mediterranean France.* Berkeley: University of California Press.

Dietler, M., and B. Hayden, ed. 2001. *Feasts: Archaeological and Ethnographic Perspectives on Food, Politics, and Power.* Washington, DC: Smithsonian Institution Press.

Dietler, M., and C. López-Ruiz, ed. 2009. *Colonial Encounters in Ancient Iberia: Phoenician, Greek, and Indigenous Relations.* Chicago: University of Chicago Press.

Dietrich-Weibel, B., G. Lüscher, and T. Kilka. 1998. *Posieux-Châtillon-sur-Glâne.* Archéologie fribourgeoise 12. Fribourg Suisse: Éditions Universitaires.

Die Welt Der Kelten: Zentren Der Macht—Kostbarkeiten Der Kunst. 2012. Ostfildern: Jan Thorbecke Verlag.

Diodorus Siculus. 1939. *The Library of History, Volume III, Books 4.59–8.* Translated by C.H. Oldfather. Loeb Classical Library 340. Cambridge, MA: Harvard University Press.

Dobres, M. A., ed. 2000. *Agency in Archaeology.* London: Routledge.

Domínguez, A. J. 1999. "Hellenisation in Iberia? The Reception of Greek Products and Influences by the Iberians." *Ancient Greeks West and East.* Mnemosyne Supplement: 301–329.

———. 2001. "Cerámica Griega en la Ciudad Ibérica." *Anales de Prehistoria y Arqueología* 17–18: 189–203.

————. 2002. "Greeks in Iberia: Colonialism without Colonization." In *The Archaeology of Colonialism*, edited by C. L. Lyons and J. K. Papadopoulos. Los Angeles: Getty Publications.

————. 2003a. "Archaic Greek Pottery in the Iberian Peninsula: Its Presence in Native Contexts." In *Griechische Keramik im Kulturellen Kontext: Akten des Internationalen Vasen-Symposions in Kiel vom 24. bis 28.9.2001, Veranstaltet durch das Archäologische Institut der Christian-Albrechts-Universität zu Kiel*, 201–204. Münster: Scriptorium.

————. 2003b. "Fenicios y Griegos en Occidente: Modelos de Asentamiento y Interaccion." In *Contactos en el Extremo de la Oikouméne: Los Griegos en Occidente y Sus Relaciones con los Fenicios. XVII Jornadas de Arqueología Fenicio-Púnica*, 19–59. Treballs Del Museu Arqueològic d'Eivissa i Formentera 51. Eivissa: Museo Arqueològico de Ibiza y Formentera.

————. 2009. "El Final del Arcaismo y la Transformación de los Mecanismos de Intercambio en el Mediterraneo." *Gerión* 27 (1): 127–146.

————. 2013a. "Mobilità Umana, Circolazione di Risorse e Contatti di Culture nel Mediterraneo Arcaico." In *Il Mondo Antico*, edited by M. Giangiulio, 3:131–175. Storia d'Europa e del Mediterraneo 2. Rome: Salerno Editrice.

————. 2013b. "Los Primeros Griegos en la Península Ibérica (s. IX-VI a.C.): Mitos, Probablidades, Certezas." In *El Oriente Griego en la Península Ibérica: Epigrafía e Historia*, edited by M. Paz de Hoz and G. Mora, 11–42. Bibliotheca Archaeologica Hispana 39. Madrid: Real Academia de la Historia.

Domínguez, A. J., and C. Sánchez Fernández. 2001. *Greek Pottery from the Iberian Peninsula: Archaic and Classical Periods*. Edited by G. R. Tsetskhladze. Leiden: Brill.

Dougherty, C. 1993. *The Poetics of Colonization: From City to Text in Archaic Greece*. New York: Oxford University Press.

Douglas, M., and B. Isherwood. 1996. *The World of Goods: Towards an Anthropology of Consumption*. 2nd ed. London; New York: Routledge.

Dubosse, C. 1998. *Musée national d'Ensérune*. Edited by J.-J. Maffre. Corpus vasorum antiquorum France 37. Paris: Diff. de Boccard.

Dunbabin, T. J. 1948. *The Western Greeks: The History of Sicily and South Italy from the Foundation of the Greek Colonies to 480 B.C.* Oxford: Oxford University Press.

Dunn, R. G. 2008. *Identifying Consumption: Subjects and Objects in Consumer Society*. Philadelphia: Temple University Press.

Duval, A., J.-P. Morel, and Y. Roman, ed. 1990. *Gaule Interne et Gaule Méditerranéenne aux IIᵉ et Iᵉʳ Siècles avant J.-C: Confrontations Chronologiques*. Revue Archéologique de Narbonnaise Supplément 21. Paris: CNRS.

Duval, S. 2006. "Mobilier, Céramique et Commerce à Destination D'habitats Indigènes en Provence Occidentale, du VIᵉ s. au debut du Vᵉ s. av. J.-C." In *Gli Etruschi da Genova ad Ampurias: Atti del XXIV Convegno di Studi Etruschi ed Italici, Marseille, Lattes, 26 settembre–1 ottobre 2002*, 103–120. Atti di Convegni (Istituto Nazionale di Studi Etruschi e Italici), 24. Pisa/Rome: Istituti editoriali e poligrafici internazionali.

École du Louvre. 1988. *Les Princes celtes et la Méditerranée*. Paris: Documentation française.

Éluère, C. 1997. "Das Gold der Kelten." In *Die Welt der Kelten: Dia-Vortragsreihe in Hochdorf/Enz 1991–1997: 30 Vorträge—Zusammenfassung*, edited by T. Bader, 11–16. Hochdorf an der Enz: Keltenmuseum.

Emberling, G. 1999. "Review of *Ethnic Identity in Greek Antiquity*, by Jonathan M. Hall, and *The Archaeology of Ethnicity: Constructing Identities in the Past and Present*, by Siân Jones." *American Journal of Archaeology* 103 (1): 126–127.

Engels, H.-J. 1972. "Der Fürstengrabhugel von Rodenbach." *Bonner Hefte zur Vorgeschichte* 3: 25–52.

Escacena, J. L. 2004. "Tartessos (des)orientado." In *Colonialismo e Interacción Cultural: El Impacto Fenicio Púnico en las Sociedades Autóctonas de Occidente. XVIII Jornadas de Arqueología Fenicio-Púnica, 7–55.* Treballs Del Museu Arqueològic d'Eivissa i Formentera 52. Eivissa: Museo Arqueolo`gico de Ibiza y Formentera.

Escacena Carrasco, J. L. 1989. "Los Turdetanos o la Recuperación de la Identidad Perdida." In *Tartessos: Arqueología Protohistorica del Bajo Guadalquivir,* edited by M. E. Aubet Semmler, 433–476. Sabadell: Editorial AUSA.

Etrusker nördlich von Etrurien: etruskische Präsenz in Norditalien und nördlich der Alpen sowie ihre Einflüsse auf die einheimischen Kulturen. Akten des Symposions von Wien-Schloss Neuwaldegg 2.–5. Oktober 1989. 1992. Vienna: Verl. d. Österr. Akad. d. Wiss.

Euzennat, M. 1980. "Ancient Marseille in the Light of Recent Excavations." *American Journal of Archaeology* 84 (2): 133–140.

Facchetti, G. M. 2005. "The Interpretation of Etruscan Texts and Its Limits." *Journal of Indo-European Studies* 33: 359–388.

Fehr, B. 1990. "Entertainers at the Symposion: The Akletoi in the Archaic Period." In *Sympotica: A Symposium on the Symposion,* edited by O. Murray, 185–195. Oxford: Oxford University Press.

Fernández, J. H. 1992. *Excavaciones en la necrópolis del Puig des Molins (Eivissa): Las campañas de D. Carlos Román Ferrer, 1921–1929.* Palma: Conselleria de Cultura, Educació i Esports, Govern Balear.

Fernández-Miranda, M. 1991. "Tartessos: Indígenas, Fenicios y Griegos en Huelva." In *Atti del il Congresso Internazionale di Studi Fenici e Punici, Roma, 9–14 Novembre 1987,* 1:87–96. Rome: Consiglio Nazionale delle Ricerche.

Fischer, J. 1990. "Zu Einer Griechischen Kline und Weiteren Südimporten aus dem Fürstengrabhügel Grafenbühl, Asperg, Kreis Ludwigsburg." *Germania* 68: 115–127.

Ford, J. A. 1938. "A Chronological Method Applicable to the Southeast." *American Antiquity* 17: 260–264.

Foxhall, L. 1998. "'Cargoes of the Heart's Desire': The Character of Trade in the Archaic Mediterranean World." In *Archaic Greece: New Approaches and New Evidence,* edited by N. Fisher and H. van Wees, 295–309. London and Swansea: Duckworth and The Classical Press of Wales.

Freeman, E. A. 1891. *The History of Sicily from Earliest Times.* 2 vols. Oxford: Clarendon Press.

Furtwängler, A., K. Reichhold, and A. Huber. 1924. *Griechische Vasenmalerei: Auswahl hervorragender Vasenbilder aus dem gleichnamigen großen Werke.* Munich: Bruckmann.

Gale, N. H., ed. 1991. *Bronze Age Trade in the Mediterranean: Papers Presented at the Conference Held at Rewley House, Oxford, in December 1989.* Jonsered, Sweden: Paul Astroms Forlag.

García, A., A. Domínguez, F. González de Canales, and L. Serrano. 2009. "Una Inscripción Griega Arcaica Hallada en el Cabezo de San Pedro (Huelva)." *Spal* 18: 93–103.

Garcia, D. 1993. *Entre Ibères et Ligures: Lodécois et Moyenne Vallée de l'Hérault Protohistoriques.* Revue Archéologique de Narbonnaise Supplément 26. Paris: CNRS.

García-Gelabert Pérez, M. P., and J. M. Blázquez. 1988. *Castulo, Jaén, España.* 2 vols. BAR International Series 425. Oxford, England: Archaeopress.

García Martín, J.M. 2003. *La distribución de cerámica griega en la Contestania ibérica: El puerto comercial de La Illeta dels Banyets.* Alicante: Instituto Alicantino de Cultura Juan Gil-Albert.

Garnsey, P. 1999. *Food and Society in Classical Antiquity.* Key Themes in Ancient History. Cambridge, UK; New York: Cambridge University Press.

Garnsey, P., K. Hopkins, and C.R. Whitaker, ed. 1983. *Trade in the Ancient Economy*. London: Chatto and Windus.

Garrido Roiz, J.P., and E.M. Orta García. 1966. "Hércules de La Isla Saltés (Huelva)." In *IX Congreso Nacional de Arqueología*, 255–256. Madrid: Congresos Arqueológicos Nacionales, Secretaría General.

———. *El Hábitat Antiguo de Huelva (períodos Orientalizante y Arcaico). La Primera Excavación Arqueológica en la Calle del Puerto*. Excavaciones Arqueológicas en España 117. Madrid: Ministerio de la Cultura.

Garrido Roiz, J.P., and J. Ortega. 1994. "A Propósito de Unos Recientes Hallazgos Cerámicos Griegos Arcaicos y Orientalizantes En Huelva." In *Iberos y Griegos: Lecturas desde la Diversidad*, 1: 49–66. Huelva Arqueológica 13.

Gebhard, R., F. Marzatico, and P. Gleirscher. 2011. *Im Licht des Südens: Begegnungen antiker Kulturen zwischen Mittelmeer und Zentraleuropa*. Lindenberg: Kunstverlag Josef Fink.

Gericke, H. 1970. *Gefässdarstellungen auf Griechischen Vasen*. Berlin: Hessling.

Gersbach, E., H. van den Boom, H. Drescher, and J. Wahl. 1995. *Baubefunde der Perioden IVc–IVa der Heuneburg*. Forschungen und Berichte zur Vor- und Frühgeschichte in Baden-Württemberg 53. Stuttgart: Theiss.

Gill, D. W. J. 1988a. "Silver Anchors and Cargoes of Oil: Some Observations on Phoenician Trade in the Western Mediterranean." *Papers of the British School at Rome 56*: 1–12.

———. 1988b. "Trade in Greek Decorated Pottery: Some Corrections." *Oxford Journal of Archaeology 7*: 369–370.

———. 1990. "Reflected Glory: Pottery and Precious Metal in Classical Greece." *Jahrbuch des Deutschen Archäologischen Instituts 105*: 1–30.

———. 1991. "Pots and Trade: Spacefillers or Objets d'Art?" *Journal of Hellenic Studies 111*: 29–47.

———. 1994. "Positivism, Pots, and Long-Distance Trade." In *Classical Greece: Ancient Histories and Modern Archaeologies*, edited by I. Morris, 99–107. New Directions in Archaeology. Cambridge: Cambridge University Press.

Gori, S, and M.C. Bettini, eds. 2006. "Gli Etruschi da Genova ad Ampurias." In *Atti del XXIV convegno di studi etruschi ed italici, Marseille, Lattes, 26 settembre–1 ottobre 2002*. Pisa/Rome: Istituti editoriali e poligrafici internazionali.

Gracia Alonso, F. 2000. "El Comercio Arcaico en el Nordeste de la Península Ibérica. Estado de la Cuestión y Perspectivas." In *Ceràmiques Jònies D'època Arcaica: Centres de Producció Comercialització Al Mediterrani Occidental. Actes de La Taula Rodona Celebrada a Empúries, Els Dies 26 al 28 de Maig de 1999*, 257–276. Barcelona: Museu d'Arqueologia de Catalunya—Empúries.

Graeber, D. 2011. *Debt: The First 5,000 Years*. Brooklyn, NY: Melville House.

Graells I Fabregat, R. 2006. "El Aryballos Corintio de la Necrópolis de Milmanda (Vimbodí, Tarragona) y Su Cronología." *Archivo Español de Arqueología 79*: 207–216.

Grafen, A. 1990a. "Biological Signals as Handicaps." *Journal of Theoretical Biology 144*: 517–546.

———. 1990b. "Sexual Selection Unhandicapped by the Fisher Process." *Journal of Theoretical Biology 144*: 473–516.

Graham, A.J. 1983. *Colony and Mother-City in Ancient Greece*. Chicago: Ares.

Gran-Aymerich, J.M. 1986. "Céramiques Locales et Influences Exteriures en Mediterranee Occidentale: Exemples Pris en Etrurie et a Tartessos." In *Céramiques: Les Problemes de L'autochtonie*, 31–53. Nantes: Université de Nantes.

———. 1997. "Les Premiéres Importations Mediterranées de Bourges." In *Vix et les Éphèmérès Principautés Celtiques: Les VIe et Ve Siècles avant J.-C. en Europe Centre-occidentale. Actes du Colloque de Châtillon-sur-Seine (27–29 Octobre 1993)*, edited by P. Brun and B. Chaume, 201–211. Paris: Editions Errance.

Greco, G. 2005. "Sulle Tracce dei Focei." In *AEIMNHΣTOΣ: Miscellanea di Studi per Mauro Cristofani*, 93–102. Florence.

Gruen, E. S., ed. 2011. *Cultural Identity in the Ancient Mediterranean*. Los Angeles: Getty Research Institute.

Gudeman, S. 2001. *The Anthropology of Economy: Community, Market, and Culture*. 1st ed. Oxford: Wiley-Blackwell.

Guggisberg, M.A. 2004. *Die Hydria von Grächwil: Zur Funktion und Rezeption mediterraner Importe in Mitteleuropa im 6. und 5. Jahrhundert v.Chr. Akten des Internationales Kolloquium anlässlich des 150. Jahrestages der Entdeckung der Hydria von Grächwil, organisiert durch das Institut für Archäologie des Mittelmeerraumes der Universität Bern, 12.-13. Oktober 2001*. Bern: Verlag Bernisches Historisches Museum.

———. 2011. "Griechische Keramik nördlich der Alpen. Kontext und Funktion." In *Im Licht des Sudens: Begegnungen antiker Kulturen zwischen Mittelmeer und Zentraleuropa. Ausstellungskataloge der archäologischen Stattssammlung*, 163–165. Lindenberg: Kunstverlag Josef Fink.

Hall, J.M. 2000. *Ethnic Identity in Greek Antiquity*. Cambridge, UK; New York: Cambridge University Press.

———. 2005. *Hellenicity: Between Ethnicity and Culture*. Chicago: University of Chicago Press.

Hammer, D. 2004. "Ideology, the Symposium, and Archaic Politics." *American Journal of Philology* 125: 479–512.

Hannestad, L. 1996. "Athenian Pottery in Italy c. 550–470: Beazley and Quantitative Studies." In *I Vasi Attici ed Altre Ceramiche Coeve in Sicilia*, 2: 211–216. Catania: Università di Catania.

Harrison, T., ed. 2001. *Greeks and Barbarians*. London; New York: Routledge.

Hellström, P. 1975. "The Assymetry of the Pinakotheke—Once More." *Opuscula Atheniensia* 11: 87–92.

Hermary, A. 2002a. "Les Naïskoi Votifs de Marseille." In *Les Cultes Des Cités Phocéennes: Actes du Colloque International Aix-en-Provence/Marseille 4–5 Juin 1999*, 119–133. Etudes Massaliètes 6. Aix-en-Provence: Edisud: Centre Camille Jullian.

———. 2002b. "The Greeks in Marseilles and the Western Mediterranean." In *The Greeks beyond the Aegean: From Marseilles to Bactria*, edited by V. Karageorghis, 59–77. New York: Alexander S. Onassis Public Benefit Foundation (USA).

Hermary, A., A. Hesnard, and H. Tréziny. 1999. *Marseille grecque: 600–49 av. J.-C.: La cité phocéenne*. Paris: Editions Errance.

Hesnard, A. 1992. "Nouvelles Recherches sur les Épaves Préromaines en Baie de Marseille." In *Marseille Grecque et La Gaule: Actes du Colloque Internationale D'histoire et de Archéologie et du Vᶜ Congrès Archéologique de Gaule Meridionale*, edited by M. Bats, G. Bertucchi, G. Congès, and H. Tréziny, 235–243. Lattes: ADAM.

Hodder, I. 2012. *Entangled: An Archaeology of the Relationships between Humans and Things*. Malden, MA; Oxford;West Sussex, UK: Wiley-Blackwell.

Hodos, T. 1999. "Intermarriage in Western Greek Colonies." *Oxford Journal of Archaeology* 18: 61–78.

———. 2006. *Local Responses to Colonization in the Iron Age Mediterranean*. 1st ed. London; New York: Routledge.

———. 2009. "Local and Global Perspectives in the Study of Social and Cultural Identities." In *Material Culture and Social Identities in the Ancient World*, edited by S. Hales and T. Hodos, 3–31. Cambridge: Cambridge University Press.

Holloway, R.R. 2006. "The Tomb of the Diver." *American Journal of Archaeology* 110 (3): 365–388.

Hoving, T. 1994. *Making the Mummies Dance: Inside the Metropolitan Museum of Art*. New York: Simon and Schuster.

Hurst, H., and S. Owen, ed. 2005. *Ancient Colonizations: Analogy, Similarity, and Difference*. London: Duckworth.

Hurwit, J. 1977. "Image and Frame in Greek Art." *American Journal of Archaeology* 81 (1): 1–30.

Jacobs Solmonson, L. 2012. *Gin: A Global History*. London: Reaktion.

Jacobsthal, P. "Bodenfunde griechischer Vasen nördlich der Alpen." *Germania* 18: 14–19.

Jacoby, F. 1923–1998. *Die Fragmente der Griechischen Historiker*. 4 parts. Berlin/ Leiden: Weidmannische Buchhandlung/Brill.

Jameson, M. 1990. "Private Space and the Greek City." In *The Greek City: From Homer to Alexander*, edited by O. Murray and S. R. F. Price, 171–195. Oxford: Clarendon Press.

Joachim, H.-E. 1997. "Waldalgesheim: Das Grab Einer Keltischen Fürstin." In *Die Welt der Kelten: Dia-Vortragsreihe in Hochdorf/Enz 1991–1997: 30 Vorträge—Zusammenfassung*, edited by T. Bader, 105–110. Hochdorf an der Enz: Keltenmuseum.

Joffroy, R. 1954. *Le Trésor de Vix (Côte-d'Or)*. Paris: Presse Universitaire de France.

———. 1957. "Considérations sur la Tombe Princière de Vix (Côte-d'Or) et les Tombes à Char du Premier Âge du Fer." In *Mélanges Pittard, Offerts au Professeur Eugène Pittard par Ses Collègues et Ses Amis en L'honneur de Son 90ᵉ Anniversaire, 5 Juin 1957*, 175–180. Brive: Nizet.

———. 1960. *L'Oppidum de Vix et la Civilisation Hallstattienne Finale dans l'est de la France*. Publications de l'Université de Dijon 20. Dijon: Université de Dijon.

———. 1979. *Vix et Ses Trésors*. Paris: Librairie Jules Tallendier.

Johnston, A. W. 1979. *Trademarks on Greek Vases*. Warminster, Wiltshire, UK: Aris & Philips.

———. 1991a. "Greek Vases in the Marketplace." In *Looking at Greek Vases*, edited by T. Rasmussen and N. Spivey, 203–232. Cambridge: Cambridge University Press.

———. 1991b. "The Vase Trade: A Point of Order." *Acta Hyperborea* 3: 403–409.

Jones, J. E. 1976. "Hives and the Honey of Hymettus: Beekeeping in Ancient Greece." *Archaeology* 29: 80–91.

Jones, J. E., A. J. Graham, and L. H. Sackett. 1973. "An Attic Country House below the Cave of Pan at Vari." *Annual of the British School at Athens* 68: 355–453.

Jones, S. 1997. *The Archaeology of Ethnicity: Constructing Identities in Past and Present*. London: Routledge.

Jost, L. 2006. "Entropy and Diversity." *Oikos* 113 (2): 363–375.

Jully, J.-J. 1982. *Céramiques Grecques ou de Type Grec et Autres Céramiques en Languedoc Méditerranéen, Roussillon et Catalogne, VIIᵉ—IVᵉ s. avant Notre Ère et Leur Contexte Socio-Culturel*. Centre de Recherche D'histoire Ancienne 46. Paris: Les Belles Lettres.

Jung, M. 2007. "Kline Oder Thron? Zu den Fragmenten eines griechischen Möbelpfostens aus dem späthallstattzeitlichen 'Fürstengrab' Grafenbühl in Asperg (Kr. Ludwigsburg)." *Germania* 85: 95–107.

Jurado, J. F. 1989. "La Orientalización de Huelva." In *Tartessos: Arqueología Protohistorica del Bajo Guadalquivir*, edited by M. E. Aubet Semmler, 339–373. Sabadell: Editorial AUSA.

———. 2000. "Minería y Metalurgia en Tartessos." In *Argantonio, Rey de Tartessos*, 137–146. Seville: Fundacio El Monte.

———. 2002. "The Tartessian Economy: Mining and Metallurgy." In *The Phoenicians in Spain*, edited by M. R. Bierling, 241–262. Winona Lake, IN: Eisenbrauns.

Karageorghis, V., ed. 2002. *The Greeks beyond the Aegean: From Marseilles to Bactria*. New York: Alexander S. Onassis Public Benefit Foundation (USA).

Kenfield, J. 1990. "An East Greek Master Coroplast at Late Archaic Morgantina." *Hesperia* 59: 265–274.

———. 1993a. "A Modelled Terracotta Frieze from Archaic Morgantina: Its East Greek and Central Italian Affinities." In *Deliciae Fictiles: Proceedings of the First Architectural Conference on Central Italic Architectural Terracottas at the Swedish Institute in Rome*, 21–28. Stockholm: Swedish Institute.

———. 1993b. "The Case for a Phokaian Presence at Morgantina as Evidenced by the Site's Archaic Architectural Terracottas." In *Les grands ateliers d'architecture dans le monde égée du VIe siècle av. J.-C.*, edited by J. des Courtiles and J.-C. Moretti, 261–269. Paris: Diff. de Boccard.

Kimmig, W. 1983a. "Die griechische Kolonisation im westlichen Mittelmeergebiet und ihre Wirkung auf die Landschaften des westlichen Mitteleuropa." *Jahrbuch des römisch-germanischen Zentralmuseums Mainz* 30: 5–78.

———. 1983b. *Die Heuneburg an der oberen Donau*. 2nd ed. Führer Zu Archäologischen Denkmälern in Baden-Württemberg 1. Stuttgart: Theiss.

———, ed. 1988a. *Das Kleinaspergle: Studien zu einem Fürstengrabhügel der frühen Latenezeit bei Stuttgart*. Forschungen Und Berichte Zur Vor- Und Fruhgeschichte in Baden-Wurttemberg 30. Stuttgart: Theiss.

———. 1988b. "La Heuneburg sur le Danube Súperieur et Ses Relations Avec les Pays Méditerranéens." In *Les Princes Celtes et la Méditerranée*, 145–154. Paris: La Documentation Francaise.

———. 1992. "Etruskischer und griechischer Import im Spiegel westhallstattischer Fürstengraber." In *Etrusker nördlich von Etrurien: Etruskische Präsenz in Norditalien und nördlich der Alpen sowie ihre Einflüsse auf die einheimischen Kulturen: Akten des Symposions von Wien-Schloss Neuwaldegg 2.–5. Oktober 1989*, 281–328. Vienna: Verl. d. Österr. Akad. d. Wiss.

Kimmig, W., and E. Böhr. 2000. *Importe und mediterrane Einflüsse auf der Heuneburg*. Heuneburgstudien 11; Römisch-germanische Forschungen Bd. 59. Mainz am Rhein: V. Zabern.

Knappett, C. 2011. *An Archaeology of Interaction: Network Perspectives on Material Culture and Society*. Oxford; New York: Oxford University Press.

Korres, G. 1976. "Tumboi, tholoi, kai taphikoi tēs Messenias." In *Proceedings of the First International Conference of Peloponnesian Studies*, Vol. 2, 337–369. Athens: Society for Pelopnnesian Studies.

———. 1984. "The Relations between Crete and Messenia in the Late Middle Helladic and Early Late Helladic Period." In *The Minoan Thalassocracy: Myth and Reality*, edited by R. Hägg and N. Marinatos, 141–152. Athens: Swedish Institute at Athens.

Krause, R., E. Böhr, and M. Guggisberg. 2005. *Neue Forschungen zum frühkeltischen Fürstensitz auf dem Ipf bei Bopfingen, Ostalbkreis (Baden-Württemberg)*. Berlin: de Gruyter.

Krausse, D. 1999. "Der 'Keltenfürst' von Hochdorf: Dorfältester Oder Sakralkönig? Anspruch Und Wirklichkeit Der Sog. Kulturanthropologischen Hallstatt-Archäologie." *Archäologisches Korrespondenzblatt* 29 (3): 339–358.

———. 2004. "Komos und Kottabos Am Hohenasperg? Überlegungen zur Funktion Mediterraner Importgefässe Des 6. Und 5. Jahrhunderts Aus Südwestdeutschland." In *Die Hydria von Grächwil: Zur Funktion und Rezeption mediterraner Importe in Mitteleuropa im 6. und 5. Jahrhundert v. Chr.*, 193–201. Bern: Bernisches Historisches Museum.

Krausse, D., and N. Ebinger-Rist. 2012. "Jenseits der Donau: Das neue 'Fürsteinnengrab' von der Heuneburg." In *Die Welt der Kelten—Zentren der Macht, Kostbarkeiten der Kunst*, 124–126. Stuttgart: Thorbecke.

Krausse, D., and M. Fernández-Götz. 2012. "Die Heuneburg: Neue Forschungen zur Entwicklung einer späthallstattzeitlichen Stadt." In *Die Welt der Kelten—Zentren der Macht, Kostbarkeiten der Kunst*, 116–123. Stuttgart: Thorbecke.

Krausse, D., and G. Längerer. 1996. *Hochdorf. III, Das Trink- und Speiseservice aus dem späthallstattzeitlichen Fürstengrab von Eberdingen-Hochdorf (Kr. Ludwigsburg)*. Stuttgart: K. Theiss.

Kroeber, A. 1916. "Zuñi Potsherds." *Anthropological Papers of the American Museum of Natural History* 18: 1–38.

Kurke, L. 1999. *Coins, Bodies, Games, and Gold: The Politics of Meaning in Archaic Greece*. Princeton, NJ: Princeton University Press.

Kurz, S. 2007. *Untersuchungen zur Entstehung der Heuneburg in der späten Hallstattzeit*. Forschungen und Berichte zur Vor- und Frühgeschichte in Baden-Württemberg 105. Stuttgart: Theiss.

Kurz, S., and H. Drescher. 2000. *Die Heuneburg-Aussensiedlung: Befunde und Funde*. Forschungen und Berichte zur Vor- und Frühgeschichte in Baden-Württemberg 72. Stuttgart: Theiss.

Lacroix, W. F. G. 1998. *Africa in Antiquity: A Linguistic and Toponymic Analysis of Ptolemy's Map of Africa, Together with a Discussion of Ophir, Punt and Hanno's Voyage*. Saarbrücken: Verlag für Entwicklungspolitik Saarbrücken.

Laurence, R. 1998. "Land Transport in Roman Italy: Costs, Practice, and the Economy." In *Trade, Traders, and the City*, 129–148. London: Routledge.

Leighton, R. 1993. *Morgantina Studies IV: The Protohistoric Settlement on the Cittadella*. Princeton, NJ: Princeton University Press.

———. 1999. *Sicily before History: An Archaeological Survey from the Palaeolithic to the Iron Age*. Ithaca, NY: Cornell University Press.

———. 2012. *Prehistoric Houses at Morgantina. Excavations on the Cittadella of Morgantina in Sicily, 1989–2004*. Specialist Studies on Italy 15. London: Accordia.

Lenerz–de Wilde, M. 1995. "The Celts in Spain." In *The Celtic World*, edited by M. J. Green, 533–551. London; New York: Routledge.

Lepore, E. 1970. "Strutture della Colonizzazione Focea in Occidente." *La Parola Del Passato* 130–133: 19–54.

Lepore, E., and G. Nenci, ed. 1983. *Modes de Contacts et Processus de Transformation dans les Sociétés anciennes-Forme di Contatto e Processi Trasformazione nelle Società Antiche*. Collection de L'École Française de Rome 67. Pisa/Rome: Scuola normale di Pisa/École française de Rome.

Lewis, D.M. 1986. "Temple Inventories in Ancient Greece." In *Pots & Pans: A Colloquium on Precious Metals and Ceramics in the Muslim, Chinese and Graeco-Roman Worlds,* edited by M. Vickers, 71–95. Oxford: Oxford University Press.

Lissarrague, F. 1987. *Un flot d'images: Une esthétique du banquet grec*. Paris: A. Biro.

———. 1990a. "Around the Krater: An Aspect of Banquet Imagery." In *Sympotica: A Symposium on the Symposion*, 196–209. Oxford: Oxford University Press.

———. 1990b. *The Aesthetics of the Greek Banquet: Images of Wine and Ritual*. Princeton, NJ: Princeton University Press.

———. 1999. *Vases grecs: Les athéniens et leurs images*. Paris: Hazan.

Long, L. 1987. "Quelques Précisions sur le Conditionnement des Lingots de L'épave Antique Bagaud 2." In *Mines et Métallurgie en Gaule et dans les Provinces Voisines*, 149–163. Caesarodunum 22. Paris.

———. 1990. "Amphores Massaliètes: Objets Isolés et Gisements Sous-marins du Littoral Française Méditerranéen." In *Les Amphores de Marseille Grecque: Chronologie et Diffusion (VIᵉ-Iᵉʳ s. av. J.-C.),* edited by M. Bats, 27–70. Études Massaliètes 2. Lattes: ADAM.

Long, L., L.-F. Gantés, and M. Rival. 2006. "L'épave Grand Ribaud F: Un Chargement de Produits Étrusques du Début du Vᵉ s. av. J.-C." In *Gli Etruschi da Genova ad Ampurias: Atti del XXIV Convegno di Studi Etruschi ed Italici, Marseille, Lattes, 26 Settembre–1 Ottobre 2002,* 455–495. Pisa: Istituti editoriali e poligrafici internazionali.

Long, L., J. Miro, and G. Volpe. 1992. "Les Épaves Archaiques de La Pointe Lequin (Porquerolles, Hyères, Var): Des Données Nouvelles sur le Commerce de Marseille à la Fin du VIe S. et dans le Première Moitié du Ve S. Av. J.-C." In *Marseille Grecque et La Gaule: Actes du Colloque Internationale D'histoire et de Archéologie et du Ve Congrès Archéologique de Gaule Meridionale,* edited by M. Bats, G. Bertucchi, G. Congès, and H. Tréziny, 199–234. Lattes: ADAM.

Long, L., P. Pomey, and J.-C. Sourisseau. 2002. *Les Étrusques en Mer: Épaves d'Antibes à Marseille.* Aix-en-Provence: Edisud.

López-Ruiz, C. 2009. "Tarshish and Tartessos Revisited: Textual Problems and Historical Implications." In *Colonial Encounters in Ancient Iberia: Phoenician, Greek, and Indigenous Relations,* edited by M. Dietler and C. López-Ruiz, 255–280. Chicago: University of Chicago Press.

Lyons, C. L. 1996a. *Morgantina Studies V: The Archaic Cemeteries.* Princeton, NJ: Princeton University Press.

———. 1996b. "Sikel Burials at Morgantina: Defining Social and Ethnic Identities." In *Early Societies in Sicily: New Developments in Archaeological Research,* 177–188. Accordia Specialist Studies on Sicily 5. London: University of London.

———. 2007. "Nola and the Historiography of Greek Vases." *Journal of the History of Collections* 19 (11): 239–247.

Lyons, C. L., and J. K. Papadopoulos. 2002. *The Archaeology of Colonialism.* Los Angeles: Getty Publications.

Maffre, J.-J., and L.-F. Gantés. 2003. "Les Coupes Attiques." In *La Tombe Princière de Vix,* edited by C. Rolley. Paris: Picard et Société des amis du musée du Châtillonais.

Malkin, I. 1987. *Religion and Colonization in Ancient Greece.* Leiden: Brill.

———. 2011. *A Small Greek World: Networks in the Ancient Mediterranean.* New York: Oxford University Press.

Maluquer de Motes, J. 1985. *La Civilización de Tartessos: Historia.* Biblioteca de Cultura Andaluza 18. Seville: Editoriales Andaluzas Unidas.

Marshall, Y., and A. Maas. 1997. "Dashing Dishes." *World Archaeology* 28 (3) (February 1): 275–290.

Martín Ortega, M. A. 2000. "L'Oppidum del Puig de Sant Andreu d'Ullastret: Aportació de Les Intervacions Arqueològiques Recents al Coneixement dels Sistemes Defensius i de l'Urbanisme." In *L'hàbitat Protohistòric a Catalunya, Rossellói Llenguadoc Occidental: Actualitat de L'arqueologia de L'edat Del Ferro: Actes Del XXII Col·loqui Internacional Per a L'estudi de l'Edat Del Ferro,* 107–121. Monografies Emporitanes 11. Barcelona: Museu d'Arqueologia de Catalunya, Generalitat de Catalunya.

Martín Ortega, M. A., R. Buxó, J. López, and M. Mataró, ed. 1999. *Excavacions Arqueològiques a l'Illa D'en Reixac (1987–1992).* Monografies d'Ullastret 1. Girona: Museu d'Arqueologia de Catalunya, Ullastret.

Maschner, H. D. G., and C. Chippindale. 2005. *Handbook of Archaeological Methods.* Lanham, MD: Altamira.

Mateos Cruz, P. 2009. *Santuarios, Oppida y Ciudades: Arquitectura Sacra en el Origen y Desarrollo Urbano del Mediterráneo Occidental.* Anejos de Archivio Español de Arqueología 45. Mérida: Consejo Superior de Investigaciones Científicas, Instituto de Arqueología de Mérida.

Matthäus, H. 1998. "The Greek Symposion and the Near East: Chronology and Mechanisms of Cultural Exchange." In *Classical Archaeology towards the Third Millennium: Proceedings of the XVth International Congress of Classical Archaeology, Amsterdam, July 12–17, 1998,* 256–260. Amsterdam: Allard Pierson Museum.

McGovern, P., B. Luley, N. Rovira, A. Mirzoian, M. Callahan, K. Smith, G. Hall, T. Davidson, and J. Henkin. 2013. "Beginning of Viniculture in France." *Proceedings of the National Academy of Sciences of the United States of America* 110 (25): 10147–10152.

Megaw, J. V. S. 1966. "The Vix Burial." *Antiquity* 40: 38–44.

Milcent, P.-Y. *Bourges-Avaricum: Un Centre Proto-Urbain Celtique du V. s. av. J.-C.; les Fouilles du Quartier de Saint-Martin-des-Champs et les Decouvertés des Etablissements Militaires.* Bourges: Editions de la Ville de Bourges, service d'archéologie municipal.

Miller, D. 1995. "Consumption and Commodities." *Annual Review of Anthropology* 24: 141–161.

Miller, M. C. 1986. "Perserie: The Arts of the East in Fifth-Century Athens." Dissertation, Ann Arbor: University of Michigan.

———. 1993. "Adoption and Adaptation of Achaemenid Metalware Forms in Attic Black-Gloss Pottery of the Fifth Century B.C." *Archäologische Mitteilungen aus Iran* 26: 109–146.

———. 1997. *Athens and Persia in the Fifth Century B.C.: A Study in Cultural Receptivity.* Cambridge; New York: Cambridge University Press.

———. 2011. " 'Manners Makyth Man': Diacritical Drinking Practices in Achaemenid Anatolia." In *Cultural Identity in the Ancient Mediterranean,* edited by E.S. Gruen, 97–134. Issues & Debates. Los Angeles: Getty Research Institute.

Miró i Alaix, M. T. 2011. *La Ceràmica Àtica de Figures Roges de La Ciutat Grega d'Emporion.* Empúries: Museu d'Arqueologia de Catalunya, Empúries.

Moliner, M. 2001. "Orientations Urbaines dans Marseille Antique." In *Marseille: Trames et Paysages Urbains de Gyptis au Roi René: Acted du Colloque de Marseille 1999,* 101–120. Études Massaliètes 7. Aix-en-Provence: Edisud: Centre Camille Jullian.

Molist i Capella, N., and D. Asensio. 2008. *La Intervenció al Sector 01 del Conjunt Històric d'Olèrdola: De la Prehistòria a l'Etapa Romana (Campanyes 1995–2006).* Monografies d'Olèrdola 2. Barcelona: Museu d'Arqueologia de Catalunya; Generalitat de Catalunya, Departament de Cultura i Mitjans de Comunicació.

Morel, J.-P. 1983a. "Greek Colonization in Italy and the West: Problems of Evidence and Interpretation." In *Crossroads of the Mediterranean: Papers Delivered at the International Conference on Early Italy, Haffenreffer Museum, Brown University, 8–10 May 1981,* edited by T. Hackens, R. R. Holloway, and N. D. Holloway, 123–161. Providence-Louvain-la-Neuve: Brown University–Institut supérieur d'archéologie et d'histoire de l'art.

———. 1983b. "La Céramique comme Indice du Commerce Antique (Réalités et Interprétations)." In *Trade and Famine in Classical Antiquity,* edited by Peter Garnsey and C.R. Whitaker, 66–74. Cambridge: Cambridge Philological Society.

Morelli, G., and G. Frizzoni. 1890. *Kunstkritische Studien über italienische Malerei.* Leipzig: F. A. Brockhaus. http://archive.org/details/kunstkritischest01more.

Morris, I. 1996. "The Strong Principle of Equality and the Archaic Origins of Greek Democracy." In *Dēmokratia: A Conversation on Democracies, Ancient and Modern,* edited by J. Ober and C. Hedrick, 19–48. Princeton, NJ: Princeton University Press.

———. 2000. *Archaeology as Cultural History: Words and Things in Iron Age Greece.* Malden, MA: Blackwell.

———. 2003. "Mediterraneanization." *Mediterranean Historical Review* 18 (2): 30–55.

Mötsch, A. 2011. *Der Späthallstattzeitliche "Fürstensitz" auf dem Mont Lassois: Ausgrabungen des Kieler Instituts für Ur- und Frühgeschichte, 2002–2006.* Bonn: R. Habelt.

Müller-Scheessel, N. 2000. *Die Hallstattkultur und ihre Räumliche Differenzierung: Der West- Und Osthallstattkreis aus Forschungsgeschichtlich-Methodologischer Sicht.* Tübinger Texte—Materialen zur Ur- und Frühgeschichtlichen Archäologie 3. Tübingen: VML Verlag Marie Leidorf.

Mullins, P. R. 2011. "The Archaeology of Consumption." *Annual Review of Anthropology* 40: 133–144.

Murray, O., ed. 1990. *Sympotica: A Symposium on the Symposion.* Oxford: Clarendon Press.

Murray, O. 1995. "Forms of Sociality." In *The Greeks,* 2nd ed., edited by J.P. Vernant, 218–253. Chicago: University of Chicago Press.

Murray, O., and S. R. F. Price, eds. 1990. *The Greek City: From Homer to Alexander.* Oxford: Clarendon Press.

Napoli, M. 1970. *La Tomba del Tuffatore.* Spazio e Tempo. Bari: De Donato.

Neils, J. 1995. "The Euthymides Krater from Morgantina." *American Journal of Archaeology* 99: 427–444.

Neiman, F. 1997. "Conspicuous Consumption as Wasteful Advertising: A Darwinian Perspective on Spatial Patterns in Classic Maya Terminal Monument Dates." *Archeological Papers of the American Anthropological Association* 7 (1): 267–290.

Nevett, L.C. 1999. *House and Society in the Ancient Greek World.* Cambridge: Cambridge University Press.

Nickels, A. 1982. "Agde Grecque: Les Recherches Recentes." *La Parola del Passato:* 269–279.

———. 1983. "Les Grecques en Gaule: L'example du Languedoc." In *Modes de Contacts et Processus de Transformation dans les Sociétés Anciennes: Actes du Colloque de Cortone (24–30 Mai 1981),* 409–428. Collection de l'École Française de Rome 67. Pisa/Rome: Scuola normale di Pisa/École Française de Rome.

———. 1989. "La Monédière à Bessan (Hérault): Le Bilan des Recherches." *Documents d'Archéologie Mérdionale* 12: 51–120.

———. 1995. "Les Sondages de la Rue Perben à Agde." In *Sur les Pas des Grecs en Occident: Hommages à André Nickels,* 59–98. Etudes Massaliètes, 4, Travaux du Centre Camille Jullian, 15. Lattes/Paris: Association pour la diffusion de l'archéologie méridionale /Errance.

Northover, P. 1984. "Iron Age Bronze Metallurgy in Central Southern England." In *Aspects of the Iron Age in Central Southern Britain,* edited by B. Cunliffe and D. Miles, 126–145. Oxford: Oxford University Press.

Obeyesekere, G. 1997. *The Apotheosis of Captain Cook: European Mythmaking in the Pacific.* Princeton, NJ: Princeton University Press.

Oliva Prat, M. 1950. "Actividades de La Comisaria (1) Provincial de Excavaciones Arqueológicas de Gerona en 1950." *Anales del Instituto de Estudios Gerundenses.* Excavaciones Arqueológicas en la Ciudad Ibérica de Ullastret (Gerona): 267–270.

———. 1953. "Actividades de la Comisaria (4) Provincial de Excavaciones Arqueológicas de Gerona en 1953." *Anales del Instituto de Estudios Gerundenses.* Excavaciones Arqueológicas en la Ciudad Ibérica de Ullastret (Gerona): 296–327.

———. 1954. "Excavaciones Arqueológicas en la Ciudad Ibérica de Ullastret (Gerona): Quinta Campaña de Trabajos." *Anales del Instituto de Estudios Gerundenses.* Excavaciones Arqueológicas en la Ciudad Ibérica de Ullastret (Gerona).

———. 1962. "Les Fouilles Archéologiques de L'oppidum d'Ullastret (Gérone, Espagne)." In *Actes du 86e Congrès National des Sociétés Savantes, Montpellier 1961. Section D'archéologie,* 61–69. Paris: Impr. nationale.

———. 1976. "Excavaciones Arqueológicas en el Yacimiento Prerromano de Ullastret, Bajo Ampurdán (Gerona). Propiedad de la Excma. Diputación Provincial." *Noticiario Arqueológico Hispánico:* 733–799.

———. "Actividades de la Delegación Provincial Del Servicio Nacional de Excavaciones Arqueológicas de Gerona en 1955." *Anales del Instituto de Estudios Gerundenses.* Excavaciones Arqueológicas en la Ciudad Ibérica de Ullastret (Gerona): 317–411.

Olmos-Romera, R. 1986. "Los Griegos en Tarteso: Replanteamiento Arqueológico-histórico del Problema." In *Actas Del Congreso <<Homenaje a Luis Siret>> (1934–1984), Cuevas del Almanzora, Junio 1984,* edited by O. Arteaga, 584–600. Seville: Consejería de Cultura de la Junta de Andalucía, Dirección General de Bellas Artes.

Olsen, B. 2013. *In Defense of Things: Archaeology and the Ontology of Objects.* Lanham: Altamira.

Olson, S.D., and A. Sens. 2000. *Archestratos of Gela: Greek Culture and Cuisine in the Fourth Century* BC. Oxford: Oxford University Press.

Orsi, P. 1919. "Gli Scavi Intorno all'Athenaion di Siracusa." *Monumenti Antichi* 25: 353–754.

Orton, C., P. Tyers, and A. Vince. 1993. *Pottery in Archaeology.* Cambridge: Cambridge University Press.

Osuna Ruiz, M., J. Bedia García, and A.M. Domínguez Rico. 2000. "El Santuario Protohistórico Hallado En La Calle Méndez Núñez (Huelva)." In *Cerámiques Jònies D'época Arcaica: Centres de Producció i Comercialitizició Al Mediterrani Occidental,* 177–188. Barcelona: Museu d'Arqueología de Catalunya.

Owen, S. 2005. "Analogy, Archaeology, and Archaic Greek Colonization." In *Ancient Colonizations: Analogy, Similarity, and Difference,* 5–22. London: Duckworth.

Pais, E. 1933. *Storia Dell' Italia Antica e Della Sicilia Per L'età Anteriore al Dominio Romano.* 2nd ed. 2 vols. Torino: Unione tipografico-editrice torinese.

Paleothodoros, D. 2007. "Commercial Networks in the Mediterranean and the Diffusion of Early Attic Red-figure Pottery (525–490 BCE)." *Mediterranean Historical Review* 22 (2): 168–182.

Pelagatti, P., and C.M. Stibbe. 1988. "Una Forma Poco Conosciuta di Vaso Laconico: Il Cratere a Campana." *Bollettino d'Arte* 73 (2): 13–26.

Pellicer, M. 1982. "Las Cerámicas del Mundo Fenicio en el Bajo Guadalquivir. Evolución y Cronología según El Cerro Macareno (Sevilla)." In *Phönizier im Westen: Die Beiträge des Internationalen Symposiums über "Die Phönizische Expansion im westlichen Mittelmeerraum" in Köln Vom 24. Bis 27. April, 1979,* 371–403. Madrider Beiträge 8. Mainz: v. Zabern.

Pellicer, M., P. Rouillard, and L. Menanteau. 1977. "Para una Metodología de Localización de Colonias Fenicias en las Costas Ibéricas: El Cerro del Prado." *Habis. Filología Clásica. Historia Antigua, Arqueología Clásica* 8: 217–251.

Pellizer, E. "Outline of a Morphology of Sympotic Entertainment." In *Sympotica: A symposium on the Symposion,* edited by O. Murray, 177–184. Oxford: Oxford University Press.

Pereira Sieso, J. 1987. "Imitaciones Ibéricas de Cráteras Áticas Procedentes de Gor (Granada)." In *XVIII Congreso Nacional de Arqueología,* 701–711. Zaragoza: Secretaría General de los Congresos Arqueológicos Nacionales, Universidad de Zaragoza Seminario de Arqueología.

———. 1988. *La Cerámica pintada a torno en Andalucía entre los siglos VI y III a. d. c.: Cuenca del Guadalquivir.* Tesis doctorales 406/88. Madrid: Universidad Complutense de Madrid. Servicio de Reprografía.

Picazo, Marina. 1977. *Las cerámicas áticas de Ullastret.* Publicaciones eventuales 28. Barcelona: Universidad, Instituto de Arqueología y Prehistoria.

Plana i Mallart, R., and M.A. Martín Ortega. 2001. "L'Organitzacio de L'espai Rural Entorn de L'oppidum d'Ullastret: Formes i Dinamica Del Poblament." In *Territori Polítics i Territori Rural Durant L'edat del Ferro a La Mediterrània Occidental: Actes de La Taula Rodona Celebrada a Ullastret,* 157–176. Girona:

Museu d'Arqueologia de Catalunya; Generalitat de Catalunya, Departament de Cultura i Mitjans de Comunicació.

Pomey, P., and L. Long. 1992. "Les Premiers Échanges Maritimes du Midi de la Gaule du VIᵉ au IIIᵉ s. av. J.-C. à travers Les Épaves." In *Marseille Grecque et La Gaule: Actes du Colloque Interntaionale D'histoire et de Archéologie et du Vᵉ Congrès Archéologique de Gaule Meridionale*, edited by M. Bats, G. Bertucchi, G. Congès, and H. Tréziny, 189–198. Lattes: ADAM.

Prats, A.G., A. García Menárguez, and E. Ruiz Segura. 2002. "La Fonteta: A Phoenician City in the Far West." In *The Phoenicians in Spain*, 113–126. Winona Lake, IN: Eisenbrauns.

Pugliese Carratelli, G. 1996. *The Greek World: Art and Civilization in Magna Graecia and Sicily*. New York: Rizzoli.

Pulak, C. 2008. "The Uluburun Shipwreck and Late Bronze Age Trade." In *Beyond Babylon: Art, Trade, and Diplomacy in the Second Millennium B.C.*, edited by J. Aruz, K. Benzel, and J.M. Evans, 288–305. New York: Metropolitan Museum of Art.

Py, M. 1990. *Culture, Économie et Société Protohistoriques dans la Région Nimoise*. 2 vols. Collection de l'École Française de Rome 131. Rome: École Française de Rome.

———. 1992. *Les Gaulois du Midi: De la Fin de l'Âge du Bronze à la Conquête Romaine*. Paris: Hachette.

———. 1993. *Dicocer: Dictionnaire des céramiques antiques (VIIᵉᵐᵉ s. av. n. è.—VIIᵉᵐᵉ s. de n. è.) en Méditerranée nord-occidentale (Provence, Languedoc, Ampurdan)*. Lattara 6. Lattes: Édition de l'Association pour la recherche archéologique en Languedoc oriental.

———. 2001. *Dicocer2: Corpus des ce´ramiques de l'Age du Fer à Lattes (fouilles 1963–1999)*. Lattara 14. Lattes: Editions de l'Association pour la recherche archéologique en Languedoc oriental.

Reim, H. 1968. "Zur Henkelplatte eines attischen Kolonettenkraters vom Uetliberg (Zurich)." *Germania* 46: 274–285.

Reusser, Christoph. 2002. *Vasen für Etrurien: Verbreitung und Funktionen attischer Keramik im Etrurien des 6. und 5. Jahrhunderts vor Christus*. Kilchberg: Akanthus—Verlag für Archäologie.

Rice, P.M. 2005. *Pottery Analysis: A Sourcebook*. Chicago: University of Chicago Press.

Ridgway, D. 1992. *The First Western Greeks*. New York: Cambridge University Press.

Roberts, S.R., and A. Glock. 1986. "The Stoa Gutter Well: A Late Archaic Deposit in the Athenian Agora." *Hesperia* 55 (1): 1–74.

Robertson, M. 1985. "Beazley and Attic Vase Painting." In *Beazley and Oxford*, edited by D.C. Kurtz, 19–30. Oxford: Oxford University Press.

Rocha Pereira, M.H. 1955. "Notícias sobre Vasos Gregos Existentes em Portugal." *Humanitas* 7: 177–194.

———. 1959. "Notícias sobre Vasos Gregos Existentes em Portugal, 2." *Humanitas* 11: 11–32.

———. 2007. *Vasos Gregos em Portugal—Aquém das Colunas de Hércules*. Lisbon: Museu Nacional de Arqueologia.

Rotroff, S.I., and J.H. Oakley. 1992. *Debris from a Public Dining Room in the Athenian Agora*. Hesperia Supplement 25. Princeton, NJ: American School of Classical Studies at Athens.

Rouet, P. 2001. *Approaches to the Study of Greek Vases*. Oxford: Oxford University Press.

Rouillard, P. 1991. *Les Grecs et la péninsule ibérique Péninsule Ibérique du VIIIᵉ au IVᵉ Siècle avant Jésus-Christ*. Publications du Centre Pierre 21. Talence, France; Paris: Université de Bordeaux III; Diffusion De Boccard.

———. 1995. "Les Emporia dans la Méditeranée Occidentale aux Époques Archaïque et Classique." In *Les Grecs et l'Occident, Actes du Colloque de la Villa "Kérylos"*, 95–108. Collection de l'École Française de Rome, 208, Cahiers de la Villa "Kérylos", No. 2. Paris: École Française de Rome.

———. 2009. "Greeks and the Iberian Peninsula." In *Colonial Encounters in Ancient Iberia: Phoenician, Greek, and Indigenous Relations*, edited by M. Dietler and C. López-Ruiz, 131–151. Chicago: University of Chicago Press.

Rouillard, P., E. Gailledrat, and H. Dridi. 2009. "Entre Phéniciens et Ibères: Le Cas de La Fonteta/Rábita à Guardamar Del Segura." In *Phönizisches und Punisches Städtewesen: Akten der Internationalen Tagung in Rom vom 21. bis 23. Februar 2007*, 485–497. Iberia Archaeologica 13. Mainz am Rhein: V. Zabern.

Rouillard, P., and A. Verbanck-Piérard. 2003. *Le Vase Grec et Ses Destins*. München: Biering & Brinkmann.

Ruby, P. 2006. "Peuples, Fictions? Ethnicité, Identité Ethnique et Sociétés Anciennes." *Revue des Études Anciennes* 108 (1): 25–60.

Ruiz, A., and M. Molinos. 1998. *The Archaeology of the Iberians*. Cambridge; New York: Cambridge University Press.

Ruiz Delgado, M.M. 1989. "Las Necrópolis Tartésicas: Prestigio, Poder y Jerarquías." In *Tartessos: Arqueología Protohistorica del Bajo Guadalquivir*, edited by M. E. Aubet Semmler, 247–286. Sabadell: Editorial AUSA.

Ruiz Mata, D., ed. 2000. *Fenicios e Indígenas en el Mediterraneo y Occidente: Modelos e Interacción*. Encuentros de Primavera en el Puerto de Santa María 3. Cádiz: Universidad de Cádiz.

Ruiz Zapatero, G. 1983–1984. "El Comercio Protocolonial y los Orígenes de la Iberización: Dos Casos de Estudio: El Bajo Aragón y la Cataluña Interior." *Kalathos* 3–4: 51–70.

Sahlins, M. 1987. *Islands of History*. Chicago: University of Chicago Press.

———. 1996. *How "Natives" Think: About Captain Cook, For Example*. Chicago: University of Chicago Press.

———. 2004a. *Stone Age Economics*. London; New York: Routledge.

———. 2004b. *Apologies to Thucydides: Understanding History as Culture and Vice Versa*. Chicago: University of Chicago Press.

Said, E. W. 1979. *Orientalism*. New York: Vintage.

Sanmartí, E., and J. Padro. 1976–1978. "Ensayo de Aproximación al Fenómeno de Iberización en las Comarcas Meridionales de Cataluña." *Ampurias* 38–40.

Sanmartí, J. 2009. "Colonial Relations and Social Change in Iberia (Seventh to Third Centuries BC)." In *Colonial Encounters in Ancient Iberia: Phoenician, Greek, and Indigenous Relations*, edited by M. Dietler and C. López-Ruiz, 49–89. Chicago: University of Chicago Press.

Sanmartí, J., and J. Santacana. 2005. *Els Ibers del Nord*. Barcelona: Rafael Dalmau.

Sanmartí-Grego, E. 1992. "Massalia et Emporion: Une Origine Commune, Deux Destins Differents." In *Marseille Grecque et la Gaule: Actes du Colloque Internationale D'histoire et de Archéologie et du Vᵉ Congrès Archéologique de Gaule Meridionale*, 27–41. Études Massaliètes. 3.

Santos, A. 2003. "Fenicios y Griegos en el Extremo NE Peninsular Durante la Época Arcaica y los Orígenes del Enclave Foceo de Emporion." In *Contactos en el Extremo de La Oikouméne: Los Griegos en Occidente y Sus Relaciones con los Fenicios. XVII Jornadas de Arqueología Fenicio-Púnica*, 87–132. Treballs del Museu Arqueològic d'Eivissa i Formentera 51. Eivissa: Museo Arqueológico de Ibiza y Formentera.

Schaaff, U. 1988. "Zu den antiken Repareturen der griechischen Schalen." In *Das Kleinaspergle: Studien zu einem Fürstengrabhügel der frühen Latenezeit bei*

Stuttgart, edited by W. Kimmig, 191–195. Forschungen und Berichte zur Vor- und Frühgeschichte in Baden-Württemberg 30. Stuttgart: Theiss.

Schmitt-Pantel, P. 1990. "Sacrificial Meal and *Symposion:* Two Models of Civic Institutions in the Archaic City?" In *Sympotica: A symposium on the Symposion,* edited by O. Murray, 14–35. Oxford: Oxford University Press.

———. 1992. *La Cité au Banquet: Histoire des Repas Publics dans les Cités Grecques.* Paris: École Française de Rome.

Schulten, A. 1959. *Geografía y Etnografía Antiguas de la Peninsula Ibérica.* 2 vols. Madrid: Consejo Superior de Investigaciones Científicas, Instituto "Rodrigo Caro" de Arqueología.

Schwab, H., and L. Kahil. 1983. "Châtillon-sur-Glâne: Bilanz der ersten Sondier-grabungen." *Germania* 61 (2): 405–458.

Schweitzer, R. 1971. "Decouverté de Tessons Attiques à Figures Noires au Britzgyberg près d'Illfurth." *Bulletin du Musée Historique de Mulhouse* 79: 39–44.

———. 1973. "Le Britzgyberg—Station du Hallstatt." *Bulletin du Musée Historique de Mulhouse* 81: 43–64.

Schweizer, B. 2003. *Die François-Vase vom Kerameikos in Athen bis ins Grab bei Chiusi. Zur Lesung griechischer Mythenbilder im Medialen und im Funktions-kontext.* Münster: Scriptorium.

———. 2012. "Bilder griechischer Tongefäße in Mittelitalien und Nördlich der Alpen. Medien der Hellenisierung oder Mediterranisierung, der Akkulturation oder der kulturellen Interaktion, der interkulturellen Kommunikation oder der Konstruk-tion kultureller." *Corpus Vasorum Antiquorum Beiheft* 5: 15–25. Munich.

Searle, J. 1995. *The Construction of Social Reality.* New York: Free Press.

Serra-Rafols, J. 1974. "Las Relaciones Comerciales entre Iberia y Grecia durante la Segunda Edad del Hierro." In *Simposio Internacional de Colonizaciones,* edited by E.R. Perelló and E.S. Grego, 217–222. Barcelona: Instituto de Prehistoria y Arqueología.

Shefton, B. B. 1982. "Greeks and Greek Imports in the South of the Iberian Penin-sula: The Archaeological Evidence." In *Phönizier im Westen: Die Beiträge des internationalen Symposiums über "Die phönizische Expansion im westlichen Mittelmeerraum" in Köln vom 24. bis 27. April, 1979,* 337–368. Madrider Beitrager 8. Mainz: v. Zabern.

———. 1994. "Massalia and Colonization in the North-Western Mediterranean." In *The Archaeology of Greek Colonisation,* 61–86. Oxford: Oxford School of Archaeology.

———. 1995. "Leaven in the Dough: Greek and Etruscan Imports North of the Alps—The Classical Period." In *Italy in Europe: Economic Relations, 700* BC–AD *50,* 9–44. London: British Museum Press.

———. 1996. "The Castulo Cup. An Attic Shape in Black Glaze of Special Signif-icance in Sicily. With Philological Addenda." In *I Vasi Attici ed Altre Cerami-che Coeve in Sicilia,* 1:85–98. Cronache di Archeologia 29–30. Catania: Istituto d'Archeologia.

Shennan, S. 1997. *Quantifying Archaeology.* Edinburgh: Edinburgh University Press.

Shepherd, G. 1999. "Fibulae and Females: Intermarriage in the Western Greek Col-onies and the Evidence from the Cemeteries." In *Ancient Greeks West and East,* edited by G. Tsetskhladze, 267–300. Leiden: Brill.

———. 2005. "The Advance of the Greek: Greece, Great Britain and the Archaeo-logical Empires." In *Ancient Colonizations: Analogy, Similarity, and Difference,* edited by H. Hurst and S. Owen, 23–44. London: Duckworth.

Simpson, E. H. 1949. "Measurement of Diversity." *Nature* 163: 688.

Sjöqvist, E. 1962. "I Greci a Morgantina." *Kokalos* 8: 52–68.

Smalls, J. P. 1994. "Scholars, Etruscans, and Attic Painted Vases." *Journal of Roman Archaeology* 7: 34–58.

Smith, E. A., M. B. Mulder, and K. Hill. 2001. "Controversies in Evolutionary Social Sciences: A Guide for the Perplexed." *Trends in Ecology and Evolution* 16 (3): 128–135.

Smith, T. J. 2000. "Dancing Spaces and Dining Places." In *Periplous: Papers on Classical Art and Archaeology Presented to Sir John Boardman,* edited by G. R. Tsetskhladze, A. J. N. W. Prag, and A. M. Snodgrass, 309–319. London: Thames and Hudson.

———. 2005. "The Beazley Archive: Inside and Out." *Art Documentation* 24 (1): 22–25.

———. 2010. *Komast Dancers in Archaic Greek Art.* Oxford; New York: Oxford University Press.

Smith, W. S. 1998. *The Art and Architecture of Ancient Egypt.* Rev. Pelican History of Art. New Haven, CT: Yale University Press.

Sparkes, B. A. 1996. *The Red and the Black: Studies in Greek Pottery.* London; New York: Routledge.

Sparkes, B. A., and L. Talcott. 1970. *Black and Plain Pottery of the 6th, 5th and 4th Centuries B.C.* 2 vols. The Athenian Agora XII. Princeton, NJ: American School of Classical Studies at Athens.

Spencer-Wood, S., ed. 1987. *Consumer Choice in Historical Archaeology.* New York: Plenum Press.

Spindler, K. 1980. "Zur Elfenbeinscheibe aus dem hallstattzeitlichen Fürstengrab vom Grafenbühl." *Archäologisches Korrespondenzblatt* 10: 239–248.

———. 1991. *Die frühen Kelten.* Ditzingen, Germany: Reclam Philipp Jun.

Stahl, A. 2002. "Colonial Entanglements and the Practices of Taste: An Alternative to Logocentric Approaches." *American Anthropologist,* New Series, 104 (3): 827–845.

Stead, I. M., and V. Rigby. 1999. *The Morel Collection: Iron Age Antiquities from Champagne in the British Museum.* London: British Museum Press.

Steinbauer, D. H. 1999. *Neues Handbuch des Etruskischen.* St. Katharinen, Germany: Scripta Mercaturae.

Sternberg, M., and H. Tréziny. 2005. "Le Territoire Marsellais et les Resources Naturelles." In *Marseille et Ses Alentours,* edited by M.-P. Rothé and H. Tréziny, 244–251. Carte Archéologique de La Gaule 13.3. Paris: CID.

Stibbe, C. M. 1972. *Lakonische Vasenmaler des sechsten Jahrhunderts v. Chr.* Amsterdam: North-Holland Publishing.

———. 1989. *Laconian Mixing Bowls: A History of the Krater Lakonikos from the Seventh to the Fifth Century B.C.* Allard Pierson Series vol. 2. Amsterdam: Allard Pierson Museum.

Strabo. 1917. *Geography.* Translated by H. L. Jones. 8 vols. Loeb Classical Library. Cambridge, MA: Harvard University Press.

Strassler, R. B. 2009. *The Landmark Herodotus: The Histories.* New York: Random House.

Strong, D. E. 1966. *Greek and Roman Gold and Silver Plate.* London: Methuen.

Tarkington, B. 1918. *The Magnificent Ambersons.* Lexington, KY.

Tartaron, T. F. 2013. *Maritime Networks in the Mycenaean World.* Cambridge: Cambridge University Press.

Themelis, P. G. 2002. "Contribution to the Topography of the Sanctuary at Brauron." In *Le Orsi di Brauron: Un Rituale di Iniziazione Femminile nel Santuario di Artemide,* B. Gentili and F. Perusino, eds. Pisa: ETS. 103–116.

Thomas, N. 1991. *Entangled Objects: Exchange, Material Culture and Colonialism in the Pacific.* Cambridge, MA: Harvard University Press.

Tomlinson, R.A. 1990. "The Chronology of the Perachora Hestiatorion and Its Significance." In *Sympotica: A Symposium on the Symposion*, 95–101. Oxford: Oxford University Press.

Topper, K. 2009. "Primitive Life and the Construction of the Sympotic Past in Athenian Vase Painting." *American Journal of Archaeology* 113 (1): 3–26.

Topper, K. 2012. *The Imagery of the Athenian Symposium.* New York: Cambridge University Press.

Travlos, J. 1971. *Pictorial Dictionary of Ancient Athens.* London: Thames and Hudson.

Tréziny, H. 2001. "Les fortifications de Marseille dans l'Antiquité." In *Marseille: Trames et paysages urbains de Gyptis au Roi René,* edited by M. Bouiron and H. Tréziny, 45–57. Aix-en-Provence: Edisud.

Trías de Arribas, G. 1967–1968. *Cerámicas Griegas de la Península Ibérica.* 2 vols. Valencia: William L. Bryant Foundation.

Trigger, B.G. 2006. *A History of Archaeological Thought.* 2nd ed. Cambridge; New York: Cambridge University Press.

Ugolini, D., and C. Olive. 1995. "La Céramique Attique de Béziers (VIᵉ-IVᵉ s.): Approche de la Diffusion et de L'utilisation de la Vaisselle Attique en Languedoc Occidental." In *Sur les Pas des Grecs en Occident: Hommages à André Nickels,* edited by P. Arcelin, M. Bats, D. Garcia, G. Marchand, and M. Schwaller, 237–260. Paris-Lattes: Editions Errance, ADAM.

Untermann, J. 1992. "Quelle Langue Parlait-on dans l'Hérault Pendant l'Antiquité?" *Revue Archeólogique Narbonnaise* 25: 19–27.

Van den Boom, H. 2006. "Remarks on Some Less-Known Greek Imports at the Heuneburg." In *I Celti e il Mondo Greco*, 13–19. Bologna: Università di Bologna, Dipartimento di archeologia.

Van der Leeuw, S.E. 1999. "Exchange and Trade in Ceramics: Some Notes from the Potter's Point of View." In *The Complex Past of Pottery: Production, Circulation and Consumption of Mycenaean and Greek Pottery (Sixteenth to Early Fifth Centuries BC). Proceedings of ARCHON International Conference, Amsterdam, 8–9 November 1996,* edited by J.P. Crielaard, V. Stissi, and G.J. Van Wijngaarden, 115–136. Amsterdam: J.C. Gieben.

van Dommelen, P. 1997. "Colonial Constructs: Colonialism and Archaeology in the Mediterranean." *World Archaeology* 28 (3) (February 1): 305–323.

———. 2002. "Ambiguous Matters: Colonialism and Local Identities in Punic Sardinia." In *The Archaeology of Colonialism,* edited by C.L. Lyons and J.K. Papadopoulos, 121–150. Los Angeles: Getty Publications.

Veblen, T. 1899. *Theory of the Leisure Class: An Economic Study of Institutions.* New York: Macmillan.

Vickers, M.J. 1999. *Skeuomorphismus, oder die Kunst, aus Wenig Viel zu Machen.* Trierer Winckelmannsprogramme 16. Mainz: v. Zabern.

Vickers, M.J., and D.W.J. Gill. 1994. *Artful Crafts: Ancient Greek Silverware and Pottery.* Oxford: Oxford University Press.

———. 1995. "They Were Expendable: Greek Vases in the Etruscan Tomb." *Revue des Études Anciennes* 97: 225–249.

Vickers, M.J. O.R. Impey, and J.W. Allan. 1986. *From Silver to Ceramic: The Potter's Debt to Metalwork in the Graeco-Roman, Oriental and Islamic Worlds.* Oxford: Ashmolean Museum.

Villard, F. 1959. *La Céramique Grecque de Marseille (VIᵉ-IVᵉ siècle); Essai d'histoire Économique.* Paris: E. de Boccard.

Vitali, D., ed. 2008. *I celti e il mondo Greco.* Bologna: Università di Bologna, Dipartimento di archeologia.

Vives-Ferrándiz, J. 2010. "Mobility, Materiality, and Identities in Iron Age East Iberia: Appropriation of Material Culture and the Question of Judgement." In

Material Connections in the Ancient Mediterranean: Mobility, Materiality, and Identity, edited by P. van Dommelen and A.B. Knapp, 190–209. New York: Routledge.

Von Reden, S. 2003. *Exchange in Ancient Greece.* London: Duckworth.

Voss, B., and R. Allen. 2010. "Guide to Ceramic MNV Calculation Qualitative and Quantitative Analysis." *Technical Briefs in Historical Archaeology* 5: 1–9.

Voza, G. 1973a. "Thapsos." In *Archeologia nella Sicilia Sud-Orientale,* edited by P. Pelagatti and G. Voza, 30–53. Naples: Centre Jean Bérard.

———. 1973b. "Villasmundo—Necropoli in Contrada Fossa." In *Archeologia nella Sicilia Sud-Orientale,* edited by P. Pelagatti and G. Voza, 57–63. Naples: Centre Jean Bérard.

Wagner, C. 1995. "Fenicios y Autóctonos en Tartessos. Consideraciones sobre las Relaciones Coloniales y la Dinámica de Cambio en el Suroeste de la Península Ibérica." *Trabajos de Prehistoria* 52 (1): 109–126.

Wallace, D.F. 2009. *This Is Water: Some Thoughts, Delivered on a Significant Occasion, About Living a Compassionate Life.* New York: Little, Brown.

Wallerstein, I. 1974. *The Modern World-System.* New York: Academic Press.

Walsh, J. 2006. "Ethnicity, Daily Life, and Trade: Domestic Assemblages from Fifth-Century BCE Morgantina, Sicily." Dissertation, Charlottesville: University of Virginia.

———. 2009. "Exchange and Influence: Hybridity and the Gate Reliefs of Thasos." In *Structure, Image, Ornament: Architectural Sculpture in the Greek World,* edited by P. Schultz and R. von den Hoff, 174–187. Oxbow Books.

———. 2011–2012. "Urbanism and Identity at Classical Morgantina." *Memoirs of the American Academy in Rome* 56/57: 115–136.

———. 2013. "Consumption and Choice in Ancient Sicily." In *Regionalism and Globalism in Antiquity: Exploring Their Limits,* edited by F. De Angelis, 229–246. Ancient West and East, Colloquia Antiqua 7. Leuven: Peeters.

Walsh, J., and C.M. Antonaccio. 2014. "Athenian Black Gloss Pottery: A View from the West." *Oxford Journal of Archaeology* 33 (1).

Watkins, C. 1995. "Greece in Italy outside Rome." *Harvard Studies in Classical Philology* 97: 35–50.

Watson, P. and C. Todeschini. 2006. *The Medici Conspiracy: The Illicit Journey of Looted Antiquities From Italy's Tomb Raiders to the World's Greatest Museums.* New York: Public Affairs.

Wehgartner, I., and H. Zoller. 1995. *Luxusgeschirr Keltischer Fürsten: Griechische Keramik nördlich der Alpen: Sonderausstellung des Mainfränkischen Museums Würzburg in Verbindung mit der Antikenabteilung des Martin-von-Wagner-Museums der Universität Würzburg und der prähistorischen Staatssammlung München, 14. Juni–13. August 1995.* Mainfränkisches Heft 93. Würzburg: Mainfränkisches Museum Würzburg.

Wells, P. 1979. "West-Central Europe and the Mediterranean: The Decline in Trade in the Fifth Century BC." *Expedition* 21 (4): 18–24.

———. 1981. *Culture Contact and Culture Change: Early Iron Age Central Europe and the Mediterranean.* Cambridge; New York: Cambridge University Press.

———. 1995. "Trade and Exchange." In *The Celtic World,* edited by M.J. Green, 230–243. London: Routledge.

———. 2001. *Beyond Celts, Germans and Scythians: Archaeology and Identity in Iron Age Europe.* Duckworth Debates in Archaeology. London: Duckworth.

Wheatley, D., and M. Gillings. 2002. *Spatial Technology and Archaeology: The Archaeological Applications of GIS.* New York: Taylor & Francis.

Wilkins, J., D. Harvey, and M. Dobson. 1995. *Food in Antiquity.* Exeter, UK: University of Exeter Press.

Wilkins, J., and S. Hill. 2006. *Food in the Ancient World*. Malden, MA; Oxford: Blackwell.

Zahavi, A. 1975. "Mate Selection: A Selection for Handicap." *Journal of Theoretical Biology* 53: 205–214.

———. 1977. "The Cost of Honesty (Further Remarks on the Handicap Principle)." *Journal of Theoretical Biology* 67: 603–605.

Zeller, K. W. 1997. "Die Salzherren vom Dürrnberg." In *Die Welt der Kelten: Dia-Vortragsreihe in Hochdorf/Enz 1991–1997: 30 Vorträge—Zusammenfassung*, edited by T. Bader.

Zürn, H. 1975. "Der Grafenbühl, ein späthallstattzeitlicher Fürstengrabhügel bei Asperg." In *Ausgrabungen in Deutschland, Gefördert von der deutschen Forschungsgemeinschaft, 1950–1975. Teil 1, Vorgeschichte. Römerzeit*, 216–220. Mainz: Verlag des Römisch-Germanischen Zentralmuseums.

Index

For Product Safety Concerns and Information please contact our EU
representative GPSR@taylorandfrancis.com
Taylor & Francis Verlag GmbH, Kaufingerstraße 24, 80331 München, Germany

www.ingramcontent.com/pod-product-compliance
Ingram Content Group UK Ltd.
Pitfield, Milton Keynes, MK11 3LW, UK
UKHW020940180425
457613UK00019B/483